8.95

D1557145

THE UFO ENIGMA

PUBLISHED BOOKS:

THE UFO ENIGMA, Donald H. Menzel and Ernest H. Taves

THE WORLD OF FLYING SAUCERS, Donald H. Menzel and Lyle G. Boyd

FLYING SAUCERS, Donald H. Menzel

WRITING A TECHNICAL PAPER, Donald H. Menzel, Howard Mumford Jones, and Lyle G. Boyd

THE FRIENDLY STARS, Martha Evans Martin and Donald H. Menzel

PRINCIPLES OF ATOMIC SPECTRA, Bruce W. Shore and Donald H. Menzel

STELLAR INTERIORS, Donald H. Menzel, P. L. Bhatnagar, and H. K. Sen

THE NATURE OF THE LUNAR SURFACE, Wilmot N. Hess, Donald H. Menzel, and John A. O'Keefe

By Donald H. Menzel:

OUR SUN

ASTRONOMY

STARS AND PLANETS

MATHEMATICAL PHYSICS

THE UNIVERSE IN ACTION

FUNDAMENTAL FORMULAS OF PHYSICS

FIELD GUIDE TO THE STARS AND PLANETS

THE UFO ENIGMA

The Definitive Explanation
of the UFO Phenomenon

Donald H. Menzel & Ernest H. Taves

Introduction by DR. FRED L. WHIPPLE
former Director of the Smithsonian Astrophysical Observatory

DOUBLEDAY & COMPANY, INC.
GARDEN CITY, NEW YORK   1977

ISBN: 0-385-03596-9
Library of Congress Catalog Card Number 76-16255
Copyright © 1977 by Florence Menzel, Executrix of the Estate of Donald H. Menzel, and Ernest H. Taves
Printed in the United States of America

Library of Congress Cataloging in Publication Data

Menzel, Donald Howard, 1901–
  The UFO enigma.

  Includes bibliographical references and index.
  1. Flying saucers. I. Taves, Ernest Henry, 1916–   joint
author. II. Title.
TL789.M458   001.9′42

This is for
Florence
Judith
&
Margot

ACKNOWLEDGMENTS

For permission to quote from copyrighted material, the authors gratefully make acknowledgment to the publishers and copyright owners noted on the copyright page of this book. We are grateful also to the United States Air Force for permission to publish extensive excerpts from their voluminous files concerning unidentified flying objects and to the Houghton Library of Harvard University for permission to reproduce photographs of illustrations in *Meteorologia Philisophico-politica* (1709), by Franz Reinzer.

We also wish to express our gratitude to Mr. Chuck Baker, for permission to reproduce one of his astronomical photographs; to Ms. Doris Beaudoin for tireless and efficient work in the preparation of the manuscript; to Dr. Whitfield J. Bell, Jr., and the staff of the library of the American Philosophical Society, and particularly to Mr. Carl F. Miller, for invaluable assistance in our study of the Condon papers; to Lyle G. Boyd for her cooperative interest; to Dr. Bernard D. Davis for helpful suggestions in respect of Chapter 15, on extraterrestrial life; to Dennis di Cicco for his fine photograph of parhelia; to Dr. Alistair B. Fraser, for interesting conversations about theological optics and for permission to reproduce one of his copyrighted photographs; to Mr. J. Robert Hamilton, for line drawings of parhelic phenomena; to Mr. Philip Klass, for stimulating ufological discussion and for providing us with copies of materials from his files; to Frederick John Rosenthal of the Library of Congress for skillful bibliographic assistance; and to Mr. Robert Sheaffer for comment and discussion about hoax photography and other subjects.

TABLE OF CONTENTS

LIST OF ILLUSTRATIONS

Many people believe a tenacious myth: that the scientific "establishment" has a built-in bias against evidence for the existence of extraterrestrial intelligence, UFOs, or even extraterrestrial life. Actually, most of the scientists who become even peripherally involved in the UFO question are creative people, highly imaginative themselves and open to imaginative ideas of others. They would be excitedly delighted to find any semisatisfying evidence that supports the reality of intelligent life outside our planet. I, for one, have been a science-fiction buff for over fifty years. My first technical article on artificial satellites appeared in 1946, at which time I invented the meteor bumper now used extensively in space probes. My major contact with UFOs occurred when the United States Air Force sent me a list of numerous unexplained sightings. I made a preliminary analysis and sent back a report, correlating a significant fraction of the sightings with the occurrence of Venus and the moon in the sky, usually near the horizon. Receiving no reply to my report, I terminated my UFO research. I have other reasons to believe that the U. S. Air Force took its protective role seriously, leaning over backwards in an attempt to establish the reality of possible external hazards to our national security, a laudable approach to the problem in view of their mission.

The authors of this book place unusually high value on imaginative activity, not only having widely read but also having written science fiction. They have been active supporters of the space program, a superb enterprise, broadening our horizons in the search for extraterrestrial life. I share their firm belief that extraterrestrial life and intelligence are relatively frequent in the universe. But a belief or a hope is a far cry from scientific supporting evidence.

As a team the authors are eminently prepared for the task of evaluating the evidence concerning UFOs. Professor Menzel has enormous competence and experience in observational techniques and in the areas of astronomy, atmospheric phenomena, and military activities. Dr. Taves, in addition to being an electronics expert, has especial competence in the subtle evaluation of human reporting and motivation. Anyone who believes that either of these authors would leave a stone unturned to find evidence for extraterrestrial intelligence is simply misguided. I am certain that they, like myself, would devote the rest of their lives to the detailed study of the subject if they had reason to believe that there was even a 30 per cent chance of finding or helping to find evidence for extraterrestrial intelligence. Their contribution in assembling information and in making it easily readable in this book must be judged honestly as a massive effort to find positive evidence, an effort which has ended in failure. They might well have devoted their time to some other activity with guaranteed success, except for their intense desire to find the truth about UFOs.

In these days of violent cultural change and uncertain futures for man and his works, I can readily understand why so many of our youth are turning to the supernatural and the occult, attempting to escape even the modicum of rationality with which most of us try to guide our lives. This urge is a powerful defense mechanism for the preservation of personal integrity in a highly disturbed cultural environment. I do not begrudge anyone his beliefs, however bizarre or unrealistic, if they give him comfort and confidence in this uncertain and threatening world. On the other hand, I am certain in my own mind that the only hope for the future of mankind lies in rationality. This book is a solid steppingstone out of the morass of unconscious yearning for supernatural intervention.

—Dr. Fred L. Whipple

June 16, 1976

CHAPTER 1

FRIGHT AND FLYING SAUCERS

AND HE WAS AFRAID, AND SAID,
HOW DREADFUL IS THIS PLACE!

Genesis 28:17[1]

Flying saucers, whatever they are, are by no means a new phenomenon. Records throughout the ages have clearly shown that weird apparitions in the sky have frightened man since prehistoric times. The Bible contains dozens of references to such apparitions. And when man cannot understand what he is seeing, he will invent an explanation to satisfy his questions and, perhaps, to partially quell his fears.

The myths that have come down to us through the ages are examples of what might be called primitive science. Lightning was a thunderbolt cast by the hand of Zeus, or Jupiter. Earthquakes were produced by the struggles of a giant chained to rock in some subterranean cavern. Volcanic lava flowed from the forge of Vulcan. The winds were produced by giants who lined the horizon, cheek by jowl, blowing vigorously, their lungs like bellows.

Primitive people the world over have generally believed in the existence of demons, ghosts, elves, goblins, dragons, sea serpents, fairies, leprechauns, and witches—to mention just a few of the more common fantasies.

Many people have believed in such things either because they themselves thought they had seen them or because they knew someone who had seen them. Some people still believe that these mythical creatures are real, as witness a 1974 news story from Ireland. This report blamed the then-current drought at Waterville on the bulldozing of an area thought to be frequented by good fairies. The fairies, in retaliation for being thus rudely dislocated, turned off the heavenly waters and caused the drought. The story was widely accepted and believed. It provided a natural and easily understood explanation for the dry spell.

Fairies! Who would believe in fairies today? Yet, to the foregoing example we must add the case of the eminent British writer, Sir Arthur Conan Doyle, who was once cleverly hoaxed by a couple of "innocent" children who produced, for his scrutiny, photographs of fairies. (The gullible Doyle was also an enthusiastic believer in spirit photography.)

Most of us no longer believe in ghosts, witches, or leprechauns. We regard anyone who holds such beliefs as perhaps a bit "touched"—or, at the least, very superstitious. Yet, during the last few years we have seen a tremendous resurgence of belief in many manifestations of the occult. Witchcraft is again widely practiced in various areas of the world. Astrology is in vogue. Exorcism has, in some localities, become commonplace.

And, for more than a quarter of a century, people have been seeing what were originally called "flying saucers," but which are now more commonly referred to as "unidentified flying objects," or UFOs.

There is no question but that many of the UFO sightings are of the same variety that have frightened people throughout the ages. And, like our forebears, we have devised a mythology to explain the phenomena. In 1947, when the modern age of flying saucers began, we were only talking about space travel, about visiting the moon and the planets. Since then we have in fact set foot on the moon, have sent numerous vehicles to the planets, and have made space travel a reality. If we earthlings are visiting the moon and are sending spacecraft to other planets, why should not the theoretical inhabitants of our other planets or of the planets of other planetary systems be involved in space travel to the earth?

This is a reasonable question, and it deserves a serious answer.

Many people, however, seem to think that, because such a question is reasonable, the answer must be in the affirmative. Why should the earth be the only inhabited planet? And if, perchance, the other planets of our solar system should be devoid of life, how about the millions and billions of stars in our Milky Way system alone, let alone those in the innumerable other galaxies? Some of these stars must surely have planets. And if they do, why are not the inhabitants of at least some of these planets so much more advanced than we that they have overcome the problems of space travel over the tremendous distances involved and have come to visit us?

We shall concern ourselves with these questions in a later chapter. Let us say here, however, that we readily grant the possibility that it may be as natural for some types of stars to have planets as for a cat to have kittens. If we conservatively limit ourselves to the stars most likely to have habitable planets, say the main-sequence stars lying between spectral types F2 through K1 inclusive, we can reasonably expect that our galaxy contains something like 650 million planets upon which life might exist.

We must grant, that is to say, that conditions favorable to the development of life and the evolution of intelligent beings could hardly be restricted to the microcosm we call Earth. Man, as a sentient being, is of relatively recent origin. His history probably does not go back more than three or four million years. If Earth has been in existence for, let us say, five billion years, man has been on the scene for about seven ten-thousandths of that time. If, for comparison, we compress the story of the origin and evolution of Earth into a three-hour drama, man has been on the stage for less than eight seconds. We tend to think that we are stealing the show or, indeed, are the show, but isn't it a little too early to tell? We shall presently discuss some of the flying saucers of history, but for the moment we return to the beginning of the present age of UFOs, which started in a simple and unheralded manner.

On June 24, 1947, Kenneth Arnold, a businessman from Boise, Idaho, was making a routine flight from Chehalis, Washington, to Yakima, Washington, in his private plane. The official United States Army Air Force report recounts Arnold's story in some detail, which can be summarized as follows:

As Arnold neared Mount Rainier and was admiring the grandeur of one of the highest peaks in the United States, he saw with a start what appeared to be a chain of unfamiliar aircraft flying close to the mountain.

"I could see their outline quite plainly against the snow as they approached the mountain," he said. "They flew very close to the mountain tops, directly south to southeast down the hogback of the range, flying like geese in a diagonal chainlike line, as if they were linked together.

"They were approximately twenty or twenty-five miles away, and I couldn't see a tail on them. I watched for about three minutes —a chain of saucerlike things at least five miles long, swerving in and out of the high mountain peaks. They were flat like a pie pan and so shiny they reflected the sun like a mirror. I never saw anything so fast."[2]

Arnold estimated that the objects were slightly smaller than a DC-4 that happened to be conveniently near at hand for comparison. He clocked the speed at about 1,200 miles an hour, a figure that seems to be inconsistent with the length of time he estimated them to be in view. From his previous statement, they could scarcely have traveled more than twenty-five miles during the three minutes he watched them. This gives about 500 miles an hour, which is still a figure large enough to be startling.

Arnold, on arrival at his destination, naturally reported what he had seen—thus touching off what eventually proved to be a chain reaction that soon attained fantastic and frightening proportions. The saucer story caught the public eye and, although the newspapers tended at first to scoff at or ridicule the tale, as the reports of other sightings increased the saucers became front-page news everywhere.

Arnold himself felt keenly the criticism of the press and said the papers could call him anything they liked—Einstein, Flash Gordon, or just a screwball—but he was absolutely certain of what he had seen. He added that no matter what else he might see in the sky in the future, even if it were a ten-story building flying through the air, he would shut his eyes and completely disregard it.

Arnold's story, coupled with the other incidents that soon followed, was of such a nature as to require an official investigation.

The Air Force stepped into the picture, setting up "Project Saucer" to investigate the sightings in general and to study the various phenomena from a number of angles. Professor J. Allen Hynek, then an astrophysicist at Ohio State University, became a consultant to advise the Air Force on the possible astronomical character of these incidents. His report on the Arnold sighting stated that it could not possibly be attributed to any known astronomical phenomenon and finally concluded, "It appears probable that whatever objects were observed were traveling at subsonic speeds, and may therefore have been some sort of known aircraft."

In later reports Arnold departed from his original description of his UFOs as being "flat like a pie pan." In his later descriptions the objects were crescent-shaped, with swept-back wings, not unlike flying birds. These were not his exact words, but are an accurate description of the graphic picture he drew of the objects.

The first thing to study in the investigation of any UFO report is the question whether some natural phenomenon, usual or unusual, could possibly be responsible for the sighting. Hynek's evaluation in this case did not seem particularly responsive, in view of Arnold's experience as a flyer. Arnold could scarcely have mistaken a squadron of DC-4s or other similar aircraft for the objects he saw. Reflections of sunlight from clouds of ice crystals were among the phenomena originally proposed by one of us (DHM), who later observed a phenomenon strikingly similar to that reported by Arnold. His report follows:

On 13 September 1972 I was flying into the famous airport, Schiphol, near Amsterdam, Netherlands. The plane was a DC-9, and I was sitting in an aisle seat on the left-hand side of the plane. Seat belts had been fastened, and the NO SMOKING sign had been turned on. I was staring out of the window, casually looking at the beautifully green Dutch landscape, when suddenly I noted that we were overtaking three shiny aircraft, seemingly flying in formation.

The striking thing was that I could see no detail whatever on the aircraft, only the silvery swept-back wings. They vanished abruptly as they reached the left-hand edge of the window. I leaned forward but could not see them again.

However, a new group of four or five planes appeared, also drifting backward.

I was suddenly reminded of the Arnold sighting. But I could not figure out what these peculiar objects flying in formation might be.

With an effort I refocused my gaze upon the surface of the window. To my surprise those brilliant UFOs shrank in size to become tiny raindrops, drifting slowly across the outer curved surface of the window. The force of the slipstream made each drop appear something like a tiny horseshoe. These drops picked up light from the distant sky, and looked exactly like planes with swept-back wings, flying in formation. I could regain the illusion by focusing my eyes on the distant landscape. As we descended, the number of raindrops increased and the illusion vanished. When we landed at the airport I found that a light rain was falling.

I cannot, of course, say definitely that what Arnold saw were merely raindrops on the window of his plane. He would doubtless insist that there could have been no rain at the altitude at which he was flying. But many queer things happen at different levels in the earth's atmosphere. Temperature inversions produce warm layers of air, which would melt any ice crystals. And even contact with the body of the plane, heated in the sunlight, could produce such melting.

Kenneth Arnold's spectacular description of the mysterious flying disks hit the headlines on a day that otherwise found the news unusually dull. Additional reports of sightings immediately swept the nation, flooding eastward like a tidal wave. Like Arnold's, most of these early reports concerned daylight observations. To see a flying saucer, apparently all one had to do was look at the sky for a reasonable length of time, whereupon a saucer would obligingly skim into view.

Everybody wanted to get into the act. The early stories caused some wonderment in London and other foreign capitals; a leading scientist commented on the gullibility of the American public with respect to these "hallucinations." But within a few weeks, sightings from England and other countries began to pour in. The saucers did not recognize national boundaries.

In the United States, behind the scenes, there was considerable consternation. The Air Force (then the U. S. Army Air Forces, but later in 1947 the United States Air Force), charged with the responsibility of defending the country from air attack, was mystified. There was an immediate concern, highly classified of course, that the sightings were related to some secret weapon, possibly Russian in origin. World War II had ended only two years before, and memories of the top-secret Japanese fire balloons were still vivid. These objects had been released in Japan, to cross the Pacific. It was intended that when they reached the North American continent they would descend and ignite huge forest fires. These balloons were not tremendously successful, but they did cause some conflagrations in western United States and Canada. Were the flying saucers an indication of a similar activity on the part of the Soviet Union?

Air Force personnel rushed about the country, investigating first this sighting and then that. They hastily organized a classified project to analyze the incoming reports. It is significant that not one of the individuals chosen to study the observations had any training in the important and relevant field of meteorological optics. No one familiar with this field could possibly have failed to identify the nature of an UFO* observed only a few days after the Arnold sighting—a disk over Boise, Idaho. The disk was described as semicircular in shape; it clung to a cloud and was bright and silvery in appearance, like a mirror reflecting the rays of the sun. This was, beyond all question, a sundog, or mock sun, produced by a layer of ice crystals in the upper atmosphere. But the Air Force investigators were confused by this sighting, as they were by many others.

The evidence indicates that during those early days the Air Force lumped the flying saucers into three general classifications: misidentified material objects such as planes, balloons, and kites; astronomical objects such as fireballs, meteors, and planets; and psychological phenomena, including hallucinations.

---

* Pronounced *oofo*. See p. 9.

That some of the sightings came from Finland and Sweden, near the borders of communist nations, caused concern in high circles in Washington. A security lid was clamped on because of the remote possibility that the reported sightings might in some way result from unknown activities behind the Iron Curtain. The proximity of some of the sightings to Russian-controlled Peenemünde, where the Germans had developed the V-1 flying bombs and V-2 rockets during World War II, was also disquieting.

Saucers were seen by day and by night, from the ground, from the sea, and from the air. Some moved rapidly, some were stationary. The inexperienced and mystified Air Force investigating teams exchanged reports with one another in an atmosphere of hushed excitement and extreme security. Though they might brush off the report of a mere civilian, they had to take seriously the reports of experienced airline and military pilots.

Nighttime saucers began to dominate the reports; this was not surprising, since bright lights in the sky are easier to observe during the hours of darkness. The news media contributed substantially to the general confusion. UFO reports were big stories.

The rational explanation of a sighting, no matter how spectacular the original occurrence had been, drew practically no attention. The field was ripe for hack writers, who found profit in exploiting the public with sensational stories about ships from outer space.[3] The air was filled with strange objects, and the public lapped up the new reports. Flying-saucer societies were formed around the world, each with its own publication and run by a select few at the top who preyed upon the gullible public for years.

THE ELUSIVE UFO

"YES," I ANSWERED YOU LAST NIGHT;
   NO," THIS MORNING, SIR, I SAY:
COLORS SEEN BY CANDLELIGHT
   WILL NOT LOOK THE SAME BY DAY.

Elizabeth Barrett Browning[1]

Not all things seen at night are illusions, but many of them are, and among these we include many UFOs, or flying saucers. In some circles the term "flying saucer" fell into disrepute shortly after the contemporary interest in these objects arose in 1947. The original Air Force investigation, known successively by the code names Project Saucer and Project Sign (1947), Project Grudge (early 1949), and Project Blue Book (mid-1951), experimented for a time with alternative names for the phenomena, most of them corruptions of "unidentified flying object." The original abbreviation, UFOB, pronounced *youfob,* was too cumbersome, and was shortly discarded in favor of UFO. Some simply pronounced the letters separately: *U-F-O.* Others said *youfo.* For a reason we shall give later, we have adopted the pronunciation preferred by Dr. Edward U. Condon, director of the Air Force investigation at the University of Colorado, which led to the famous (or infamous, according to the point of view) Condon Report. He pronounced the word *oofo.* Hence, as the reader will note, we speak of "an UFO" rather than of "a UFO."

The term "unidentified flying object" has been translated into

many tongues. The Spanish, for example, refer to OVNI, signifying *"objecto volador no identifacado."* Similar acronyms appear
in other languages.

For a time, some members of the Air Force group referred to
"anomalous phenomena" and sometimes to "aerial phenomena,"
but these terms were shortly abandoned, though some amateur organizations adopted the phrases as part of their own acronyms.
Chief among these was NICAP, a Washington-based organization
known as the "National Investigative Committee on Aerial
Phenomena." There were also APRO (Aerial Phenomena Research Organization) and BUFORA (British Unidentified Flying
Object Research Association). Certainly the best acronym to
emerge was SAUCERS, for "Saucers and Unexplained Celestial
Events Research Society," a contemporary organization.

Various problems of terminology have arisen. When, for example, an UFO is identified, does it become an IFO, an "identified
flying object"? Hynek employs this designation; we do not approve
of it. Our motto is "Once an UFO, always an UFO." For, if a
sighting is confusing to one individual, it will often remain so, even
though a second individual may be able to make a scientific interpretation of the sighting, thus removing it from the "unidentified"
category. In addition, many ufologists reject the identifications
made by others, clearly wishing to keep as many cases as possible
in the "unidentified" area. We employ the term UFO to designate
the phenomenon, using the qualifying adjectives "unknown" or
"known," a notation consistent with general Air Force practice.

Saucers have been seen in the daytime, flashing like silver in the
sunlight. Others have been seen at night—luminous globes or disk-
shaped blobs of light. Sometimes they stand still, and at other
times they move or veer with tremendous speed. Estimates of size
have varied all the way from a few feet to more than a thousand
feet in diameter, with fifty feet being somewhere near the average.
Saucers have been seen from the ground and from planes. Some
saucers have skimmed along the horizon; others have soared to
great heights. And saucers have been frequently seen on radar
screens—a phenomenon we shall discuss later.

One cause of major concern in the early days of UFOs was the
number of sightings from the neighborhood of a highly secret

atomic laboratory located in the desert country of the southwest United States. The famous U-2 incident—when the high-flying stratospheric spy plane was shot down over the U.S.S.R.—was then ten years in the future, but our military intelligence was certainly aware of the possibility that the Russians might be sending high-flying spy planes or satellites over our secret military installations. Accordingly, the U.S. intelligence people doubled the watches by night and by day, and then doubled them again. The number of UFOs observed increased proportionally, and the worries grew.

At one of the atomic laboratories in New Mexico, an antiaircraft gun was once brought into play in a vain attempt to shoot down what had been identified as a spy balloon shining brilliantly in the clear daytime sky. Faces were red when qualified astronomers identified the UFO as the planet Venus, at that time near maximum brightness. But even then there were observers who insisted, in spite of identification by experts, that the UFO must have been other than a planet, because it had seemed to move more rapidly than a planet should.

In the same general area, throughout the Southwest, UFO sightings were increasing, particularly in the nighttime. But no one thought to connect this increase with the fact that the watch had been intensified. Also, the clear atmosphere of the Southwest, with its dark nighttime skies, made the area a much better observing post than the bright cities. These are simple facts, but they were overlooked during the era of greatest concern.

Then there were the bright green fireballs, also reported from several sites in New Mexico, including the White Sands Proving Ground, the Holloman Air Force Base, and Los Alamos. One of us (DHM) had the good fortune to see one of these bright fireballs over the White Sands National Monument. He and several other astronomers present observed the bright green object as it slowly traversed the northern sector of the heavens, moving from east to west; they quickly and unequivocally identified it as a meteor, or bolide—a piece of interplanetary debris, heated by friction and glowing as it passed through the earth's atmosphere.*

---

* Generally, a "meteor" is the fiery streak in the sky caused by the incandescence of an entering body. "Fireballs" may be informally defined as

The object was widely observed, from Colorado to California. Observations from Colorado and New Mexico showed that the object was (like most meteors) at an altitude of from 75 to 100 miles above the surface of the earth. However, one airline pilot reported that the object came so close to his plane that the aircraft was deflected by the wake of the fiery object. Hence Air Force investigators rejected the conclusion of the scientists in favor of that of the pilot—for how could a meteor at an altitude of 75 miles possibly rock a plane? We shall show elsewhere how other pilots have similarly misidentified other proven meteors.

The green color was thought, by the Air Force investigators, to be unusual. It is, however, well known that burning copper emits a characteristic green flame. The Air Force analysts concluded that the UFOs were made of copper.

New methods of chemical analysis, developed primarily in connection with secret research on atomic weapons, were now put to use. These new techniques made it possible to detect the slightest traces of chemical substances. A number of samples of air collected over White Sands were sent to Los Alamos for analysis. And, surprisingly enough, traces of copper were found. The Air Force now believed that they had definite evidence of the correctness of their supposition that the UFOs from outer space were composed of copper.

DHM was then spending considerable time in the Sacramento Mountains, not far from the Holloman Air Force Base, building a major solar observatory under Air Force auspices. He therefore was close to the studies being undertaken in respect of UFOs, and was frequently consulted—although his advice and suggestions were usually strongly discounted.

He pointed out, in this case, that one of the large mines of the Kennecott Copper Corporation was near Silver City, New Mexico, only about 130 miles to the west. There huge stacks belched out clouds of smoke, carrying measurable amounts of copper into the atmosphere—a pollution which, with the prevailing wind, would drift directly over the White Sands area. Copper-mining operations

---

meteors bright enough to be reported in the newspapers. "Bolides" are unusually bright fireballs. They are usually *heard* at ground level, and they frequently explode.

were also present near El Paso, Texas, about 80 miles to the south.

Furthermore, he pointed out, more than fifteen years earlier a Canadian astrophysicist, Peter M. Millman, then a graduate student at Harvard University, had carried out a spectroscopic study of light from fireballs. He had concentrated his attention on those having an unusual green color and had discovered that the particular shade came from magnesium rather than copper. Millman's data had been available in the scientific literature years before UFOs became popular.

DHM was then asked, as a favor to the Air Force, to build a spectrograph that could be used to determine the spectrum, and thus the chemical composition, of the green objects they had been observing. He designed and built such an instrument, checking it out for reliability on man-made sources of radiant energy, including neon signs in the distant city of Alamogordo, New Mexico. He trained several airmen at Holloman AFB in its operation. These men patrolled the sky for nearly six months, but there was now a singular dearth of the green fireballs. DHM heard someone say that the operators of the alien vehicles must have learned about the surveillance and moved their maneuvers elsewhere. In the end the program was discontinued. And, as luck would have it, the very next night a green fireball was observed. But, of course, no spectrum was obtained.

For this service, it should be said for the record, DHM received no compensation. This fact is recorded here because several writers have accused DHM of being "an Air Force stooge"—for a sum, of course. The fact is that he never received a single cent of compensation from the Air Force or from any other government agency for work in the field of UFOs. Instead, he contributed generously of his time to advise the Air Force on certain difficult cases that neither their consultants nor any of their personnel were able to solve.

In those early days, from about 1949 to 1952, the personnel in charge of Project Grudge and its mid-1951 successor, Project Blue Book, became quite convinced that the extraterrestrial hypothesis (ETH) was the only one that could explain the observations. Among the higher officers connected with the projects, only General John A. Samford and Colonel John O'Mara were receptive to

DHM's theories and suggestions. The others, especially Captain Edward J. Ruppelt, who was nominally in charge of day-to-day operations, directly refused to carry out some simple experiments that would have helped resolve some of the problems.

The main problem arose from the fact that airline and military pilots, persons whose reliability was presumably unquestioned, time and again reported seeing what appeared to be "material objects," frequently described as "metallic." They moved at "fantastic speeds." They often appeared to take "evasive action." And there were reports of UFOs seen on radar, a subject we shall consider in a later chapter.

The difficulty with these reports lay in the fact that the investigators failed to distinguish between what the observer really saw and the conclusions that he drew from his sighting. His report that the phenomenon seen visually was an actual material object, that it was metallic, or that it took evasive action represents not facts of observation, but conclusions of the observer.

The case of the bright green bolide, or meteor, previously discussed, is a case in point. Which observer are we to believe? The pilot who claimed it rocked his plane or the scientist whose objective measurements from the ground placed the source of illumination at an altitude of more than 75 miles? We should not be too critical of the Air Force personnel suddenly confronted with the need to analyze such problems. They simply had no proper background for undertaking such investigation. Granted the context, it was perhaps predictable that they would prefer to accept the conclusion of an "experienced" pilot, who was right up there, over that of some scientist on the ground.

The basic fact, as we shall presently establish, is that even the experienced observer is easily misled. Consider, for example, such a simple phenomenon as a shadow. How could anyone be so naïve as to mistake his shadow for something material and "real"? The old saying "Afraid of his own shadow" indicates that the error must be fairly common. Indeed, an old and well-known apparition known as the "Specter of the Brocken" falls into this category. We shall describe it later, in Chapter 10.

As for the ability of the eye to judge size, ask yourself or someone else this question: "How large an object would you have to hold at arm's length to just cover the rising full moon? A washtub? A dinner plate? A saucer? A teacup? A fifty-cent piece? A quarter? A nickel? A dime? An average-sized pea?

Tests have shown that in this simple case estimates of size usually range between that of a dinner plate and that of a teacup. Few people initially believe the correct answer, which is "an average-sized pea." The experiment is well worth trying.

Moreover, that same full moon is always perceived as being larger on the horizon than it appears when overhead. In fact, the moon near the horizon is slightly smaller in apparent diameter than the full moon as seen near the zenith. The difference in apparent size is quite small, about 2 per cent, but it is by no means negligible. The apparently larger size of the moon on the horizon is caused by the "moon illusion"—a well-known, much-discussed, and still-controversial phenomenon. All too easily a major misjudgment of size, speed, or distance can result from human error. Consider the following incident, which happened some years ago to one of us (DHM):

While walking along a country road he chanced to look upward and saw what appeared to be a distant plane, traveling soundlessly and at enormous speed. His first and natural reaction was, "So we have a new type of plane." In a matter of seconds the plane was nearly overhead, and then it suddenly began to falter and fall. He tried to run from the scene because the plane seemed about to crash. And indeed it did, almost in his face. He stooped to pick it up; it was a tiny, powered model. Its owner suddenly appeared, running across a field, waving to indicate that the fallen aircraft was his.

This was, of course, a compound perceptive error. Both size and distance were misjudged. If either had been perceived correctly, there would have been no error. The distance of the small aircraft was no doubt within the normal limits within which humans can make a fair judgment of distance. But the observer saw an airplane and perceived it as being of normal airplane size. The necessary distance was then added by complex neural events not directly related to the sense of sight as such.

In the absence of clues, such as would be provided by an intervening foreground or background of familiar objects, human eyes are able to judge distance only by virtue of stereoscopic vision, which is based upon the fact that when one looks at a near object the retinal images of the two eyes are not quite the same. This is because each eye is in a different place. The limit of stereoscopic vision according to J. P. C. Southall is about a quarter of a mile, and this distance depends largely upon the interpupillary distance of the individual.[2] This distance in humans ranges from about 50 to 74 millimeters, a substantial range. The farther apart the eyes, the better the depth perception. As we have said, the human nervous system can and does make use of other clues, but the main foundation of distance judgment is stereoscopic vision, and beyond a distance of about a quarter of a mile it just doesn't work.

Especially in the air, then, no one—not even the most experienced pilot—can infallibly tell, beyond that critical distance, whether an object is something small and close at hand or large and far away.

Edgar Allan Poe, in "The Sphinx," uses this inability of the human eye to judge both size and distance as a basic theme for a horror story. The plot is a bit farfetched, but certainly relevant.

The story is laid against a background of death during an epidemic of cholera. Taking refuge in the home of a friend, a man looks up from his reading to regard through a window the naked face of a hill, whereupon he sees a living monster of tremendous proportions. The apparition is described in vivid terms:

> Estimating the size of the creature by comparison with the diameter of the large trees near which it passed—the few giants of the forest which had escaped the fury of the land-slide —I concluded it to be far larger than any ship of the line in existence. I say ship of the line, because the shape of the monster suggested the idea—the hull of one of our seventy-fours might convey a very tolerable conception of the general outline. The mouth of the animal was situated at the extremity of a proboscis some sixty or seventy feet in length, and about as thick as the body of an ordinary elephant. Near the root of this trunk was an immense quantity of black shaggy hair—more than could have been supplied by the coats of a score of buffaloes; and projecting from this hair downwardly

and laterally, sprang two gleaming tusks not unlike those of
the wild boar, but of infinitely greater dimension. Extending
forward, parallel with the proboscis, and on each side of it,
was a gigantic staff, thirty or forty feet in length, formed
seemingly of pure crystal, and in shape a perfect prism,—it
reflected in the most gorgeous manner the rays of the declin-
ing sun. The trunk was fashioned like a wedge with the apex
to the earth. From it there were outspread two pairs of wings
—each wing nearly one hundred yards in length—one pair
being placed above the other, and all thickly covered with
metal scales; each scale apparently some ten or twelve feet in
diameter. I observed that the upper and lower tiers of wings
were connected by a strong chain. But the chief peculiarity of
this horrible thing was the representation of a *Death's Head,*
which covered nearly the whole surface of its breast, and
which was as accurately traced in glaring white, upon the
dark ground of the body, as if it had been there carefully designed by an artist. While I regarded this terrific animal, and
more especially the appearance on its breast, with a feeling of
horror and awe—with a sentiment of forthcoming evil, which
I found it impossible to quell by any effort of the reason, I
perceived the huge jaws at the extremity of the proboscis suddenly expand themselves, and from them there proceeded a
sound so loud and so expressive of woe, that it struck upon
my nerves like a knell, and as the monster disappeared at the
foot of the hill, I fell at once, fainting, to the floor.

For some time the narrator keeps the matter from his host, but
eventually decides to describe the apparition in minute detail. The
host recognizes what it actually is: the sphinx moth. He leans
forward and places himself in the exact position where his friend
had just seen a reappearance of the creature:

"Ah, here it is!" he presently exclaimed—"it is reascending
the face of the hill, and a very remarkable looking creature I
admit it to be. Still, it is by no means so large or so distant as
you imagined it; for the fact is that, as it wriggles its way up
this thread, which some spider has wrought along the win-

dow-sash, I find it to be about the sixteenth of an inch in its extreme length, and also about the sixteenth of an inch distant from the pupil of my eye."

The story is not really scientific, because no one could possibly see the details as described in an object only one sixteenth of an inch away from the eye. It would be completely out of focus.

Still, it is relatively easy to produce the effect of an UFO in a manner not too different from that described by Poe. Such phenomena may well account for a fair number of saucer sightings.

A single thread from a spider web hanging in a graceful horizontal loop between two branches or across a window is almost invisible except when the full sunlight falls upon it. Its surface is like that of a curved mirror, so that we see a brilliant reflection from only a small portion of the loop. If the strand of web is near the eye, the out-of-focus effect may make it look like a brilliant saucer against the sky or distant scene. If a slight breeze disturbs it, the image will dance around and seem to veer, as the saucers have been reported to do.

To study the effect on a slightly larger scale, look at the bright reflection of the sun in a shiny, round lead pencil or fountain pen, preferably of dark color. Fine silk or nylon thread or a fisherman's leader reproduces the effect even better. Note that each eye sees a different image. If one tries to focus on the reflection so as to see a single object, the pencil will be out of focus. Thus the saucer seems to be far away. Windborne cobwebs may thus be one more cause of unexplained UFOs.

DHM's sighting of raindrops moving across the window of an airplane, previously described, is another example of the same phenomenon. Uncorrected myopia or astigmatism in the observer's eye can enhance the illusion.

FLYING SAUCERS OF THE BIBLE

GOD DRIVES A FLYING SAUCER

Current book title[1]

Some of the earliest references to UFOs appear in the Scriptures. The natural phenomena that give rise to saucer sightings are by no means unique to our times. Many people today seeing these strange apparitions in the sky are confused, puzzled, and often enough frightened. The ancients were no doubt even more confused.

We should not be too critical of the ancients, who lacked access to modern science. We cannot accuse them of lack of perception, though we feel that they were often overimaginative in their vivid descriptions of certain phenomena. The Bible dramatically records many meteorological observations, including those of storms, thunder, lightning, and rainbows.

There exist in the Bible numerous cases of primitive science. Rain, for example, was a mysterious and almost miraculous phenomenon. Whence came the heavenly waters? The ancients visualized great oceans or bodies of water in the sky, held back from the earth by a crystal globe in which were many windows. A rainstorm was merely a leaky window. When the Flood occurred, "the windows of heaven were opened."[2] The Flood ended when "the fountains also of the deep and the windows of heaven were stopped, and the rain from heaven was restrained."[3]

The rainbow was regarded as a symbol of God's promise to man,[4] and the rainbow ever since has by many been held in superstitious awe.

A somewhat similar phenomenon is recorded in Exodus.[5] A flame appeared in the middle of a bush and, to the surprise of Moses, did not consume the bush, though the bush burned. We believe that the Burning Bush, often enough identified as an UFO, is the meteorologists' St. Elmo's fire—an electrical discharge. This is a spectacular and frightening apparition indeed, but no miracle. It has often appeared in the rigging of sailing ships.*

The crossing of the Red Sea by the Israelites may be attributed to a well-known phenomenon of meteorological optics, an inferior mirage. (We discuss mirages further in Chapter 10.) A person standing on a slight elevation in the desert on a hot, clear day will often see the sky spread out *below* him, giving the appearance of a lake. As he walks forward through this apparent body of water, the blue recedes, appearing to open a path of dry land before him. Persons coming from behind will seem to be swallowed up and drowned as the "water" closes over them. The phenomenon is not unusual and certainly would have been judged by anyone encountering it in biblical times as a sort of miracle.

The legend of Jesus walking on the water can be similarly explained, as Alistair B. Fraser has suggested.[6] Where a mirage exists, an individual can appear to walk on water when his feet are actually on dry land—as shown in one of Fraser's photographs in Plate 1. Note that the figures appearing to walk on the water seem larger than those in the boat. In fact, they were standing on a sand spit about as far beyond the boat as the boat was from the camera. This magnifying effect is generally found in such mirages.

The same phenomenon may be seen on a highway on a hot day; a mirage of the sky causes the pavement ahead to appear wet. A

---

* Our attention has recently been drawn to a description of St. Elmo's fire in Shakespeare: "A common slave . . . held up his left hand, which did flame and burn like twenty torches join'd; and yet his hand, not sensible of fire, remain'd unscorch'd." (*Julius Caesar*, I, iii, 15–18)

car driving ahead of you may appear to be floating or moving on the water.

Another biblical apparition that we readily recognize is described vividly in Genesis 28, where Jacob dreams of an enormous ladder set on the earth, leading up to heaven, with the angels of God ascending and descending upon it. As a possible meteorological explanation of this, we shall later describe the "corona," a remarkable formation that occasionally occurs in association with the aurora borealis. This phenomenon is caused by electrons and atoms that come from the sun, and are then focused by the earth's magnetic field, producing the appearance of an enormous ladder or barrel stretching upward into the sky toward the magnetic zenith. The apparition is frequently accompanied by flickering lights, which could readily be interpreted as movements of angels.

Finally, we come to the spectacular visions of Ezekiel (Chapter 1, verses 4–28):

And I looked, and, behold, a whirlwind came out of the north, a great cloud, and a fire infolding itself, and a brightness was about it, and out of the midst thereof as the colour of amber, out of the midst of the fire.

Also out of the midst thereof came the likeness of four living creatures. And this was their appearance; they had the likeness of a man.

And every one had four faces, and every one had four wings.

And their feet were straight feet; and the sole of their feet was like the sole of a calf's foot: and they sparkled like the colour of burnished brass.

And they had the hands of a man under their wings on their four sides, and they four had their faces and their wings.

Their wings were joined one to another; they turned not when they went; they went every one straight forward.

As for the likeness of their faces, they four had the face of a man, and the face of a lion, on the right side: and they four had the face of an ox on the left side; they four also had the face of an eagle.

Thus were their faces: and their wings were stretched upward; two wings of every one were joined one to another, and two covered their bodies.

And they went every one straight forward: whither the spirit was to go, they went; and they turned not when they went.

As for the likeness of the living creatures, their appearance was like burning coals of fire, and like the appearance of lamps; it went up and down among the living creatures; and the fire was bright, and out of the fire went forth lightning.

And the living creatures ran and returned as the appearance of a flash of lightning.

Now as I beheld the living creatures, behold one wheel upon the earth by the living creatures, with his four faces.

The appearance of the wheels and their work was like unto the colour of a beryl: and they four had one likeness: and their appearance and their work was as it were a wheel in the middle of a wheel.

When they went, they went upon their four sides: and they turned not when they went.

As for their rings, they were so high that they were dreadful; and their rings were full of eyes round about them four.

And when the living creatures went, the wheels went by them; and when the living creatures were lifted up from the earth, the wheels were lifted up.

Whithersoever the spirit was to go, they went, thither was their spirit to go; and the wheels were lifted up over against them: for the spirit of the living creature was in the wheels.

When those went, these went; and when those stood, these stood; and when those were lifted up from the earth, the wheels were lifted up over against them: for the spirit of the living creature was in the wheels.

And the likeness of the firmament upon the heads of the living creature was as the colour of the terrible crystal, stretched forth over their heads above.

And under the firmament were their wings straight, the one toward the other; every one had two, which covered on this side, and every one had two, which covered on that side, their bodies.

And when they went, I heard the noise of their wings, like the noise of great waters, as the voice of the Almighty, the voice of speech, as the noise of an host: when they stood, they let down their wings.

And there was a voice from the firmament that was over their heads, when they stood, and had let down their wings.

And above the firmament that was over their heads was the likeness of a throne, as the appearance of a sapphire stone; and upon the likeness of the throne was the likeness as the appearance of a man above upon it.

And I saw as the colour of amber, as the appearance of fire round about within it, from the appearance of his loins even upward, and from the appearance of his loins even downward, I saw as it were the appearance of fire, and it had brightness round about.

As the appearance of the bow that is in the cloud in the day of rain, so was the appearance of the brightness round about. This was the appearance of the likeness of the glory of the Lord. And when I saw it, I fell upon my face . . .

As well he might.

The second vision, recounted in Ezekiel 10, is almost identical. The question is, Just what did the prophet really see? Our view is that the agreement between Ezekiel's vision and a modern description of a deluxe-model display of mock suns with attendant glories is completely convincing.

As a key to the scriptural interpretation, compare Figures 1 and 2. The first is a schematic drawing combining observed features of well-known solar halos complete with mock suns, or sundogs, and "glories," phenomena produced by ice crystals in the upper atmosphere (see Chapter 10). The second is an imaginative sketch that attempts to interpret the biblical account. In Plate 2 we show another such interpretation. In Plate 3 we reproduce a black-and-white photograph of a well-developed parhelion. The upper outward arc, one of the "glories," shows particularly well. The mock sun to the left of the viewer is clearly delineated. No photograph or reproduction can compare with an eyewitness observation, but

Figure 1. Schematic diagram of sundogs and associated halos, the prototype of Ezekiel's wheels. *Courtesy of Harvard University Press*

it is not difficult to understand how such an apparition could indeed electrify the imagination of a viewer in biblical times.

The similarity of Ezekiel's apparition to the solar halo is remarkable. True, the phenomenon of mock suns varies according to the type and size of the ice crystals, their density and distribution in space, the relative quiescence of the different air layers containing these crystals, and finally the altitude of the sun. The character of the display can range from a simple unadorned halo or a single mock sun to the super-deluxe model known as the "St. Petersburg phenomenon," because the St. Petersburg (now Leningrad) astronomer Johann Tobias Lowitz was the first to observe and describe it, in 1794. We have compromised on a somewhat simpler form, a minor modification of the so-called "Roman phenomenon," one of the earlier records of parhelic phenomena observed and described by the Jesuit priest Christoph Scheiner at Rome in 1630.

The two separate visions of Ezekiel refer to independent apparitions, which naturally accounts for some of the observed differences.

One of the main features of the apparition of "a wheel in the middle of a wheel" requires no assistance from the imagination, consisting as it does of two concentric circles around the sun. The

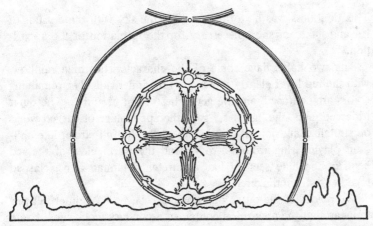

Figure 2. Ezekiel's visualization of the apparition: four winged angels. *Courtesy of Harvard University Press*

"four living creatures" are the mock suns themselves, whose "appearance was like burning coals of fire, and like the appearance of lamps." The reported flickering is common to such sundogs. Many of them seem to be composed of myriads of twinkling sparks. These are the "faces."

From the description we clearly see that the figure contained a cross centered on the sun. The arms of the cross looked like the spokes of a wheel; each formed the body of a figure, each mock sun itself representing the head. In early times it was customary to carve the spokes of chariot wheels into the forms of animals or human beings.

The description leads us to suppose that the apparition occurred not long after sunrise, and presumably these columns, the spokes of the wheel, carried some of the dawn-pink glow. They seem to have a feathery appearance, and very little imagination would be required to see them as "wings" covering the body of the figure. And the foot of each figure, where it stands on the sun, broadened by its brightness, could readily suggest the "straight" image like "a calf's foot," sparkling with "the colour of burnished brass." The sun itself, perhaps even dimmer than its mock companions, contributed the brassy glow.

The biblical text describes a whirlwind coming from the north.

This doubtless was a storm that filled the sky with the crystals of ice and flakes of snow necessary for the formation of the apparition.

The two halos have some of the characteristics of a rainbow, with the red layer clearly showing on the inner side. The remaining colors are confused, and we get at best a tint of amber. The outer iridescent arcs, the "glories," gave the appearance of curved wings outstretched and joined together to make the full circle, like children playing ring-around-a-rosy. And the warm glow of the red band of the halo seemed like outstretched human arms, clasped together to form the circle.

We read that the outer ring possessed "eyes." We interpret this to mean that the apparition contained secondary mock suns, a rare phenomenon.

Commentaries point out that the same Hebrew word in Ezekiel, chapter 1, verse 24, is rendered both as "voice" and "noise." And indeed the rushing noises may belong to the storm itself. The Scriptures frequently refer to thunder as "the voice of the Almighty." Thunder is uncommon in a snowstorm, but we are by no means sure that the apparition occurred in winter. If the cold region is highly elevated, the phenomenon can be seen at almost any time of the year.

Part of the apparition is described as a throne of "sapphire." This throne would seem to be the arc tangent to the outer wheel, and the description of its color fits almost uniquely; of all the bows and arcs associated with a fully developed apparition of mock suns, the upper arc is the *only* one that is plainly blue.

The wheels did not turn but were "lifted up," and the living creatures went with them. In other words, as the sun rose the great wheels and the entire apparition moved with it.

The only obscure passage in the whole description relates to the faces; these were supplied by vivid imagination—the face of a man in front, the face of a lion to the right, the face of an ox to the left, with the face of an eagle invisibly turned away. Many authorities have called attention to the similarity between this wheeled throne and the chariot—perhaps the "chariot of fire" that carried up Elijah "by a whirlwind into Heaven."[7]

Other visions described in the Scriptures suggest that mock suns or mock moons were their inspiration.[8]

Some commentaries on Ezekiel, referring to the construction of a "wheel in the middle of a wheel," have supposed that these two wheels were like hoops set at right angles to one another, and some of the more famous illustrated Bibles depict Ezekiel's wheels in this way. The Italian Renaissance master Raphael also illustrated the vision, but without wheel or chariot.

Without some guidance from meteorology, the artists were unable to interpret the confused images. With meteorology as a guide, the whole description falls into place, and—whatever religious significance one may wish to assign to it—the origin of the vision becomes clear. In fact, Ezekiel proves to take high rank as an observing scientist and recorder of important meteorological phenomena.

Recently a number of writers have taken to interpreting the visions of Ezekiel and similar sights as evidence that the earth was visited thousands of years ago by supermen from outer space. There is no rational basis for such belief, as we shall show later, in Chapter 20.

CHAPTER 4

"STRANGE SIGNES FROM HEAVEN"

. . . FEARFUL THUNDERBOLTS AND HORRIBLE
FIERY DRAGONS WERE SEEN PASSING THROUGH THE AIR,
FOREBODING A MIGHTY FAMINE AND
DREADFUL SLAUGHTER OF THE PEOPLE.

Roger de Wendover[1]

The further back we try to trace flying saucers, the more confused the record becomes. Part of the difficulty, of course, arises because original records are difficult to find. But a more important reason is that early observers of meteorological phenomena lumped together almost everything seen in the atmosphere into a single category called "meteors." Our present use of the word "meteorology" recalls this early usage, though now we rarely apply the term "meteor" to other than "shooting stars" or "bolides."

If the early observers made any distinction at all, it was between "aerial meteors," which included phenomena like whirlwinds; "aqueous meteors," such as fog, rain, hail, snow, and clouds; and "luminous meteors," which, in addition to shooting stars, included lightning bolts, sundogs, the aurora borealis, and comets.

With such spectacular phenomena as comets, bright fireballs, lightning, solar halos, and even eclipses to compete with, the flying saucers had little chance—unless they proved to be exceptional. Thus, whenever we do find an apparition whose description identifies it clearly as a flying saucer, the details are sometimes

more useful than those of modern sightings because of their viv-
idness.

However, the imagination of the observer was often a hindrance
to accurate presentation. We have to remember that these early
observers were uneducated and generally illiterate. Even the most
intelligent people of the times, say, in the early seventeenth century, had no idea what a comet really was. Their textbooks described a comet as an "exhalation of the earth." Superstitious people believed that any celestial apparition was a sign from Heaven,
presaging some catastrophic event on the earth—death, war, pestilence, or even the end of the world. Thus fortunetellers, oracles,
and soothsayers flourished, preying upon the superstitious ignorance of their fellow men.

We show in Plate 4 an eighteenth-century woodcut showing a
man, serpents, and other animals fleeing from the rising sun, which
is accompanied by no less than seven comets. The comets—which
are drawn accurately, with their tails pointing away from the sun—
are portents of dire events.

Increase Mather, in the early 1680s, gave a series of sermons to
his Puritan flock in Massachusetts, in which he tried to prove that
strange heavenly apparitions did presage terrible events. He took
special issue with the passage in Jeremiah (10:2): "Thus saith the
Lord, Learn not the way of the heathen, and be not dismayed at
the signs of heaven; for the heathen are dismayed at them." Instead, Mather expounded his views in a sermon, "Heaven's Alarm
to the World," calling comets "God's sharp razors on mankind,
whereby he doth poll, and his scythe whereby he doth shear down
multitudes of sinful creatures . . . Doth God threaten our very
heavens? O pray unto him that he would not take away stars and
send comets to succeed them."

And as Isaac Newton, in England, began to establish order in
the universe through his law of gravitation, Increase Mather tried
to counter the suggestion that "signs" were natural phenomena. As
proof of his contention he refers to the total solar eclipse of August 22, 1672. During that year Harvard College "was eclipsed by
the death of the learned president there, Mr. Chauncy; and two
colonies—namely, Massachusetts and Plymouth—by the death of
two governors, who died within a twelvemonth after . . . Shall,

then, such mighty works of God as comets are be insignificant things?"[2]

But signs of the times prevailed over signs in the heavens, and by 1726 we find Increase Mather's famous son, Cotton, taking issue with his father: "Perhaps there may be some need for me to caution you against being dismayed at the signs of the heavens, or having any superstitious fancies upon eclipses and the like . . . I am willing that you be apprehensive of nothing portentous in blazing stars. For my part, I know not whether all our worlds, and even the sun itself, may not fare the better for them."

Thus, by degrees, comets, eclipses, halos, and other "meteors" came under natural law, as parts of an ordered universe. We shall find that flying saucers will follow the same pattern.

One small seventeenth-century book by an anonymous English author throws a great deal of light upon the reactions of our ancestors to mysterious apparitions. The title page of this book reads: "*STRANGE SIGNES FROM HEAVEN;* Seene and heard in *Cambridge, Suffolke, and Norfolke,* in and upon the 21 day of May last past in the afternoone, 1646. *MIRACULOUS WONDERS,* seene at *Barnstable, Kirkham, Cornwall,* and *Little Britain,* in *London. Whereunto is annexed SEVERALL APPARITIONS,* seene in the aire, at the *Hague* in *Holland,* upon the 21/31 day of May last past, about one of the clocke in the Afternoone." These signs, so the introduction states, are specifically "to warne and awaken the Eastern Association, with the Southerne Parts of the Kingdom."

The text begins:*

Incredulity hath always been the forerunner of misery ever since the Creation; the old World would not be warned by Noah's building the Ark until the flood came. Pharaoh would not be warned by God's judgments till he was swallowed up of the Red Sea . . . The Lord, who is slow to wrath and of much mercy, gave Signs from Heaven unto the Jews, to forewarn them of their approaching destruction, but they regarded it not. The *Blazing Star* seen in our Horizon so many

* For the convenience of the reader, we use modern spelling.

years ago, which began toward *Germany,* fetched its compass
to *Ireland,* and whose blazing bush tail hung over *England,*
was but a nine days wonder, although those countries hath
since found the effects thereof, the Almighty divert his Judgments from us if it be his will, which we may justly fear hang-
eth over our heads, by reason of our continual crying sins,
notwithstanding the many tokens of his anger showed unto us
by strange and fearful apparitions seen in the air (the 21 of
May last past) in many parts.

About *New-Market,* in the County of *Cambridge,* there
were seen by diverse honest, sober, and civil persons, and
men of good credit, three men in the air, striving, struggling,
and tugging together, one of them having a drawn sword in his
hand, from which Judgment God in his mercy preserve these
three Kingdoms of *England, Scotland,* and *Ireland,* from further conflicts and effusion of blood.

Betwixt *New-Market* and *Thetford* in the County of *Norfolke,* there was observed a pillar or cloud to ascend from the
earth, with the bright hilts of a sword toward the bottom of
it, which pillar did ascend in a pyramidal form, and fashioned
itself into the form of a spire or broach steeple, and there descended also out of the Sky in the form of a Pike or Lance,
with a very sharp head or point to encounter with it.

Also at a distance, there appeared another Spear or Lance,
with a very acute point out of the Sky . . . The first Spear,
which came down from Heaven point blank, was after a
while clean elevated higher, and that spire or spear which
went up from the earth, ascended after it, to encounter with it
the second time.

This continued about an hour and a half.

At *Sopham,* in the County of *Cambridge* aforesaid, a ball
of wild-fire fell upon the earth, which burnt up and spoiled
about an Acre of Grain, and when it had rolled and run up
and down to the terror of many people and some townsmen
that see it, it dissolved and left a most sulphurous stink
behind it . . .

Also at *Brandon* in the County of *Norfolke* was seen at the

same time, a Navy or Fleet of Ships in the Air, swiftly passing under sail, with Flags and Streamers hanged out, as if they
were ready to give an encounter . . .

In all these places there was very great thunder, with rain
and hail stones of extraordinary bigness and round, and some
hollow within like rings.

The Lord grant that all the people of this Kingdom may
take heed to every warning Trumpet of his, that we may
speedily awaken out of our sins, and truly turn to the Lord,
fight his battles against our spiritual enemies, and get those
inward riches of which we cannot be Plundered of, and so
seek an inward Kingdom of Righteousness and Peace.

The book goes on to tell of the punishment brought down upon
a Mrs. Haughton, who swore, "I pray God that rather than I shall
be a Round-head, or bear a Round-head, I may bring forth a child
without a head."†

The book then states that her child did not live, but rumors
about its physical appearance attained such proportions that the
minister of the parish finally "caused the grave to be opened, and
the child to be taken up and laid to view, and found there a body
without an head . . . only the child had a face upon the breast of it,
the two eyes near unto the place where the paps usually are, and a
nose upon the chest, and a mouth a little above the navel, and two
ears, upon each shoulder one." The book concludes with a description of strange sights seen in Holland.

First, came a little round thing about the bigness of a table
or board, like unto gray paper: and without it was seen the
likeness of a Lion and a Dragon which furiously fought together, which Dragon after a while did spit fire furiously, but
was overcome by the Lion; and yet the Lion appeared in
sight.

2. Appeared by the Lion a multitude of soldiers, with another Dragon likewise, and with a multitude of soldiers both

---

† Roundheads were supporters of Parliament—i.e., antimonarchists—during
the English civil war.

foot and horse . . . and the Lion and the Dragon continued
still in sight.

3. There appeared also a King with three crowns on his
head . . . but the Lion and Dragon abode still in sight.

4. There appeared also a number of peoples heads, and
one great head amongst them: and a multitude of bodies
without heads which vanished away, yet the Lion and Dragon
abode as before continuing in sight.

5. There appeared yet likewise one man sitting upon a
horse, which shot himself through (as with a pistol) and fell
backward, and so vanished away.

Lastly, there appeared a mighty fleet of ships in the Southeast, by the Lion and the Dragon, where the fight was, with a
multitude of men aboard the ships, with half their bodies to
be seen above board, which we saw perfectly hoisting up their
sails, and driving to and fro, and as it were continued all
standing still, till the Lion and the Dragon embraced one another and so fell backward, and disappeared: whereupon
there appeared a great cloud which was not there before, and
so drove away with the wind.

This curious collection of natural and undoubtedly fictitious
phenomena—the incident of the child with no head appears to be
highly questionable—illustrates the reaction of people to strange
events.

Remember that these objects reported as visible in the sky must
have been unusual. They occurred in the daytime and hence could
have had no relation to the aurora borealis. The widespread apparition of the spears, lances, or steeples, clearly suggests an atmospheric condition rather than a peculiar cloud formation. This phenomenon was probably a fata morgana, a type of mirage in which
astigmatic vertical magnification of distant objects occurs. This
kind of mirage frequently produces apparitions of steeples, castles,
towers, cities, ships, and armies waging war. We show an early
woodcut of such an apparition in Plate 5.

The "ball of wild-fire" was probably ball lightning, or perhaps a
sundog, an image brought to Earth by optical illusion characteristic
of some types of atmospheric reflection. The "little round thing"

Plate 1. Walking on the waters of Puget Sound, a lesson in theological optics. It has been suggested that the phenomenon shown here, an ordinary inferior mirage, may explain the legend of Jesus walking on the water. Note that the mirage magnifies. The figures apparently walking on water are about twice as far from the camera as the boat. © *Alistair B. Fraser 1975*

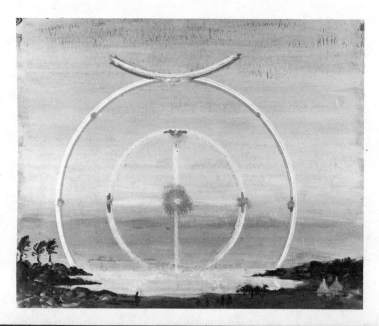

Plate 2. *top:* Artist's impression of sundogs and associated halos—the prototype of Ezekiel's wheels. *Charles Bittinger*

Plate 3. *bottom:* A well-developed parhelion. The upper outward arc, one of the "glories," shows particularly well. The mock sun to the left of the viewer is clearly delineated. *Photo by Dennis di Cicco of* Sky and Telescope *Magazine*

Plate 4. Man, serpents, and other animals fleeing from the rising sun and accompanying comets. The comets are portents of dire events. Note that they are accurately depicted, with their tails pointing away from the sun. Eighteenth-century woodcut. *The Houghton Library, Harvard University*

Plate 5. *left:* Armies waging war in the sky. This apparition is the result of a fata morgana, one of many kinds of mirages. *The Houghton Library, Harvard University*

Plate 6. *right:* A sundog, or mock sun, explained as a reflective phenomenon. This early eighteenth-century view was incorrect. Mock suns are caused by the refraction of sunlight by ice crystals in the upper atmosphere. *The Houghton Library, Harvard University*

Plate 7. A contemporary "dragon" threatening a high-rise apartment building in Cambridge, Massachusetts. The object is a rather spectacular kite, photographed with a Nikon camera and Perkin-Elmer 680-mm f12 compact telephoto lens. *Photo by Donald H. Menzel*

was the first appearance of a mock sun. The apparition then grew to a full-scale display of circles and crowns, as will be discussed further in Chapter 10.

Fully as important as the nature of the apparitions is the fright of the people at seeing something unknown: "strange signes in the skye" forecasting portentous events. Sometimes the predicted event, possibly a retribution, was long delayed, but eventually it would come, even after three years, so say some of the records.

Among the ancient volumes alluding to flying saucers the most outstanding is one by a Jesuit, Franz Reinzer, whose *Meteorologia Philosophico-politica* was published in Augsburg in 1709.[8]

In this remarkable book Reinzer discusses all kinds of "meteors" and gives instructions how to act in various circumstances so as to turn these strange apparitions to one's advantage. The basic theme of this meteorological philosophy seems to be that when someone loses a battle, someone else must win. Hence, if a sign appears in the sky, regard it as a bad omen for your enemies but a good omen for yourself and hold yourself in readiness to take advantage of the developing situation. Thus, in the meteorological sense, Reinzer is preaching the doctrine that "it's an ill wind that blows nobody good."

Apparently this book enjoyed wide popularity, for the original Latin was soon translated into German. It is, moreover, beautifully illustrated with wood engravings, some of which appear in this book (Plates 4, 5, 6, 8, and 14). From the fact that Reinzer rarely makes statements of scientific import or even gives detailed descriptions of the observed phenomena, one judges that his concern was much more with philosophy than with nature. To each phenomenon he gives a moral as well as a natural interpretation. Consequently, the book has no great scientific significance other than indicating the trend of the times.

Reinzer does, however, pose the question, "Do meteors come from natural causes or do they forebode something?" But he avoids any well-reasoned answer. He advises people in high office thus:

A statesman sees how the sky darkens and how cloudbursts descend amid great thunder and lightning. He sees how the moon and stars become eclipsed. He learns how dragons fly and how fountains of fire spurt their glowing sparks. Lightning shines terribly. Comets appear. Swords and lances flash in the clouds. The sky opens and pours forth a deluge.

When the statesman sees such strange happenings, should he not be afraid? No! These apparitions and events are only "love-kisses" of the sky. No matter what appears, everything is for the best, all to some useful purpose. Fear of thunderstorms or meteors denotes weakness.

Though Reinzer adopts this attitude for the statesman, he also supports the view that strange sights in the sky forebode terrible happenings on the earth.

The year 1462, for example, was outstanding for its strange celestial warnings. Someone saw "a monk who fought with a king and after a while was vanquished and fell down from the sky. This strange apparition occurred in the vicinity of the moon. And in the selfsame year, in small Poland, a crucifix and shifting sword, which caused great consternation among the people, whereupon terrible robberies and lootings and other evil things occurred in Poland."

Here we might note, parenthetically, that the crucifix and sword commonly accompany a display of mock suns.

"But," asks Reinzer, "if one sees in the air such sights which forebode the spilling of blood, how can the statesman avoid this bad luck that seems to beset the entire country?" Reinzer has a simple answer:

Arrows seen in advance can do little harm. Take heed of the warning in the sky. Terrifying and frightening as it seems, it really is not so terrible after all.

He cites an instance:

In 1478 in Switzerland, the populace saw a fight in the air, followed, two months later, with all sorts of crosses and fiery balls striking the earth and leaving behind them invisible signs to baffle the curious, as Lycosthenes tells in the Basle

Chronicles. In the very same year the Swiss had a great victory over the Prince of Milan, vanquishing 1,400 of their enemies and finding rich loot.

Bad as this omen was for the prince, it was a good one for the Swiss, primarily because it appeared in Switzerland. The author fails to point out the conflict in his logic concerning the lootings in Poland. But, after all, we should not expect people to show greater logic in 1700 than some people do today in the matter of flying saucers.

Reinzer describes other interesting phenomena, to most of which he adds political overtones. He mentions the double sun, for example, and explains it as a reflection, as shown in Plate 6. (We know now that mock suns are refractive, not reflective, phenomena.) Reinzer then notes that to fight a battle under such a sun takes greater courage than even Hercules possessed.

Reinzer talks about flying and falling stars and says that a real meteor is not something moving, but something burning like a flame consuming a thread, moving uniformly along the thread as it burns. He compares the formation of a shooting star to the progress of a flame along a trail of gunpowder. And again he addresses the statesman: "The more it rains, the greater the threats and menaces, the greater should be the love sparks which you yourself irradiate." He tries at the same time to transfer the natural characteristics of any atmospheric phenomenon to man and to endow the meteor with human or moral characteristics. His reasoning is hard to follow, but a few more references will clarify his meaning.

He says, "Fire observed on the head and clothing of people, on their hair, or on the fur of animals, is not a true fire, but imitation. Such an appearance is regarded by the ancient philosophers as a sign of great happiness, a sort of exhalation from the free spirit of animals."

Such "fire" we readily identify as St. Elmo's fire, an electrical discharge. Reinzer recognizes that these mock fires might come from within as well as from without. "They may be due," he says, "not only to natural emotion, or anger, or excessive drinking of wine, but also to fever and illness. Thus an observer seeing 'spots before his eyes' may view them as luminous spots against the sky."

But he does not explain how to distinguish between these fires from within and the lights that come from without, except to identify the latter as "flying dragons." These luminous apparitions that fly mysteriously through the night arise from

> condensations of sulphur emanation from the sky, because there are, of course, real dragons existing on the surface of the earth . . . Dragons are visible only when they are awake because when they are asleep the luminosity is withdrawn into themselves. The fiery dragon is a hot but not thick nebulosity. It shines either because of the dragon's motion or by the vomiting of its internal fires. These lights are more abundant in summer because their emanations rise more readily to the upper atmosphere.

These dragons, Reinzer notes, signify pestilence, disease, and an air saturated with infection:

> But the political figure should recognize that he stands too high to be infected. These infections are like darts, which the rabble tend to shoot at those in elevated stations. But neither dart nor poison can be effective. If you ignore the arrows, they will be no more harmful than a will-o'-the-wisp or a mirage. Nevertheless, the statesman should beware and take a lesson from this effect. It demonstrates that the honor you pursue can lead you astray.

The flying dragons probably comprise a number of overlapping phenomena as, indeed, UFOs do today. However, the flying saucer, if observed at all back in the fifteenth to seventeenth centuries, would undoubtedly have been classified as a flying dragon.

Reinzer asked a very interesting question:

> Can one make a flying dragon by artificial means? My answer is definitely 'Yes.' The recipe is simple. Take a long, thin strip of leather, steep it in brandy wherein [spirits of] camphor is dissolved, and then dust it with finely pulverized gunpowder. Now carry it to the top of a high cliff, ignite it,

and throw it into the air. And there you have the flying dragon!

And there, we might add, we also have probably the first set of instructions for the fabrication of a fake UFO. In Plate 7 we show a contemporary "dragon" flying over Cambridge, Massachusetts.

Another remarkable book, *Flowers of History,* by Roger de Wendover (d. 1236), chronicles the history of England from A.D. 447 to 1235. Its pages abound with dragons, miracles, heavenly signs, evil spirits, and visions. One man, "restored to life from the pains of purgatory" in 699, described his descent into the abyss:[4]

As we went on through the gloom, on a sudden there appeared before us great globes of murky flames, rising, as it were, out of a great pit, and falling back into the same . . . As these globes of fire continued, now to rise on high and then to sink to the bottom of the abyss, I observed that the wreaths of flame, as they ascended, were full of human spirits . . . glaring on me with their eyes of flame, and distressing me much with the stinking fire which they breathed from their mouth and nostrils.

And then the comets:

In the year 729 there appeared about the sun two terrible stars; one of which went before the rising sun, the other followed him when he set, as it were presaging destruction to the east and west; or at least, since one of them was the forerunner of the day, and the other of the night, signifying that mortals were threatened with calamities at both seasons. They extended their fiery tails to the northwest, and, appearing in the month of January, continued nearly fifteen days. At this time, a terrible visitation of pagans ravaged the Gauls and Spain with miserable slaughter; but they not long after received in that country the reward due to their wickedness.

In . . . 747 stars were seen to fall from heaven, insomuch

that all who saw them thought the end of the world was at
hand.

In . . . 776 fiery and fearful signs were seen in the
heavens after sunset; and serpents appeared in Sussex, as if
they had sprung out of the ground, to the great astonishment
of all.

In . . . 794 dreadful prodigies terrified the miserable English nation; for fearful thunderbolts and horrible fiery dragons
were seen passing through the air, foreboding a mighty famine and dreadful slaughter of the people.

If the reasoning of early observers seems obscure, unduly superstitious, and highly influenced by the imagination, we should not
feel too superior because of our modern viewpoint. We now present some reactions, considerably more modern—in fact, from the
year 1877—that speak for themselves. The first description is most
likely that of a mirage-type flying saucer; the second probably is of
a cloud. Neither has much significance except to show that many
people even in the late nineteenth century still attached religious
significance to "strange signes in the heavens," though they may
have been nothing more than peculiar cloud formations.

COLUMBUS, SOUTH CAROLINA. Last Sunday evening, just
before sunset, Miss Ida Davis and her two younger sisters
were strolling through the woods, when they were suddenly
startled by the appearance of a huge serpent moving through
the air above them. The serpent was distant only two or three
rods when they first beheld it, and was sailing through the air
with a speed equal to that of a hawk or buzzard, but without
any visible means of propulsion. Its movements in its flight
resembled those of a snake, and it looked a formidable object
as it wound its way along, being apparently about fifteen feet
in length. The girls stood amazed and followed it with their
eyes until it was lost to view in the distance. The flying serpent was also seen by a number of people in other parts of
the country early in the afternoon of the same day, and by
those it is represented as emitting a hissing noise which could

be distinctly heard . . . Religious revival meetings have been inaugurated . . . and many declare that the day of judgment is near at hand.[5]

To the editor of the *New York Sun*. Sir: On Tuesday afternoon of this week, a few minutes after 6 o'clock, I noticed from my window a very peculiar, solitary, vapory object in the heavens. Its position was about where the constellation of the dipper would be at that hour. Viz, due north, and 35 degrees above the horizon. In magnitude and contour it in a marked degree resembled a human form, head, body, and nether limbs, the body and limbs robed in shadowy drapery. The head, which was of brighter luminosity on the crown and forehead, had thick flowing hair, and the whole figure was extended horizontally with the head eastward and the front downward. But there was another feature quite as marked, and that was in appearances of wings projecting upward and backward from the shoulders . . . this last named feature gave the entirety the appearance of an angel.

Flying in mid-heaven, considered as a cloud, it was remarkable that it kept the same outline continuously (which is uncommon in those vapory objects). While I had it in view for a considerable time, it progressed swiftly toward the east. The luminosity of the shadowy angel was of a golden white, and presented a very beautiful appearance against the blue background of the sky. In addition to the startling outline of the object, the interest in it was greatly increased by its being at the time the only one visible in the whole northern heavens, except some low-lying black clouds on the horizon. I called the attention of several persons to it, one of whom discovered himself the resemblance I did.

Query—Was this a presage of a coming event? It reminded me of the words recorded in Mark 13:27: "Then shall he send his angels and gather his elect from the four winds"; and those in Daniel 9:21: "Gabriel . . . being caused to fly swiftly, touched me about the time of the evening oblation." William H. Smith, Brooklyn, September 19.[6]

One of the earliest extensive discussions of natural phenomena occurs in Pliny's *Natural History,* written about A.D. 75. Pliny divides comets—"shaggy stars with bloody locks"—into a number of classes, according to their appearance. One variety he calls *discei*—simply disks of amber color, emitting but few rays. He also describes "a white comet, with silver hair, so brilliant it can scarcely be looked at, exhibiting, as it were, the aspect of a Deity in human form."

Pliny also mentions a

celestial flame . . . of a bloody appearance (and nothing is more dreaded by mortals) which falls down upon the earth, such as was seen in the third year of the 103rd Olympiad, when King Philip was disturbing Greece. But my opinion is that these, like everything else, occur at stated natural periods, and are not produced, as some persons imagine, from a variety of causes, such as their fine genius may suggest. They have indeed been the precursors of great evils, but I conceive that the evils occurred, not because the prodigies took place, but that these took place because the evils were appointed to occur at that period. Their cause is obscure in consequence of their rarity, and therefore we are not as well acquainted with them as we are with the rising of the stars, which I have mentioned, and with eclipses and many other things.

Pliny also discusses halos, rainbows, and mock suns and moons:

Our ancestors have frequently seen three suns at the same time, as was the case in [various] consulships . . . And we have ourselves seen one during the reign of the late Emperor Claudius. We have no account transmitted to us of more than three having been seen at the same time.

He reports other mysterious happenings, as in the following account, which may refer to the aurora borealis: "A bright light has been seen proceeding from the heavens in the night time . . . so that there has been a kind of daylight in the night." He then refers to stars that "move about in various directions, but never without some cause, nor without violent winds proceeding from the same quarter."

Of interest is his reference to "Castor and Pollux." He does not refer here to the two stars we now call by these names, but to a meteorological phenomenon that calls to mind the "unknown lights of Japan," discussed in Chapter 5. Pliny says:

These stars occur both at sea and at land. I have seen, during the night-watches of the soldiers, a luminous appearance, like a star, attached to the javelins on the ramparts. They also settle on the yardarms and other parts of ships while sailing, producing a kind of vocal sound, like that of birds flitting about. When they occur singly they are mischievous, so as even to sink the vessels, and if they strike on the lower part of the keel, setting them on fire. When there are two of them they are considered auspicious, and are thought to predict a prosperous voyage, as it is said that they drive away that dreadful and terrific meteor named Helena. On this account their efficacy is ascribed to Castor and Pollux, and they are invoked as gods. They also occasionally shine round the heads of men in the evening, which is considered as predicting something very important. But there is great uncertainty respecting the cause of all these things, and they are concealed in the majesty of nature.

Some of these references clearly are to St. Elmo's fire—the electric sparking or discharge essentially similar to the sparks that jump from one's finger when one touches metal in cold, dry weather—for example the "star" settling in the rigging of vessels. The "terrific meteor named Helena" is in fact a single St. Elmo's light, while "Castor and Pollux" is the name given to a double St. Elmo's light. Plate 9 is an eighteenth-century depiction of both of these.

One of the earliest meteorological references we have found is in a book written in 1602 by William Fulke and printed in London in 1640. This volume is surprisingly scientific in outlook and refreshingly modern in its skeptical treatment of the more superstitious items. The book's modest title is *A Most pleasant Prospect. INTO THE GARDEN of Natural Contemplation, to behold the natural causes of all Kindes of Meteors. As well fiery and aerie, as waterie and Earthly: of which sort the blazing Starres, shooting Starres, Flames in the Aire, &c. Thunder, Lightning, Earthquakes, &c. Raine, Dew, Snow, Clouds, Springs, &c. Stones, Metals, and Earths: To the glory of God, and the profit of his Creatures.*

A few quotations are useful to show the beliefs of those times, with special reference to fiery meteors and lights in the sky:

> Vapor, as the philosopher saith, is a certain watery thing and yet is not water, so exhalation hath a certain earthly nature, yet it is not earth.‡

The author talks about vapors being drawn up by the sun, there to be released in the sky to fall as rain:

> Exhalations are as smokes that be hot and dry, which because they be thin and lighter than vapors, pass the lowest and middle region of the air and are carried up even to the highest region, where for the excessive heat by a nearness of the fire, they are kindled and cause many kinds of impressions. They are also sometimes viscous, that is to say clammy, by reason whereof they cleaving together and not being dispersed, are set on fire and appear sometimes like dragons, sometimes like goats, sometimes like candles and sometimes like spears.
>
> Fiery meteors . . . are therefore divided into flames and apparitions. Flames are they, which burn indeed, and are kindled with fire. According to their diverse fashions, they have diverse names: For they are called burning stubble, torches dancing or leaping goats, shooting or falling stars, firebrands, lamps, flying dragons, or fire drakes, painted pillars or broached steeples, or blazing stars called comets.

---

‡ Here also we use modern spelling.

Although the foregoing list contains much more than what we would today call flying saucers or UFOs, the highly descriptive names by which they are known are of great interest. The author continues:

> The time when these impressions do most appear is the night season for if they were caused in the daytime they could not be seen no more than the stars be seen, because the light of the Sun, which is much greater, dimmeth the brightness of them being lesser.

Fulke describes the "flying dragons or, as Englishmen call them, Fire Drakes," as vapors ignited between two clouds. He continues:

> This dragon . . . flieth along in the air. Sometimes it turneth to and fro if it meet with a cold cloud to beat it back, to the great terror of them that behold it. Some call it a Fire Drake; others say it is the devil himself, and so make report.
>
> More than 47 years ago on May Day, when many young folk went abroad early in the morning, I remember by five of the clock in the forenoon, there was news come to London that the Devil, the same morning, was seen flying over the Thames: afterward came word that he lighted at Stratford, and there was taken and set in the Stocks, and that though he would fain have dissembled the matter by turning himself into the likeness of a man, yet was he known well enough by his cloven foot.
>
> I knew some then living that went to see him and returning affirmed that he was indeed seen flying in the air, but was not taken prisoner. I remember also that some wished he had been shot at with guns or shafts as he flew over the Thames. Thus do ignorant men judge of these things that they know not. As for the Devil, I suppose it was a flying Dragon whereof we speak, very fearful to look upon as though he had life, because he moveth, whereas he is nothing else but clouds of smoke. So mighty is God that he can fear his enemies with these and with such like operations, whereof some examples may be found in Holy Scriptures.

This is really an astonishing record of a flying saucer seen before 1600. The report, in addition to showing a saucer debunker in action, illustrates the tendency of men throughout the ages to endow such apparitions with life of some sort, be it visitors from interplanetary space or the Devil himself.

The author discusses other strange lights:

It seemeth to go before men, or to follow them, leading them out of their way unto waters and other dangerous places. It is also very often seen in the night of them that sail the sea. Sometimes it will cleave to the mast of the ship or other high part till it go out or else be quenched in the water . . . On land [this] is called ignis fatuus, "foolish fire" that hurteth not but only feareth fools. That which is seen on the sea, if it be but one, is named Helena, if it be two, it is called Castor and Pollux.

The first of these lights, the *ignis fatuus,* is the will-o'-the-wisp, or friar's lantern, commonly seen in marshy areas. This phenomenon has been the source of innumerable UFO reports. The second light is the same St. Elmo's fire as described by Pliny. The author then distinguishes between the truly fiery meteors and "apparitions":

An apparition is an exhalation in the lowest or highest region of the air, not thoroughly burning, but by refraction of light either of the Sun or the Moon, seemeth as though it burned.

Here, indeed, is an outstandingly clear and altogether modern description of many kinds of saucer phenomena, as we shall see in a later chapter. The author then discusses "fired whirlwinds." Sometimes, he writes,

a whirlwind is set on fire within the cloud, then breaking forth flyeth round like a great cart-wheel terrible to behold, burning and overthrowing all dry things that it cometh near as houses, woods, corn, grass.

The author then discusses mock suns, or sundogs:

It is strange and marvelous to behold the likelihood, which Alexander the Great, sending word to Darius, said to be impossible, that two suns should rule the world. But often times men have seen, as they thought, in the firmament, not only two suns but oftener three suns, and many more in number though not so often appearing. These, how wonderful so ever they appear, proceed of a natural cause, which we will endeavor to express. They are nothing else but idols or images of the Sun, represented in a equal, smooth and watery cloud placed on the side of the Sun and sometimes on both sides, into which the beams are being received, as in a glass. They express the likeness of fashion and light that is in the sun, appearing as though there were many suns, whereas indeed there is but one, and all the rest are images.

They are most often seen in the morning and evening, about the rising or going down of the sun. Seldom at noontime, or about the midst of the day, because the heat will soon dissolve them. Yet have there been some seen, which began in the morning and continued all day long, into the evening. Sometimes there appear many little suns, like unto little stars, which are caused after the same sort as we do see a man's face to be expelled in the pieces of a broken glass.

For a supernatural significance, they have oftentimes been noted to have portended the contention of princes for kingdoms.

A good example of a reasonable man attacking some of the superstitions of his time. Fulke goes on, then, to point out that the moon also displays mock moons, and he raises the significant question whether stars might also have similar images about them. He concludes that indeed it is possible, although he decides that the light will be much weakened by reflection. Finally, he further explicates his philosophical views about apparitions and signs in the sky:

We will close this book with a brief declaration of the nat-

ural causes of many things that are seen in the air, very wonderful and strange to behold, to the great admiration of all
men, not without the singular providence of God, to forewarn
us of many dangers that hang over us in these most perilous
times.

The apparitions of which, as it is most wonderful, so the
searching of the cause to us is most hard and difficult, a great
deal the rather because no man hath hitherto enterprised (to
my knowledge) to take out any cause of them; but all men
have taken them as immediate miracles, without any natural
means or cause to procure them.

And I truly do acknowledge that they are sent of God as
wonderful Signs to declare his power, and move us to amend-
ment of life, indeed miraculous, but not yet so, that they want
a natural cause. For if they be well weighed and considered
. . . they differ little from such miracles as are recorded in
the Scripture and admitted of divines. So that, as I abhor the
opinion of epicures, to think that such things could come by
chance, but rather by the determined purpose of God's providence; so I consent not with them that suppose when anything is derived from any natural cause, God the best cause
of all things is excluded.

Some of these wonderful apparitions consist of circles and
rainbows, of diverse fashions and placings, as one within another, the edge of one touching another, some with the ends
upward, some downward, some aside, and some across, but
all for the most part in uniform order—pleasant to behold.
Such a like apparition is made with the sun or sun's images
formed into these circles.

Another sort no less often beheld within these few years—
but a great deal more strange and wonderful to look upon—
are the sights of armies fighting in the air, of castles, cities,
and towns, with whole countries, having in them hills, valleys,
rivers, woods, and also beasts, men, and fowls, wonders of
which there are no such kind on earth and finally all manner
of things and actions that are on the Earth, as burials, processions, combats, men, women, children, horses, armies of certain noblemen, weapons . . . sometimes stars. Angels as they

are painted with the image of Christ crucified, the besieging of castles and towns . . . etc.

All these wonderful apparitions may be caused in two manner of ways: the ones artificially and the others naturally. Artificially, by certain glasses and instruments made according to a secret part of that knowledge which is called Catoptric [the science of mirrors and reflections] . . . but for the most part naturally, when the disposition of the air hath been such that it had received the image of many things placed and done on Earth.

CHAPTER 5

THE UNKNOWN LIGHTS OF JAPAN

THERE ARE MORE THINGS IN HEAVEN AND
 EARTH, HORATIO,
THAN ARE DREAMT OF IN YOUR PHILOSOPHY.

Shakespeare[1]

Our search of ufological literature has uncovered a most startling and descriptive article in the May 25, 1893, issue of a prestigious British scientific magazine which contains data important to the understanding of the flying-saucer problem.[2] The article tells of multiple lights that followed a ship throughout the night. The story is interesting enough to quote in its entirety. The phenomenon occurred in February 1893, when the oceans were extremely cold, although somewhat warmer breezes might have been blowing from the land.

During a recent wintry cruise in H.M.S. *Caroline* in the North China Sea, a curious phenomenon was seen which may be of interest to your readers. The ship was on passage between Shanghai and the western entrance of the famous inland sea of Japan. On 24th February, at 10 P.M., when in latitude 32°58′ N., longitude 126°33′ E., which, on reference to the map, will be seen to be sixteen to seventeen miles south of Quelpart island (south of the Korean peninsula), some unusual lights were reported by the officer of the watch between the ship and Mount Auckland, a mountain 6,000 feet high. It was a windy, cold, moonlight night. My first impression was that they were either some fires on shore, apparently higher from the horizon than a ship's masthead, or some junk's "flare up" lights raised by mirage.

To the naked eye they appeared sometimes as a mass; at others spread out in an irregular line, and, being globular in form, they resembled Chinese lanterns festooned between the masts of a lofty vessel. They bore north (magnetic) and remained on that bearing until lost sight of about midnight. As the ship was passing the land to the eastward at the rate of seven knots, it soon became obvious that the lights were not on the land, though observed with the mountain behind them.

On the following night, February 25th, about the same time, the ship, having cleared Port Hamilton, was steering east, on the parallel of 34°, when these curious lights were again observed on the same bearing, at an altitude of 3° or 4° above the horizon. It was a clear, still, moonlight night, and cold. On this occasion there was no land in sight on a north bearing when the lights were first observed, but soon afterwards a small islet was passed, which for the time eclipsed the lights.

As the ship steamed on at a rate of seven knots, the lights maintained a constant bearing (magnetic) of N. 2° W., as if carried by some vessel travelling in the same direction and at the same speed. The globes of fire altered in their formation as on the previous night, now in a massed group, with an outlying light away to the right, then the isolated one would disappear, and the others would take the form of crescent or diamond, or hang festoon-fashion in a curved line. A clear reflection or glare could be seen on the horizon beneath the lights. Through a telescope the globes appeared to be of a reddish colour, and to emit a thin smoke.

I watched them for several hours, and could distinguish no perceptible alteration in their bearing or altitude, the changes occurring only in their relative formation, but each light maintained its oval, globular form.

They remained in sight from 10 P.M. until daylight. When lost sight of, the bearing was one or two points to the westward of north. At daylight, land 1,300 feet high was seen to the north and north-northwest, distant fifty miles, the mirage being extraordinary.

Thus, these lights were seen first on longitude 126°33′ E., and last on longitude 128°29′ E. At first the land was behind them, but during the greater part of the distance run it was forty-five or fifty miles away to the north; and the bearing of the lights for at least three-fourths of the distance did not change.

On arrival at Kobe I read in a daily paper that the "Unknown Lights of Japan" had, as was customary at this season of the year when the weather is very cold, stormy, and clear, been observed by fishermen in the Shimbara Gulf and Japanese waters. The article went on to say that these lights were referred to in native school-books, and attributed to electrical phenomena. On mentioning the matter, however, to the leading Europeans in Yokohama and Tokio, they appeared to have no knowledge of the matter.

Captain Castle of H.M.S. *Leander,* informed me that, not long ago, the officers of his ship saw lights in the same locality which they thought at first were caused by a ship on fire. The course of the vessel was altered at once with a view of rendering assistance, but finding that the lights increased their altitude as he approached, he attributed them to some volcanic disturbance, and being pressed for time, resumed his course.

The background of high land seen on the first night dispels all idea of these extraordinary lights being due to a distant volcano. The uniformity of the bearing renders the theory of their being fires on the shore most improbable. I am inclined to the belief that they were something in the nature of St. Elmo's fires. It is probable that there are travellers among the readers of your interesting journal who have seen or heard of this phenomenon and will be able to describe its origin and the atmospheric conditions necessary for its appearance.

The observed behavior of many UFOs, but especially of "foo balls," or "foo fighters"—which term we use to designate the docile variety of lights that tend to pace aircraft—suggests very strongly the lights that followed H.M.S. *Caroline*. This behavior, in turn, suggests something that many people will have noticed: while riding on a train or in an automobile at night, looking at the moon, one easily forms the impression that the moon is following, or chasing, one. The landscape between you and the distant horizon swishes past at a rate that blurs your sense of perception. The nearby shrubbery and telephone poles flash by before you have a chance to see in detail what they actually are. But if there is a moon, it seems to follow along, pacing you, while forests, rivers, and bridges rush past. Bright stars or planets can produce a similar illusion.

Children are more sensitive to this phenomenon than grown-ups, because the average adult has become used to it. If you put a toy balloon out of the window of the car and hold it by a string, the moon and the balloon will have much in common. They keep pace with each other while the intermediate country flashes past. If the balloon is small enough, you can scarcely distinguish it from the moon. Your sense of perspective may help if the balloon is near, but if the balloon is twenty or thirty feet away you will not be able to tell, at least from a single point of observation, which of the two objects is the nearer, unless you are able to identify one or the other from surface markings or other characteristics.

The point is simply this: the moon seems to follow you at the same rate that a balloon or any other object would if attached to your moving vehicle, be it automobile, train, plane, or even yourself.

Suppose, for example, that instead of putting a balloon out the window you merely set a mirror there, so placed to catch and reflect the moonlight. You can reach out and touch the mirror. You have a sense as to the position of the image. As we show later, the sensation of distance where mirrors are concerned is entirely illusory. But let us say that you can see both the moon and its reflected image. Unless you know the mirror is there, you will not be able to tell which is the moon and which is the reflected image; they behave similarly. Indeed, if you are driving a car and if the image of the moon comes from a window, a mirror, or a fender, the image will possess many characteristics that the moon itself does. You could readily convince yourself that the moon is riding along on one of the fenders of your car.

Some would say that this phenomenon is an optical illusion. We do not class it as such because there is really no simple way of telling which object is real and which is the mirror image. We have, of course, assumed that the two are imaged perfectly. If you can have an illusion that the image is near, you can certainly have the impression that the moon itself is close—if you do not immediately recognize it as the moon.

One of the advisers to the U. S. Air Force told DHM this story: Our pilots in Korea have occasionally seen, riding along the wings of their planes, the same sort of foo balls that Allied pilots observed over Germany and Japan during the last stages of World War II. A scientific mission sent to Korea by the U. S. Air Force specially to study the foo balls and find out what they were spent many hours in the air, waiting in vain for one of the mysterious lights to put in its appearance. After many nights of fruitless search, one of the crew members suddenly called out, "Foo ball at three o'clock low!" The science mission dashed to the window and looked out. Sure enough, there was a yellow-orange ball, hanging just below the wing tip. They called for a turn to get a better look —and saw at once that the foo ball was only the rising moon. This expedition returned to the United States without having seen a single foo ball. Was this seeming avoidance of the investigating mission deliberate on the part of the foo balls? Were the mysterious objects apprised of the expedition's arrival so that they could adopt the tactic of nonappearance as the best defense, in order to retain their secrets?

We do not mean to imply that any appreciable number of foo balls are misinterpreted apparitions of the moon, though some of them, no doubt, can be attributed to reflections of the moon on the aircraft's wing. Mirages of bright stars and planets, as well as of distant lights, can produce similar effects; see Chapter 10.

The time of occurrence of these objects carries another implication. Over both Germany and Japan the foo balls appeared only during the last stages of World War II. Many of the planes partici-

pating in bomber missions had been by then partially damaged and
were considerably patched. Some of these battle scars were by no
means as aerodynamically perfect as the original wings had been.
Little eddies could form around the imperfections, forming whirlwinds that were ready to partially reflect some of the light falling
upon them, whether from the moon or from the plane's own illumination.

When air is cold and supersaturated, a sudden increase of pressure can cause fog or ice crystals to form. A cluster of these tiny
suspended particles will reflect enough light to produce the appearance of a luminous globule.

In other cases, where fine ice crystals or tiny snowflakes are already present, each individual particle is ready to act as a mirror,
if we look at it from the right direction. These tiny particles may
be invisible unless viewed by special means, because they all tend
to assume horizontal positions as they slowly fall in a quiet atmosphere. Thus, if the moon were halfway between horizon and zenith, we should see its reflection only if we were to face the moon
and look at a point 45° below the horizon, as if we were looking
downward into a sheet of water.

But if a plane, ship, car, or any moving object were to disturb
the tiny mirrors, the effect would be something like breaking a true
mirror into thousands of little pieces. The true reflection would be
tremendously reduced in brilliance, but in all directions a fraction
of the original luminosity would appear. In this manner many foo
balls originate—reflections in myriads of tiny mirrors of ice crystals
or water droplets!

As long as one moves along steadily forward, the reflected light
from a foo ball follows automatically. However, for every turn of,
say, 10°, the reflected image will appear at twice this angle, or 20°.
An angle of 45° produces a deflection of 90°, and so on. Hence, if
a pilot sees a foo ball and tries to run away from it, the reflection
will veer at twice the rate that he turns his plane.

This may easily be demonstrated. Simply hold a hand mirror
firmly against your forehead. Stand in front of a source of light
bright enough for its image in the mirror to reflect clearly on the
wall in front of you. Shift your position until the light is reflected
by the mirror directly back to the source. Now, continuing to hold

the mirror in place against your forehead, slowly turn your head to one side or the other and you will find that the reflection on the wall moves twice as fast as your head. It is this property of an image, as compared with the source of light, that has confused many pilots with respect to foo balls and given rise to the frequent reports that they execute evasive action.

Let us now turn again to the story of H.M.S. *Caroline* and note several specific points. The Nautical Almanac shows that moonlight did not persist through the night. The appearance of these lights in the direction of magnetic north suggests the aurora borealis. If the source of light was the aurora, it was probably a fairly distant one whose full brilliance was not visible from the ship even though "a clear reflection or glare could be seen on the horizon beneath the lights." This light, reflected by a thin layer of frost crystals, could have produced the "unknown lights."

The persistence of the mirage into the morning strongly suggests that the low-lying illumination of the bright horizon had been raised into the sky. Indeed, the reported altitude of 3° or 4° is large, but by no means exceptional. The disappearance of the lights when the island intervened is quite understandable; the nearby land temporarily interrupted the mirage, through production of convection currents in the atmosphere, as well as by occultation of the distant source of illumination.

The observer's description seems to rule out the suggestion made by the observer himself, namely, that the lights represented some sort of electrical disturbance, such as St. Elmo's fire.

In addition to foo balls associated with planes and ships, we have found references to similar apparitions seen from trains. For example, in 1898 a railroad postal clerk reported that he and an associate had seen a light, dull rose in color, that followed after the train.[3] The speed of the light was variable as it moved along behind the train, sometimes losing and sometimes gaining. The night was dark, the clerk said, and a heavy rain was falling. Such conditions are, of course, not conducive to the formation of an ordinary mirage. Raindrops, however, like the eyes of animals, *appear* self-luminous in the dark and send back a considerable amount of light in the direction from which the light originally came.

This experience of the clerk suggests yet another source of foo balls. When one travels in either rain or fog, a light reflected directly backward will give a surprising appearance, if one changes course, of seeming to follow after. Anyone witnessing this phenomenon might well gain the impression that someone or something out there in the dark was up to something.

We have found a reference to an incident in Canada in 1952 in which an old woman reported that as she walked along a country lane at night, a ball of fire followed her, stopping whenever she stopped and moving on as she moved.[4] Although we lack the data for complete evaluation of this event, it clearly belongs in the fooball category.

Finally, we mention an altogether different kind of luminous flying object—the "luminous owls of Norfolk." These apparitions, seen in the county of Norfolk, England, were barn owls whose feathers carried the powder of the luminous fungus *Armillaria mellea*. This widely distributed fungus infests dead trees and old stumps, where owls may roost during the day. Birds or bats so infested shine brightly in the dark. These owls were seen in the Norfolk district in 1866, 1897, 1907, 1908, 1909, 1921, and 1922. One of the owls, shot by a gamekeeper in 1897, continued to shine for several hours after its death.

THE FLYING-SAUCER SCARE
OF 1897

Boys, bicycles, and mischief are
responsible for many pranks . . .

The New York Times, April 15, 1897

The flying-saucer epidemics of 1947 and of later years were by no means the first times that strange apparitions in the sky frightened the American public. On November 22, 1896 inhabitants of Oakland, California, sighted an unfamiliar object in the sky when passengers on a streetcar saw something flying above them, a sort of winged cigar, projecting a stream of brilliant light from its head.

To understand the reactions of the Californians, we must try to recapture the mental attitude that existed at the time. Thomas Edison had made incandescent lighting practical a few years before, and the arc light was well-known to all. Two daring manufacturers had just started to build "horseless carriages." There were no such things as airplanes or airships. Some people had practiced ballooning for years, and the hot air or gas bags of that time were either spherical or pear-shaped. People had begun to talk about "steerable" or "dirigible" balloons. Contemporary patents were already picturing the rigid, cigar-shaped objects that later came into practical use as the "Zeppelins" (named for Count Ferdinand von Zeppelin, their German inventor) of World War I.

No wonder, then, that the people of Oakland were excited. The cigar-shaped body and the presence of the searchlight clearly suggested that the object was an airship of some sort.

The Oakland *Tribune* reported that "when first seen, the object seemed to be floating over San Leandro. It moved rapidly, going at least 20 miles an hour. It shot across the sky in the Northwest, then turned quickly and disappeared in the direction of Haywards." The early story emphasized the number and reliability of independent witnesses.

The excitement that gripped Oakland strongly resembled the one that swept the world after the saucer stories of 1947 appeared. Hundreds of people reported that they knew someone who had talked with somebody else who could point out the person who had built the airship. To complicate matters, the *Tribune* stated several days later that a certain reliable person named Carlson would vouch for the fact that the inventor had actually flown such a craft over the city. The *Tribune,* still not supporting the story unreservedly, warned: "This unknown Darius Green is wrapped in mystery and when he alights from his aerial flight evidently folds up his invention, tucks it under his vest and quietly goes up the back stairs so as not to have to answer embarrassing questions from his family . . . as to where he was at."

As the story spread, residents of neighboring towns also reported the appearance of the object during the early evening. Although some maintained that the mysterious thing was a star, others rejected the theory because of "its distinctly rocking motion, which was like the motion made by a kite." (This description strongly resembles many given by observers of modern UFOs.)

The *Tribune* reported: "The uncertainty of the thing has been causing much speculation and now the streets are lined with an inquisitive throng, all gazing heavenward." Charles Burckhalter, an astronomer from the Chabot Observatory, maintained that the people were seeing Mars and Venus in the evening sky. "Venus is as brilliant as an arc light and does move slowly through the heavens," he said. "The theories in regard to the airship are pure imagination, and if there were any such object in the heavens we would certainly know of it."

But the "airship" continued to fly, and on the night of November 30 many people saw it between the hours of 8:00 and 8:30. They described it as "moving in the teeth of the wind," an important point, because most balloons of the day were freely drifting, and not steerable. One of the observers reported: "No light was visible, merely the weirdly peculiar body silhouetted against the clear sky." He further stated that the object seemed at least 100 feet long, floating at an altitude of 1,500 feet. It had a triangular tail. Suddenly, he said, the object rapidly accelerated and moved at tremendous speed toward San Lorenzo, where it turned again toward San Francisco, and passed over Oakland a second time.

That report was by Case Gilson, a well-known amateur astronomer of that region. He ruled out planets and meteors and was quite sure that the object he saw was not a kite.

Fifty years later the Oakland *Tribune,* commenting on the event in its issue of May 11, 1952, stated: "No one seems to have seen the mysterious craft after that. Balloon, airplane—or flying saucer? You pays your money and you takes your choice."

But the *Tribune* was wrong. Others had seen the "aircraft," and in 1897, though the incident may have died down in Oakland, a wave of airship hysteria spread over the entire United States. In some places it caused a religious sensation, many of the superstitious believing that the end of the world was at hand. The ship, so it seemed, was gradually moving east. It appeared over Salt Lake City, Denver, Omaha, Kansas City (Kansas), and Chicago.

New York *Herald,* Sunday, April 11, 1897

THAT AIRSHIP NOW AT CHICAGO

CITY EXCITED BY THE APPEARANCE OF RAPIDLY MOVING LIGHTS IN THE SKY

ASTRONOMERS INCREDULOUS
THEY BELIEVE THAT THE LIGHTS PROCEED
FROM A STAR IN THE CONSTELLATION OF ORION

IS A DIRIGIBLE BALLOON
SO SAYS SECRETARY MAX HARMAR
OF THE CHICAGO AERONAUTICAL ASSOCIATION

(By telegraph to the *Herald*) CHICAGO, ILL., APRIL 10, 1897.
For weeks despatches have been coming in from various points

between here and California regarding an airship. At first no attention was paid to them, but they became so frequent that the public began to be interested. Then the airship was seen at Omaha, and proceeding eastward, was seen last night in Chicago. The general public believes in the airship theory, while the astronomers say it must be a star.

Late last night Professor Hough, of the Northwestern University, turned the great Dearborn telescope toward the west, and took a look at the strange visitor. The citizens who saw it said the ship displayed red and green lights, just as a vessel on the ocean would do, but the professor, after a long look, said, "Why, it must be Alpha Orionis."

"Can you read that name on the airship?" he was eagerly asked.

"Why, no," replied the Professor with a laugh, "Alpha Orionis is a star of the first magnitude, and is in the constellation Orion."

"But what about the red and green lights so many people have seen?" he was asked.

"That," said the veteran astronomer, "must be the effect of the atmosphere, which apparently causes the star to change colour." Then he added, "I think Alpha Orionis is the only airship the people have seen, but if there is another it has disappeared long ere this."

Until two o'clock this morning thousands of amazed spectators declared that the lights seen to the northwest were those of an airship or some other floating object miles above the earth, and viewed the apparent phenomenon with the deepest interest, tinged with a certain degree of awe, wonder and uneasiness.

Men of unquestioned veracity declared the moving body was an airship. Some declare they saw two cigar-shaped objects and great wings. All agree with regard to the lights. The first was white, and wonderfully resembled a searchlight. It switched from side to side, as though attempting to light up the darkness on all sides. After this came a green light, then a smaller white light, and finally a red light. Professor S. W. Burnham, a well-known astronomer, agrees with the explanation given by Professor Hough. He said: "Alpha Orionis is a star of the first magnitude. Its position in the northern sky, its parti-coloured lights, make a striking object. Shining through misty clouds and aided by refraction it would give the appearance of a rapidly moving body. One's imagination could easily give strange form to it. This star, too, looks to be but a comparatively short distance above the earth."

CHICAGO IS EXCITED

STAR OR AIRSHIP, CHICAGO AND HER SUBURBS ARE INTENSELY INTERESTED

AND THE SUBJECT IS ALMOST THE SOLE TOPIC OF CONVERSATION

That there was "something" in the northern sky there is no doubt, and it was a very curious "something." The "something" seemed to come from the mists of the lake, and, moving westward, was in plain sight of Chicago and Evanston.

The airship or star seems to be most irregular in its movements. At Kankakee, where the State Insane Asylum is located, it was observed, going in a northeasterly direction at 9 o'clock last night. It was apparently one thousand feet above the earth, and moving very rapidly. The headlight appeared as large as an ordinary electric arc light. At one time the vessel rose very rapidly, and afterwards seemed to drop a long distance. In addition to the headlight, spectators claimed to have noticed smaller lights behind, indicating that the object was of considerable size. It was apparently headed toward Chicago, and traveled very rapidly.

SAYS IT IS A REAL AIRSHIP

There is a general disposition to laugh at the theory that the object seen by so many thousands of people is really an airship, but attorney Max L. Harmar, secretary of the Chicago Aeronautical Association, does not smile at it. To him the fact of a real airship moving across the country was not a surprise.

"There is only one thing that surprises me in the presence of the airship," said Mr. Harmar. "We expected it on Sunday, and it is hard for me to believe the vessel arrived here so soon, unless the conditions were exceptionally favorable. Yes, I have a good idea concerning all this mystery. I know one of the men who is in the airship. The car contains three persons, but the exaggerated stories concerning the ship are laughable.

"Spectators have announced it as their belief that the ship was composed of steel. This was a mistake. It is paper. There is the customary inflated gas reservoir, but the inventors have discovered the secret of practical propulsion. They can steer the vessel in any direction they desire. Word was received here several weeks ago that the party had started from San Francisco, and that the ship would stop here for the purpose of registration. The end of the trip is to be at Washington City, where the ship will be brought to earth and given up to inspection. President Octave Chanute, of the Chicago Society, has full information concerning the ship. He, with a number of other wealthy men interested in the problem, has furnished the money for the venture. Mr. Chanute is in California at the present time. I would not care to furnish details as to the experiment, as it would be unfair to the inventor and would take off the edge of public interest."

We assume that the remarks of Attorney Harmar were intended irony. He said that the ship was not steel, but of "paper" and that it possessed "the customary inflated gas reservoir." Perhaps, like many of his contemporaries, he was implying that the ship was largely created from imagination—imagination fed by the newspaper stories and supported by hot air. As in later saucer flaps, hoaxers and jokers, ready to capitalize on the event, quickly entered the picture.

New York *Herald,* Monday, April 12, 1897

SNAPSHOTS OF THE AIRSHIP

TWO EXCELLENT PHOTOGRAPHS MADE WHILE THE CRAFT WAS FLYING THROUGH SPACE PRODUCED AS EVIDENCE OBTAINED BY A NEWS DEALER IN ROGERS PARK, NEAR CHICAGO, IN THE EARLY MORNING ITS INVENTOR HEARD FROM WRITES TO OFFICERS OF THE TRANS-MISSISSIPPI EXPOSITION FOR SPACE TO EXHIBIT IT

(By telegraph to the *Herald.*) CHICAGO, ILL., APRIL 11, 1897. The fact that the much talked of airship is a reality, and not a phantom, is apparently attested by two remarkable photographs, now in this city, which it is alleged were taken while the machine was in motion. Walter McCann, of Rogers Park, a town 28 miles north of here, took two snapshots with his camera at what he believed to be the airship, and secured two excellent negatives. It was early in the morning, and the vessel was scudding along at a rapid rate, but the pictures he secured are very good ones.

The work of Mr. McCann dispels any thought of an optical illusion. Three witnesses assert that they saw him take the photographs, which were obtained this morning about half-past five o'clock.

Mr. McCann is a news dealer in Rogers Park. It is his custom to get up very early in the morning, particularly on Sunday, to deliver the Chicago papers. In his store he has a small camera, the property of his young son. When McCann sighted the strange object in the sky, early this morning, he at once came to the conclusion it was the airship of which there had been so much talk and which had set so many people to thinking. He rushed into his store, seized the camera and secured a good picture of it. G. A. Oversocker, who was also looking at the ship, suggested a second snapshot, and the result was a much better negative.

PICTURES ARE GENUINE

The pictures developed from these plates were tested by acids tonight, and were pronounced genuine productions of an object in the air, and not the creations of a studio. William Hoodlees and E. L. Osborne, the latter an operator in the telegraph office of the Chicago and Northwestern Railway Co., in Rogers Park, saw McCann and Oversocker at the hour named, and asserted they not only witnessed the photographing of the object in the air, but saw the vessel.

The craft, according to the statement of all these witnesses, is an invention without wings or sails. All agree that the outlines of a man could also be seen. Through a glass they were of the opinion that they could see the man in motion, as though he were engaged in steering the vessel. The upper part of the ship apparently consisted of a cigar-shaped silken bag, attached to which was a lightly constructed framework. In the center of the framework the man was located. A propeller or rudder was attached to the framework, the rudder being shaped like the hull of a ship, except that it was sharp at both ends. Apparently the framework was composed of white metal.

Mr. McCann told his story tonight at his store on Greenleaf Ave. "I had read for some days about the airship," said he, "but I thought it must be a fake. This morning about half-past five o'clock I was attending to my usual duties when I saw a strange looking object in the sky coming from the south. It looked like a big cigar. It came nearer, and then I saw it was certainly not a balloon. Then I thought of the airship and ran for the camera. At the corner of Greenleaf Avenue and Market Street I took the first shot, while a few minutes later I took another further up from the railroad tracks. It was 500 or 600 feet from me when I photographed it, and I saw it plainly. It went north a distance and then gradually turned east."

ITS INVENTOR HEARD FROM

A despatch from Omaha tonight says that the mystery surrounding the much talked about airship promises to be cleared within a few days, through the medium of the Capitol Trans-Mississippi Exposition or a hoax is to be perpetrated on the exposition authorities.

Secretary Wakefield received a letter yesterday from Omaha and signed "A. C. Clinton." It was as follows. "To the Exposition Authorities:—My identity up to date has been unknown, but I will come to the front now, i.e., if you guarantee me 87,000 square feet of space. I am the famous airship constructor, and I will guarantee you positively of this fact within a week.

"The airship is my own invention, and as I am an Omaha man, I wish it to be heralded as an Omaha invention. It will carry safely 20 people to a height of from 10 to 20 thousand feet. I truly believe I have the greatest invention and discovery ever made. Will see you April 17 at the headquarters."

The exposition authorities will await his appearance with interest.

The first airship seen—one that seemed actually to fly and appeared to be under control of its pilot—within the last six months was near Sacramento, California. About 1 o'clock, on the morning of Monday November 16, [1896,] several persons said that they saw the object passing rapidly over that city. Several asserted they saw a cigar-shaped flying machine, and heard voices from it. According to George D. Collins, a lawyer of San Francisco, the object was a real airship. In an interview Mr. Collins said:—

"The reports about the airship are perfectly true. It was my client's airship. During the past 5 years he has spent at least $100,000 on his work. He has not secured his patent, but the application is now on file in Washington. I saw the machine at the inventor's invitation. It is made of metal, is about 150 ft. in length and is built to carry 15 persons. There was no motive power, so far as I could see; certainly no steam.

"The machine was built on the meroplane system and has two canvas wings 8 ft. wide and a rudder shaped like a bird's tail. The inventor climbed into the machine, and after he had moved the mechanism for a moment I saw the thing rise from the earth very gently. The wings flapped slowly as it arose and then a little faster as it began to move against the wind. The machine was under his full control all the time. When it reached a height of 90 ft. the inventor shouted to me that he was going to make a series of circles and then descend. He immediately did so, beginning by making a circle of about 100 yds. in diameter and then gradually narrowing until the machine got within 30 ft. of the ground. It then fell straight down and touched the ground as lightly as a falling leaf.

WENT ON LONG TRIPS

"In this recent trip the ship started from Oroville, in Butte County, and flew 60 miles in a straight line, directly over Sacramento. After running up and down over the capitol, my friend came right on a distance of 70 miles or more, and landed on a spot on the Oakland side of the Bay, where the machine now is. It is constructed on an absolutely new theory of flight."

Then came John A. Hernon, an electrician of San Jose, Cal., who in an interview on December 1, said he had been to Honolulu and back in an airship, but refused to say anything as to the inventor or the model of his machine. Hernon is the patentee of a platinum speaking apparatus. He said that six days previously he went to San Francisco to see the inventor, and went on horseback to a point on Sandy Beach, where he found the airship.

"We got on board," said he, "and rose very high, the height being measured by a meter on board ship. We traveled westward, and before daybreak we saw the lights, which the inventor said were Honolulu lights. We then turned toward the eastward again, and at dusk on Saturday evening we finished our two days' cruise and landed near our starting point. The airship rose by means of two propellers. The movement was noiseless and swift. The motive power is neither steam nor electricity."

Following this, on January 2 [1897] a despatch came from San Francisco saying that an airship on a large scale would soon be sent up from there. An order was placed with a Pittsburgh production company for a large amount of aluminum to be used in the construction of the ship, and work had been commenced. This statement was made by authority of Dr. C. A. Smith, president of the Atlantic and Pacific Aerial Navigation Co. A company was formed and 86,400 shares were authorized by the incorporators at a par value of $1.00 per share.

MYSTERIOUS CRAFT IN OMAHA

The identity of the South Omaha "thing," as it is generally called, remained a mystery, and after many attempts to gather some information regarding it, these efforts were abandoned. Then, on the night of March 29 the object was again observed, this time by the majority of the residents of Omaha. It was in the shape of a big bright light, too big for a balloon, and glowed steadily. It sailed over the city to the northwest and there disappeared. It moved very slowly and seemed to be quite near the earth. A despatch from Denver the following night said the strange visitor had been seen there, but only for a few moments.

Once more the stranger disappeared and remained out of sight until the present month, when a telephone message was received from Evanston, 11 miles north of Chicago, saying that about 20 minutes to 9 o'clock that night a mysterious light, evidently that of an airship, was seen passing rapidly over the city, going west-northwest. The light was more like an electric light than anything else. It seemed to be about a quarter of a mile above the earth.

Despatches began pouring in to Chicago from various points in Indiana, Illinois, Missouri, Iowa and Wisconsin on the night of April 9. For the first time, also, the object was seen in Chicago, and thousands stood along the lake shore and gathered at various points to view it. The moving object was first observed by Robert Lowen, of 1926 Sherman Avenue, a jeweler. He was standing in the store door when his attention was attracted by a moving light in the heavens. The light appeared to be over the lake, a short way out and was moving in a westerly direction. Mr. Lowen took a strong field glass and looked at the object. He was able to discern four lights close together and moving in unison.

The first was a bright white light, and appeared to be a search-light; directly back of this was a smaller green light further to the rear. Lowen called several passers-by to look at the light through the glasses, and all pronounced them of the colours green and white.

A later dispatch cleared up the mystery of the craft's apparent return to Omaha, which it had visited nearly two weeks earlier.

New York *Sun,* Sunday, April 11, 1897

AIRSHIP WAS A BALLOON SENT UP BY TWO PRACTICAL JOKERS OF OMAHA TO FOOL THE PEOPLE

OMAHA, NEB., APRIL 10. The "airship," which has caused such a sensation in Omaha, is now declared to be a balloon, and the men who sent it up are said to be Roy Arnold and Jack Rogers. They are practical jokers, and they bought an enormous balloon to send up on April 1, but it rained that night, so they held it off for a later day.

On last Monday night they took the balloon . . . to the hollow back of the State Institute for the Deaf, where they inflated it and sent it up.

Suspended from the balloon was a wicker basket filled with a composition resembling shavings, which they touched off just as it ascended and this was the light. The balloon struck a current of air and it carried directly over the central part of the city, and Arnold says that when they came back on the car everybody was talking of the "airship" and all were excited.

New York *Herald,* Tuesday, April 13, 1897

SURE IT'S AN AIRSHIP

OSCAR D. BOOTH THINKS HE KNOWS THE MAN
WHOSE MACHINE HAS ASTONISHED THE WEST

(By telegraph to the *Herald*.) CHICAGO, ILL., APRIL 12, 1897.
Oscar D. Booth, of 158 South Peoria Street, has constructed an
airship, and he firmly believes the strange object seen by Chicago
is another airship. He thinks the mysterious craft was made and
is being operated by an inventor named Charles Clinton residing
[in Ford County, Kansas].

The airship theory set forth in Clinton's patent papers, on file
in Washington, is a true though bungling solution of the problem,
according to Booth. The fact that the curious object was first
seen in Kansas strengthens Booth's belief. "That a machine has
already been launched and is even now soaring through the air
I have little doubt," he said. "Why, various persons have seen the
wings and the cigar-shaped car. They are not all fools, and the
reports come from so many places, too."

Referring to the Kansas ship, Booth spoke good words for his
rival. "His machine is practical, I am sure," he said. "When I
first read of the airship being seen over Kansas I ran through
the papers in my possession to see what inventor resided in
Kansas. I found the plans which this Ford County man had filed.
He has wings, or large propellers, placed at both ends of the
cigar-shaped car, and has two engines. Above is a balloon. The
general shape of the machine corresponds with the description
given of the one flying over Chicago. It is likely the same one."

The hoaxers continued to multiply in 1897. Two old soldiers reported that the airship, illuminated at both ends and moving
through space with wonderful rapidity, suddenly appeared over
Kalamazoo, Michigan. The men had scarcely time for a glimpse of
the flying machine when they heard a dull explosion and the craft
disappeared. The report, they said, was like that from a heavy can-
non, and they heard many projectiles flying through the air.
Though these men were the only ones to see the explosion, others

reported that they had heard a sound like "thunder," and two miles from the spot searchers found a large coil of heavy wire and some fused metal. How like some of the UFO reports of today! Doubtless the fees received from the exhibition of these fragments amply repaid the searchers for their trouble.

A man in Waterloo, Iowa, built an "airship" of canvas and lumber, secretly placed it in an outlying lot during the night, and put it on exhibition the following day. His audience, according to the report, numbered 5,000 persons.

The mysteries were compounded when a fisherman from Detroit reported that he had seen the airship rise from the surface of Lake Erie. He described its occupants fully and minutely. As the fisherman's boat approached, the airship rose until it stood directly above, about 500 feet from the surface, where it circled for several minutes.

Suddenly there was a tremendous splash in the water. A large swordfish had been dropped from the ship. The stunned fish was captured and placed on exhibition in the window of a local market. Presumably, the physical presence of the swordfish established beyond question the authenticity of the story.

A "respectable citizen" of Birmingham, Iowa, reported that he and others saw a ship alight in a meadow a mile from town. Before they could reach it, the ship rose and disappeared. The ship possessed a car with two occupants who waved their hands as the ship departed.

In Washington, Iowa "a half dozen reliable citizens" saw something queer in the sky—a light that changed color, with a shadow above the light. The Reverend Mr. Gray, a Baptist minister, was properly cautious. "I do not believe it was a star," he said. "I do not pretend to say that it was an airship, but I know it was something unusual. I believe something more will be heard from it. I do not believe it could have been a burned-out star. It disappeared in the southwest."

Citizens of Greensburg, Indiana, also reported the airship. A newspaper correspondent in a nearby city had warned people to be on the lookout. And, as predicted, the object appeared about three hours later, approaching from the west at a speed of ten miles an hour. No light was seen, but the ship was plainly outlined against the clear sky.

The ship reversed course and swung back from the east, this time "with three lights—a green, red, and a large white one in the center." The rest of the story, from the New York *Herald*, April 15, 1897, follows:

Professor George Keelty, who obtained a good view of it from his observatory, says the searchlight is of medium power. He probably got the best view of anyone although he did not get in his tower until it was passing away the first time. For the last two days and nights Professor Keelty has been on constant watch for the machine, thinking it would pass over this way, but he temporarily left his post tonight when it appeared. The second time he could not see it so clearly, owing to the darkness.

He says the machine is about sixty feet long, the balloon being about fifty feet long. It is cigar-shaped, the car hanging about twenty feet under the balloon. The car was entirely enclosed, it being impossible to see in it, but two men were visible in the lookout. One was apparently fifty years old, with a beard, and the other young. The oldest one wore a stiff hat and the younger a Cuban crushed hat. The lights would occasionally be changed from one color to another, and would sometimes be extinguished.

HAS GREAT SPEED

The ship would usually make about ten miles an hour, but on disappearing the last time it dashed off at the tremendous speed of fully 150 miles an hour. It went in a southwesterly direction.

Note that two of the following stories indicate the tendency of the "ship" to move ahead as it is approached—a characteristic shared by the 1947 UFOs and later models.

New York *Herald*, April 15, 1897

AIRSHIP SEEN BY DAYLIGHT

SEVERAL PERSONS AT DIFFERENT PLACES ASSERT THAT THEY SAW THIS STRANGE CRAFT ALIGHT

(By telegraph to the *Herald*.) CARLINVILLE, ILL., APRIL 13, 1897. The mysterious airship has been seen in the northern part of this county, and about half-past two o'clock Sunday afternoon alighted on [a farm] one mile north of Nilwood. It was seen by [three men]. It remained about fifteen minutes, and continued north. The craft was seen again at six o'clock alighting in a grove two miles south of Girard and a mile north of the mining camp in Green Ridge. A large crowd of miners from that place and a storekeeper . . . started to inspect the strange apparition. As they approached within a half mile, it arose and sped north.

The Chicago and Alton operators telegraphed ahead to be on the watch, and at 8 o'clock it passed over Sherman, 32 miles north of Girard, at the apparent rate of 30 miles an hour. It was last sighted over Williamsville, about 15 minutes to 9 o'clock, headed for Peoria. Those who saw the airship say it was cigar-shaped, with wings and a canopy on top. One man avers that he saw a man working about the craft, apparently fixing the machinery. The fact of its alighting twice and remaining such a long time leads to the conclusion that the machine was injured in some manner.

New York *Herald,* April 16, 1897

Two Bags of Ballast Left by
the Visitor in Lynn Grove, Iowa

(By telegraph to the *Herald.*) LYNN GROVE, IOWA, APRIL 15, 1897. The citizens of Lynn Grove are certain there is no longer any doubt of the existence of an airship. A large object was seen soon after 10 o'clock this morning slowly moving in the heavens in a northerly direction, and it seemed to be preparing to alight. [A number of men] jumped in to a wagon and started in pursuit. They saw what seemed to be an airship alight on the Jones farm, four miles north of town, but when they were within 700 yards of it, it arose and started toward the north. Two bags of ballast were thrown out, and these are now at Robertson Campbell's drug store.

The men who chased the ship are certain there were two men on board. They said the object had four wings. Every citizen of Lynn Grove saw the object as it sailed over the town, and there has been great excitement all day.

Appleton, Wis., Citizens
Too Sober Minded for Such Things

(By telegraph to the *Herald*.) Appleton, Wis., April 15, 1897. No reputable citizens here have seen any airship. This is a university town, and we are too sober minded for such things.

Since yesterday several iron arrows, with letters attached have been brought to town from the surrounding country. They purport to have been dropped from the airship, and recount its voyages from Tennessee and Colorado to Wisconsin. Boys, bicycles, and mischief are responsible for many pranks, and we who are in the secret find it difficult to enthuse properly over the heavenly visitor.

Truthful Citizens of Grand Rapids, Mich.,
Have Not Seen It

(By telegraph to the editor.) Grand Rapids, Mich., April 15, 1897. Grand Rapids' citizens are sober, law abiding and truthful. The airship has not yet been seen here.

Affidavits Made by
Eleven Residents of Anderson, Ind.,
Who Saw It

(By telegraph to the *Herald*.) Cincinnati, Ohio, April 15, 1897. A local newspaper publishes this afternoon 11 affidavits of residents of Anderson, Ind. in reference to the supposed airship said to have been seen travelling over Indiana during the last week. All the affidavits are by well-known citizens, and all refer to April 11 as the time when the object was seen.

All say they saw it at night, and that it was a strange looking object, from which at times a bright light flashed, which was larger than a star. It was moving north, at an altitude of probably 5,000 feet, and at a speed of probably 20 miles an hour. None says that it was an airship, but all agree that they cannot account for it on any other theory. This is a sample of the affidavits:

"This certifies that I, J. O. Morrison, viewed a strange body in the heavens on the evening of April 11, which I am at a loss to account. It moved in a northerly direction, and at times a strange light was flashed from it."

The fame of the airship spread abroad, where the incident found supporters and scoffers. The affair aroused a good deal of interest in Paris. French aviation authorities, arguing pro and con, generally were more con than pro.

New York *Herald,* April 15, 1897 (Editorial)

Even Paris has caught the airship contagion. The *Figaro,* according to a commercial cable despatch, publishes a special article based on the report sent from New York to the European edition of the *Herald,* which will undoubtedly furnish interest to Parisian readers for some time to come. Paris is evidently quite as anxious to get the truth about the high flier as we are, but unfortunately our western chroniclers are not inclined to take the matter as seriously as could be desired.

That the problem of aerial navigation will eventually be solved is, of course, sure, but whether this Omaha phenomenon has made the solution remains to be seen. In Europe there are at least a dozen well-known scientists working on the problem, and many half-successful efforts of flight have been made, not taking into account Hiram Maxim's [the Anglo-American inventor of the Maxim machine gun and early experimenter with airplanes] idea of spending energy uselessly in the endeavor to lift a machine into space by main force.

Poets, romanticists and dreamers have pictured the airship of the future. [Camille] Flammarion has filled his book on the "Fin du Monde" with attractive pictures of airships floating genially through space, and he followed the Hungarian Maurus Jokii, who 30 years ago made the airship the great means of communication between the various cities of the magnetic world.

Military authorities everywhere are anxious to get their balloon observatories free from the tether holding them to the earth, while custom house authorities are trembling for fear of the smugglers utilizing the new contrivance for evading [import duties]. Let us hope the Omaha airship may be tracked to its lair and another grand discovery be credited to this *fin de siècle* age.

And in the news columns of the New York *Herald* the same day, we get the French viewpoint.

The *Figaro* publishes a special article, based on the *Herald*'s cables, respecting the airship. It says:

"The news seems to be more than a canard, seeing the details and preciseness in which are related in the *Herald* the exploits of this airship. It has travelled over the new world at an average height of from 5 to 600 meters, and is stated to have been seen by thousands, and, what is more, photographed.

"About 6 months ago it was announced that the inventor, a native of Omaha, had solved the problem of aerial navigation, but no notice was taken of the assertion. It would appear that this was a mistake, as this airship has neither sails nor wings, and resembles the traditional spindle.

"With a telescope a human being was observed in the machine. In Chicago during the night, a searchlight flooded the city, with rays, which caused in some quarters such terror that many people believed the end of the world had come.

"These statements are so astounding that one doubts their reality, notwithstanding the full details given by the *Herald*. No machine exists in France that can lift its weight by screws or any other system by 1-third, without counting engineers and passengers or provisions or fuel.

"Americans are no further advanced in the science of aerostatics than the French, and to accept the statement of an airship travelling at 100 kilometers an hour we must admit the discovery of a new force or a new application of a force hither unknown to the extent of 3 or 4 times greater than any existing."

And in the same April 15 issue of the New York *Herald* appeared a story so patently a hoax that one wonders how anyone could have been deceived. But, after all, the airship was great news!

LETTER FROM THE AIRSHIP?

SAYS THE CRAFT IS CALLED THE PEGASUS
AND CAN FLY 150 MILES AN HOUR

(By telegraph to the *Herald*.) CHICAGO, ILL., APRIL 14, 1897. All sorts of telegrams come in here in regard to the alleged airship seen in this section of the country but it seems to be impossible to get anything reliable in regard to it. It has been several weeks since the agitation started but the reports did not begin to arrive in close order until the 5th of this month. Since then they have come in every night. Some of the newspapers here declare it is a nonsensical story, yet the reports in most cases have come from reliable persons. Of course, the practical joker has come to the front, and in some cases small balloons with lights attached have been sent up in various towns, but in the majority of cases the persons who saw or thought they saw an object in the sky have treated the matter in the most serious manner.

A despatch received tonight from Appleton, Wis., says that on Sunday night many persons saw an airship pass over that city. Last night, on the farm of N. B. Clark, near there a letter was picked up attached to an iron rod 18 inches long, sticking in the ground. The letter, which was not signed, was as follows:

LETTER FROM THE AIRSHIP

"Aboard the airship Pegasus, April 9, 1897
"Problem of aerial navigation has been solved. The writers have spent the past month cruising about in the airship Pegasus, and have demonstrated to their entire satisfaction that the ship is a thorough success. We have been able to attain a speed of 150 miles an hour, and have risen to a height of 2,500 feet above the sea level.

"The Pegasus was erected at a secluded point ten miles from Lafayette, Tenn., and the various parts of the machine were carried overland from Glasgow, Ky., to that point being shipped from Chicago, Pittsburgh and St. Louis. We have made regular trips of three days each from Lafayette to Yankton, and no harm has come to the Pegasus thus far.

"Within a month our application for the patents for a parallel plane airship will be filed simultaneously at Washington and the European capitals. It is propelled by steam and is lighted by electricity, and has a carrying power of 1,000 pounds."

From Grand Rapids, Wis., the report comes that the airship passed over there at 9 o'clock last evening, and was seen by a hundred reputable citizens. Similar reports come from Elkhart, Ind., Ripon, Wis., and Lake Forest.

R. J. Thompson, secretary of the Illinois Commission to the

Tennessee Centennial, says the commission will pay $25,000 for an actual airship, to exhibit at the exposition.

Oscar D. Booth, of 158 South Peoria Street, an inventor of airships, was asked tonight if he thought it likely a man could build and launch a flying machine and keep it secret.

"I judge that the flying machine seen over Chicago is one made only for a trial trip, probably a small one," he replied. "It would be very easy to take a medium sized ship to a secluded place, put together the parts and start it off. Now, with my invention I could leave Chicago without a soul knowing it. My car is only 9 feet long, and could easily be drawn to some quiet spot. I have everything ready but the balloon."

Two days later, on April 17, came the great sensation and a climax to the story. The airship dropped a message, which was found on a farm near Astoria, Illinois, the *Herald* reported. A reed three feet long, sticking in the ground and marked with a red, white, and blue streamer, carried a packet and a dirty envelope with the words: "From the airship—notice to the finder:—Please mail letter inside. Passed over here about half past two P.M. April 16, 1897, about 2300 feet high, going East and North. Excuse dirt, have just done oiling. Harris." The letter itself was addressed to Thomas A. Edison, was written in cipher, and was signed "C. L. Harris, electrician, Airship N. 3."

The final story appeared in the New York *Herald* on Tuesday, April 20, 1897:

THAT LETTER TO EDISON

"THE WIZARD" DESCRIBES THE "AIRSHIP" EPISTLE AS A FAKE AND EXPRESSES AN OPINION ON AERIAL INVENTION

That letter from the "airship" to Thomas A. Edison, a copy of which was printed in a despatch from Astoria, Illinois in the *Herald* yesterday, has not reached the distinguished inventor. The missive was dated April 16 and signed "C. L. Harris, electrician, Airship N. 3," and was found tied to a reed near Astoria. I showed Mr. Edison yesterday afternoon the letter published in the *Herald*.

"This is the latest, isn't it?" inquired he, leaning back in his chair and glancing over the letter a second time. "You can take it from me that this is a pure fake. I have had several men in my employ, but I know nothing of C. L. Harris."

Mr. Edison then grew more thoughtful and stated that he had no doubt that airships will be successfully constructed in the near future. In reference to the western "airship" he added:—

"It is absolutely absurd to imagine that a man would construct a successful airship and keep the matter secret. When I was young we used to construct big coloured paper balloons, inflate them with gas and they would float for days.

"Whenever an airship is made it will not be in the form of a balloon. It will be a mechanical contrivance, which will be raised by means of a very powerful motor of little weight. At present no one has discovered such a motor, but we never know what will happen. We may wake up some morning and hear of some invention which sets us all eagerly to work within a few hours, as was the case with the Roentgen rays.

"I am not, however, figuring on inventing an airship. I prefer to devote my time to objects which have some commercial value. At best airships would be only toys."

Significantly, this story of Edison's broke the airship bubble. Although the great inventor had in no way explained what it was people had been seeing in the sky, the mere fact that he correctly pointed out that there was no airship killed the sensation. People were interested in *airships,* not in the natural phenomena, however mysterious, that may have been producing the illusion.

About a week later there was one short message from someone in Cripple Creek, Colorado, who thought he had seen an airship. But clearly the news of Edison's pronouncement had not yet reached him.

It is perhaps even more significant, as a sign of the era, that the New York *Herald* for April 25, 1897, carried a long story, with illustrations, about the serious plans made by the Swedish aeronaut Salomon Andrée for a balloon flight over the North Pole. In July 1897 Andrée left on this daring adventure with two companions.

Nothing further was heard of their expedition, except for several messages by carrier pigeons, until in 1930 a chance landing on an

out-of-the-way island in the Arctic Ocean north of Spitzbergen led
to the discovery of the remains of the three aeronauts and their ill-
fated balloon. Thirty-three years had elapsed, but the records of
the expedition were intact. Photographs and diaries recorded how
the polar balloon, encrusted with a layer of ice, gradually lost
buoyancy and descended. The men had landed safely but had
been unable to take off again.

The 1947 scare, except for its size and duration, closely resembled that of 1897. There were the original rumors, the self-
hallucinations, the hoaxes, and the widespread interest in sky-
watching. The famous searchlight that flashed red, white, and blue
must have been a star in the majority of cases. A star that twinkles
—especially one low on the horizon—does not twinkle uniformly in
all colors. Hence the seeming effect of the flashing hues. The dark,
cigar-shaped gas bag in many cases was only a lenticular cloud or
a mirage, which would ordinarily have escaped notice except for
the special significance momentarily attached to an object of this
shape.

The similarity of the two patterns of reports also shows in the
repeated statements about the reliability of independent witnesses.
And we have the scoffing experts and the counterscoffing so-called
authorities who professed to know the real truth behind these stories and who cited names, dates, and places to substantiate their
claims.

No document indicates that the 1897 inventors referred to ever
got a patent on an airship.

THE CONDON REPORT

I CAN ONLY SAY THAT THE VAUNTED CONDON REPORT
IS A FURTHER EFFORT TO DELIBERATELY DECEIVE THE
PUBLIC . . . THE UNIVERSITY OF COLORADO WAS "USED"
AS A TOOL BY THE AIR FORCE AND THE C.I.A. . . . IT WAS
ALL A CLEVERLY RIGGED FARCE, AND VERY, VERY DISGUSTING!

Letter from private citizen to Edward U. Condon[1]

The current interest in unidentified flying objects began in June 1947 with the sighting by the Idaho businessman Kenneth Arnold, as noted in Chapter 1. What Arnold saw will never be known for certain, since there is no grist for analysis other than his report. (In Chapter 1 we have offered a reasonable conjecture to account for this sighting.)

In any case, the Arnold sighting was catalytic. In a matter of days many unidentified objects were seen flying all over the United States in the sky in widely scattered places. It was natural that such sightings would be reported to the (then) Army Air Forces, and by September 1947 the newly organized U. S. Air Force had officially begun an investigatory program, first identified as Project Saucer and quickly changed to Project Sign. In February 1949 the nomenclature was changed to Project Grudge and finally, in mid-1951, to Project Blue Book. The official involvement of the Air Force in the investigation of UFOs continued under that label until December 1969, when the Air Force got out of the UFO business.

As the Air Force inquiries and study continued into the early

1960s it became apparent to many that perhaps a primarily military investigatory body might not be the best agency to conduct
the investigation. In March 1966 an *ad hoc* committee of the
United States Air Force Scientific Board suggested to the Air
Force Office of Scientific Research (AFOSR) the probable value
of a thoroughly scientific study of unidentified flying objects
conducted entirely beyond Air Force jurisdiction, control, or influence. In consequence, AFOSR addressed itself to the University of Colorado in August 1966, asking that institution to undertake an independent scientific study of the controversial objects in
the sky. The scientists involved would have "complete freedom to
design and develop techniques for the investigation of the varied
physical and psychological questions raised in conjunction with
this phenomenon according to their best scientific judgment."[2]

The university accepted the role of grantee institution, and thus
the "Colorado Project" came into existence. The final result of this
enterprise was the so-called Condon Report—or, to give its full and
official title, the "Final Report of the Scientific Study of Unidentified Flying Objects Conducted by the University of Colorado
Under Contract to the United States Air Force." It was published
in January 1969.

The individual chosen to direct the project was Dr. Edward U.
Condon, an eminent physicist of impeccable qualifications. He had
presided over the affairs of such learned bodies as the American
Physical Society, and the American Association for the Advancement of Science. He had been director of the National Bureau of
Standards. At the University of Colorado Condon was professor
of physics at the Joint Institute for Laboratory Astrophysics.

Condon's hair was crew-cut and he had the build of a Green
Bay Packer. He had tangled successfully with the House Commit-
tee on Un-American Activities. And he was fiercely independent.
He was, by any standard, a tough customer.[3]

He was tough, but this formidably competent scientist was fair—
to a fault, as we shall see. For the Colorado Project he assembled
a staff of thirty-seven principals; these included, in addition to
Condon, Robert J. Low (the project co-ordinator), seven psychologists, one psychiatrist, five engineers, three astrophysicists, four
physicists, five meteorologists, one mathematician, one physical

chemist, one astronomer, and a group of seven writers, editors, and editorial assistants.

Among the psychologists was David R. Saunders, who was known from October 1966 onward, if not before, to be both a believer in the ETH (extraterrestrial hypothesis) and a member of NICAP (National Investigative Committee on Aerial Phenomena), an organization devoted to the proof of the extraterrestrial origin of UFOs. Yet Condon, trying too hard to be fair, retained Saunders on the project staff—a mistake, as he later learned to his cost.

During the early months of the Colorado Project, a degree of co-operation existed between the project and NICAP. This liaison rested upon a tenuous basis at best, and eventually it ended acrimoniously. With an acknowledged believer in the inner circle of the Colorado Project, this result might well have been predicted.

The believers outside the project were highly vocal in their criticism of the project, both before and after publication of the Condon Report. The epigraph at the beginning of this chapter is typical of much correspondence received by Condon commenting on his conduct of the inquiry and on the contents of the report.[4]

The serious dissension, however, occurred within the project staff. This dispute involved David Saunders, Norman E. Levine, a research associate in the team effort, and Mary Lou (Louise) Armstrong, a secretary. The focal point of the intramural row was a memorandum written by Robert Low dated August 9, 1966—before the project started.

For background, it should be said that the administration of the University of Colorado had never been wildly enthusiastic when considering the offer made to it by the Air Force to conduct the inquiry. Robert Low, then assistant dean of the Graduate School, understood well the hazards that might accompany the acceptance of the contract—having in mind, for example, the tarnish brought to the reputation of Duke University by the presence in Durham of the much-publicized work of Dr. J. B. Rhine and his staff in the Institute for Parapsychology. Accordingly, in a memorandum to the university administration, Low considered the problems that acceptance of the Air Force proposal might bring to the university.

The memorandum was written—as background information,

with suggestions to prepare the administration for forthcoming talks with representatives of the Air Force—long before the contract was signed. The memorandum, which Low no doubt later wished he had never written, was concerned primarily with the possible effects of the UFO study upon the image and reputation of the university. It had nothing to do with UFOs as such. Condon was unaware of the memorandum's existence when he became director of the project.

Levine had come across the memorandum while going through project files relating to the Air Force contract. Levine brought the memorandum to the attention of Saunders, and together they passed it on to Donald E. Keyhoe, then director of NICAP. The memo was subsequently brought to the attention of James E. McDonald, a meteorologist at the University of Arizona and a believer. Finally, the memorandum was leaked to John G. Fuller, a journalist with a taste for sensationalism.

Condon was, of course, furious when he learned what Levine and Saunders had done with the memorandum, and there was a major explosion within the project. When the dust had settled, Levine and Saunders had been summarily dismissed, Mary Lou Armstrong had resigned in protest, and Fuller had made the memorandum the focal point of a polemic article in *Look,* in the issue for May 14, 1968.[5]

The fuss centered around the Low memorandum, and we quote here its relevant passages. It must be remembered that it was meant only to provide background information to the University of Colorado administration. It set forth Low's thoughts about the possible impact of the proposed UFO study upon the university's image in the scientific community:

   In order to undertake such a project, one has to approach it objectively. That is, one has to admit the possibility that such things (UFOs) exist. It is not respectable to give serious consideration to such a possibility. Believers, in other words, would remain outcasts . . . admitting such possibilities . . . puts us beyond the pale, and we would lose more in prestige in the scientific community than we could possibly gain by undertaking the investigation.

Our study would be conducted almost exclusively by non-believers who, although they couldn't possibly prove a negative result, could and probably would add an impressive body of evidence that there is no reality to the observations. The trick would be, I think, to describe the project so that, to the public, it would appear a totally objective study, but, to the scientific community, would present the image of a group of nonbelievers trying their best to be objective but having an almost zero expectation of finding a saucer. One way to do this would be to stress investigation, not of the physical phenomena, but rather of the people who do the observing—the psychology and sociology of persons or groups who report seeing UFOs . . .[6]

The use of the word "trick" was certainly unfortunate, and the view Fuller put forth in the *Look* article was that the public had been taken in by a $500,000 trick, or fiasco, or scandal.

Public interest in the project was high at the time, and the article was widely read and discussed. Most of the readers had no way of knowing that Fuller's account was replete with misrepresentation, innuendo, and outright error. For example, Fuller stated in the article that the study had already cost the taxpayer more than half a million dollars. The facts were that at that time the total contract figure stood at less than that—$496,146—and that the amount actually spent through March was $340,645, with estimated expenditures for April bringing the figure up to about $375,000.

After the departure of Saunders, Levine, and Armstrong, the work of the project went forward. Public interest was, as we have said, high. The staff continued to receive innumerable reports of sightings. Many of these were investigated in the field, both by the project staff and by others. J. Allen Hynek, who had been hired by the Air Force as a consultant in 1947, was no longer with the Air Force, but his experience was called upon, as was that of DHM. Technical consultation of the greatest sophistication was made use of, as in, for example, complex analyses of photographs of alleged UFOs.

Later, in January 1969, when the report of this work was published, Condon was subjected to the criticism that he selected only "nutty" cases that could easily be demolished. We believe that this criticism is unjustified, as may be demonstrated by a close reading of the report. In fact, the report listed many cases as "unexplained." In the next chapter we consider *all* of these cases. (It is true, as will also be shown in the next chapter, a number of cases were included in the report that did not merit inclusion.)

Condon was also criticized, perhaps justly, for making fun of UFOs. The fact is that many of the sightings and reports did indeed have humorous aspects, and Condon had a well-developed sense of humor. He spoke frequently to a wide variety of audiences and did not hesitate to tell amusing UFO tales, such as that of the man who claimed that his wife's grandfather had immigrated to America in an UFO whose home base was in the Andromeda nebula. Widely circulated accounts of these episodes did not sit well with the critics of the project who were believers. (There were also many nonbeliever critics of the Colorado Project who thought the money could have been put to better use.)

The report was also criticized because it gave scant attention to the social and psychological aspects of the UFO phenomenon. (It will be remembered that Low, in his famous memorandum, had suggested that these aspects be emphasized.) This was in fact a matter of deliberate choice on the part of the staff, but a decision that behavioral scientists may well take issue with.

In general, however, we believe the Colorado staff did a good job. They analyzed many sightings and explained a large number of them as either natural phenomena or chicanery.

When the staff's work was finished, the Air Force, wary of potential charges by believers that they and the staff of the project had conspired to conceal the existence of UFOs—had, in effect, conducted a cover-up—requested that, before the staff's work was released to the public, the report be evaluated by the National Academy of Sciences. The academy appointed a panel of distinguished scientists to do this. The panel studied the report, did some additional homework on their own, and produced their own report, from which we quote:

We are unanimous in the opinion that this has been a very creditable effort to apply objectively the relevant techniques of science to the solution of the UFO problem. The report recognizes that there remain UFO sightings that are not easily explained. The report does suggest, however, so many reasonable and possible directions in which an explanation may eventually be found, that there seems to be no reason to attribute them to an extraterrestrial source without evidence that is much more convincing. . . . On the basis of present knowledge the least likely explanation of UFOs is the hypothesis of extraterrestrial visitations by intelligent beings.[7]

When the report was made available to the public, the believers were, predictably, outraged. Condon was the recipient of much abuse: ". . . that infamous, unscientific Condon report . . . cost us taxpayers $500,000 for the perpetration of that fraudulent study."[8]

The report did, however, command almost total respect from the scientific community (though certainly not among the few believer-scientists): "One comes away edified, amused, admiring and well satisfied . . . Science is the stronger for this sincere and expert effort to deal with a public concern."[9]

Another recipient of abuse was, of course, the supporter of the project, the U. S. Air Force. Predictably, cries of "cover-up" arose from the angry ranks of the believers. The Air Force is still subject to this continuing charge.

CHAPTER 8

THE "UNEXPLAINED" CASES

... THE BOOK LEAVES THE SAME STRANGE,
INEXPLICABLE RESIDUE OF UNKNOWNS WHICH HAS PLAGUED
THE U. S. AIR FORCE INVESTIGATION FOR TWENTY YEARS.

> J. A. Hynek,
> in a review of the Condon Report, 1969[1]

One criticism leveled against the Condon Report has been that it chose to study only easily explained cases. This accusation is curious, since no less than twenty-three of the fifty-nine cases listed in the report are classified as "unexplained"—almost 40 per cent of the cases comprising the main body of the report!

Our view is that these puzzling cases are, where adequate data are available, explicable, though some are indeed so trivial as to scarcely warrant the attempt. We shall now re-examine, seriatim, these twenty-three cases. In each instance we give first the abstract of the case as it appeared in the Condon Report, and then our analysis and comments. We use the existing abstracts from the Condon Report as a matter of convenience, and we point out here that the information given is in all essentials precisely as it was given in the Condon Report. Here and there we have deleted a sentence we thought unessential, but apart from such minor editing the texts are given here as they are in the report.

It will be noted that in many cases the locations and dates of the sightings are given only approximately, and that names are not provided. This was to protect the identities of those involved.

Where more specific information regarding these aspects of the cases is provided or has been published elsewhere, we make use of such information.

CONDON REPORT, CASE 2

The Bentwaters-Lakenheath Sightings

Abstract: In the summer of 1956 at least one UFO was tracked by air traffic control radar (GCA) [ground-controlled approach] at two USAF-RAF stations [at Bentwaters and Lakenheath] in England, with apparently corresponding visual sightings of round, white, rapidly moving objects which changed directions abruptly. Interception by RAF fighter aircraft was attempted; one aircraft was vectored to the UFO by GCA radar and the pilot reported airborne radar contact and radar "gunlock." The UFO appeared [on ground radar] to circle around behind the aircraft and followed it in spite of the pilot's evasive maneuvers. Contact was broken when the aircraft, low on fuel, returned to base.

The Bentwaters-Lakenheath case, which has frequently been cited by believers as a classic (and which baffled the Colorado team), might appear at first glance as indeed a mysterious and puzzling event. It is one of the cases cited by Hynek in his review of the Condon Report as being worthy of study in depth. And it is, beyond doubt, an example of a sighting in respect of which the Colorado staff failed to conduct anything approaching an adequate inquiry. The incident has since been studied by numerous investigators, including Philip Klass.[2]

On the evening of August 13, 1956, between approximately 9:30 and 10 P.M., three UFO-radar sightings occurred at Bentwaters, in Suffolk, England. If these sightings were what they seemed to be, material craft of some sort were moving overhead at speeds up to more than 12,000 mph. At about this same time, alerted by news of the radar sightings, Bentwaters control-tower personnel, according to the initial Bentwaters report, saw a bright light streaking over the air field at great speed; such a streaking light was also reported by the pilot of a C-47 in the vicinity.

Bentwaters radar station called the nearby station at Laken-heath to ask if their personnel had observed the UFOs. They had not. But two hours after the Bentwaters events their radar did de-tect a solitary unmoving object—which it should not have done, since it was set for full MTI (moving target indicator) and should have shown moving targets only, with no ground returns.

In consequence of the Bentwaters sightings, two aircraft were sent up in search of the targets. These were De Havilland Venoms, carrying APS-57 radar equipment. The pilot of the first airplane (and this is the only datum that made this case worthy of serious attention) reported that he had both radar and visual contact with the object and that his guns were locked on the target. He then lost the target and asked GCA where it had gone. GCA said it had circled rapidly and was behind him. The first Venom, low on fuel, then returned to the field.

That is, essentially, the outline of the Bentwaters-Lakenheath case. How, then, can it be explained in terms other than those requiring the invocation of the ETH? The relevant data are these:

1. The second Venom sent aloft in search of the mysterious ob-jects in the area found nothing.

2. Two Lockheed T-33 fighters based at Bentwaters were re-turning to base at the time of the sightings and were enlisted in the hunt. They searched the area for forty-five minutes but found nothing. (This information, though present in the original Bent-waters report, did not appear in subsequent reports of the sighting, until Klass's analysis in 1974.)

3. None of these UFOs was reported by other radar stations op-erating well within range of the alleged sightings. If the objects were material, if the targets were genuine, they would have been picked up by these other stations.

4. The incident occurred at the time of the Perseid meteor shower. In fact, Bentwaters personnel sighted many meteors that night. The account of the streaking light in the first report was ex-cised from the more detailed report written some two weeks later, suggesting that the streaking light had been identified as a meteor.

5. The APS-57 radar carried by the first Venom did not have

gunlock capability; the pilot's report is clearly in error in this respect.

6. Furthermore, the first Venom was a two-seater plane, meant to carry a pilot and a radar operator. All indications in the record are that the pilot was alone, doubling as his own radar man—an extremely difficult, if not impossible, task.

7. The sighting took place when some of today's sophisticated radar gear was still in the formative stage. The MTI, for just one example, part of highly complex circuitry, tended toward instability; the operation manual warned against this. Further, experienced radar designers, engineers, and operators, confronted with the radar data of the Bentwaters-Lakenheath case, are, to say the least, unimpressed.

8. The ground radar used at Bentwaters could not have seen the target actually circle rapidly behind the Venom, since its scan rate was such that it "looked" at the target only once every fifteen seconds. What ground radar observed was simply the disappearance of the target, followed by its reappearance behind the airplane fifteen seconds later. This must have frightened everyone concerned, and this radar sighting has remained the most inexplicable aspect of this case.

The fighter made evasive maneuvers, but was unable to shake the UFO, which continued to follow (on radar), though the pilot saw nothing behind him. Our solution to this sighting is based upon what is called "anomalous propagation" (AP), which we discuss in the next chapter. The ground radar signal bounced from the plane to some unidentified ground target, thence back to the plane. Ground radar thus registered two blips: one was directly from the plane and the other a delayed echo from the plane via the ground. However, the long-delayed *second* echo was from an earlier pulse sent out by the same transmitter on the ground. The two blips kept pace with each other because the plane (the moving target) was implicated in both signals.

We believe that this explanation of the famed Bentwaters-Lakenheath sighting is the first clear scientific account of what really happened.

CONDON REPORT, CASE 5

The RB-47 Sighting, South-Central U.S., Fall 1957

Abstract: The crew of a B-47[3] aircraft described an encounter [near Biloxi, Mississippi] with a large ball of light which was also displayed for a sustained time for both airborne radar monitoring receivers and on ground radar units. The encounter had occurred ten years prior to this study. Project Blue Book had no record of it. Attempts to locate any records of the event, in an effort to learn the identity of the encountered phenomenon, failed to produce any information. The phenomenon remains unidentified.

This is another case cited by Hynek as worthy of serious study. It is also another example of inconclusive investigation by the Colorado staff. That defect was remedied by Klass's study. Since the results of his inquiry are available elsewhere, as noted above, we shall summarize it only briefly.

The Boeing RB-47 was on a training flight from Forbes Air Force Base, Kansas. The flight would pass over a number of south-central states in the late evening and early morning of July 16–17, 1957. One aim of the mission was to test a variety of sophisticated ECM (electronic countermeasures) gear. Over Biloxi, Mississippi, one of the three radar operators, Frank B. McClure, detected a signal whose characteristics suggested that it came from an air-defense radar installation on the ground. The signal was, however, anomalous in two respects: (1) it appeared to originate from a location in the Gulf of Mexico, where there was no air-defense radar, and (2) as the flight progressed, the blip moved upward on the radar screen instead of downward, the normal direction. McClure concluded that his equipment was malfunctioning.

Shortly thereafter the pilot of the RB-47, Major Lewis D. Chase, and his copilot both saw a very bright light coming toward them from the southwest. The light crossed the plane's flight path and disappeared to the north. The flight crew began to talk of chasing an UFO, and McClure heard of the visual sighting over the plane's intercom. He wondered if the anomalous signal he had

observed over Biloxi might be related to the visual sighting, and he
tried to pick up the signal again. After a twenty-minute search he
did pick up a similar signal; its source was now roughly northwest
of the plane.

About nine minutes after that, Chase sighted a second light,
also to the northwest. He described the light as "huge" and estimated that it was about 5,000 feet below the plane. A minute
later McClure's radar signal became two separate signals at bear-
ings 30° apart; the signal source, if it were an UFO, seemed to
have split in two.

Now Chase obtained permission from the civil air-traffic control
center at Dallas to turn northwest in pursuit of the UFO, and he
enlisted the help of the USAF air-defense radar station at Duncanville, near Dallas. Then McClure's two radar signals combined into
one again, then separated again. The Duncanville station asked
where the UFO was. Chase said it was about ten miles northwest
of Dallas. The ground installation confirmed the presence of the
object on their scopes. It was now 5:50 A.M. and the plane was
over Dallas. Then the light disappeared, McClure's signals disappeared, and the blip disappeared from the ground radarscopes!

Chase, thinking he had overshot the light, executed a long turn,
trying to find the light again. At 5:51 the signal reappeared on
McClure's scope, the source being in the vicinity of Dallas. During
the next few minutes the radar signal continued to come from that
vicinity, but the pilot and copilot were unable to reacquire the
light. At 5:58 Chase did spot one more curious light, but not in
the direction the radar signal was coming from. He descended in
an attempt to close on the light, but found nothing. Fuel was now
running low, and the pilot turned toward base. McClure lost his
signal momentarily, but it was later observed, from about 6:20 to
6:40, always indicating a signal source in the general direction of
Dallas. The plane returned to base without further incident.

Here, then, was an airplane flight replete with mystifying events;
it was, inevitably, cited for years by the believers as a clincher. We
believe, however, that Klass's detective work has stripped the flight
of its mystery. The details are complex and will not be gone into
here, but the facts he developed are these:

1. The radar signals detected aboard the RB-47 were originated

by ground-based air-defense radar transmitters at Keesler AFB near Biloxi, Mississippi, and at Duncanville, Texas, near Dallas.

Radar transmitters operate on different frequencies, in different ways, for different purposes. A received radar signal is somewhat analogous to a human fingerprint; it identifies the kind of transmitter that sent it. The signals detected by McClure were characteristic of those transmitted by the two ground-based stations. (The Keesler transmitter was of a type known as CPS-6B. The one operating in Duncanville at the time of the RB-47 flight was a later version of the CPS-6B, the FPS-10. Both had the same signal characteristics.)

But McClure's first detected signal indicated a source in the Gulf of Mexico, and the blip moved the wrong way on the screen. Klass discovered that both of these anomalies can be accounted for by the temporary failure of either one of two relays in the circuitry of the airborne receiver.

How about the Dallas signal? Klass found that the signal picked on McClure's scope in the Dallas area was consistent with one transmitted from the Duncanville transmitter, a signal transmitted via a specific beam whose characteristics were such that at the RB-47's altitude the ground transmitter's radiation pattern resembled three concentric doughnuts. When in a "doughnut" area, the airborne equipment would receive a signal; out of it, it would not. Klass traced the course of the RB-47 over this radiation pattern and showed that it accounts for the on-and-off nature of the received signal.

And what of the signal splitting into two components? Klass found that the instruction book for McClure's receiving equipment specifically cautioned against the possibility of receiving at the same time both a direct signal and one reflected from a large metallic object on the ground—a subject we discuss in Chapter 9.

And how about the radar blip on the Duncanville screen? Klass discovered that in the official report filed by the commander of the Duncanville station it was denied that the object had been sighted on the Duncanville scope.

That, we think, with Klass, disposes of the radar sightings in this case. The only alternative is an alien spacecraft happening to be in the area at the same time and carrying a mass of heavy radar equipment whose characteristics matched precisely those of the ground stations at Keesler AFB and at Duncanville.

2. The description of the first bright light that flashed across the RB-47's flight path is entirely consistent with the identification of that object as a meteor or bolide.

3. The second light seen by the pilot was probably Vega, then a brilliant star in the sky in the right place at the right time.

4. The last strange light seen was probably a commercial flight (American Airlines flight #966) landing at Dallas airport.

Thus, proceeding on the assumption that the events associated with this case were *not* interrelated, Klass has found a rational solution for a long-time puzzle.

Those skeptical of the plausibility of this account of the RB-47 happenings should know that Klass's explanations have been accepted by both the pilot of the aircraft and the radar operator.

CONDON REPORT, CASE 6

Northeastern U.S., Spring 1966

Abstract: Three adult women went out on a high-school athletic field to check the identity of a bright light that had frightened an 11-year-old girl in her home nearby, and reported that one of the three lights they saw maneuvering in the sky above the school flew noiselessly toward them, coming directly overhead, 20–30 feet above one of them. It was described as a flowing, solid, disk-like, automobile-sized object. Two policemen, who responded to a telephone message that a UFO was under observation, verified that an extraordinary object was flying over the high school. The object has not been identified. *Most of the extended observation, however, apparently was an observation of the planet Jupiter.*[4]

What happened, essentially, was this: the eleven-year-old girl heard a bump outside her bedroom window about 9:00 P.M., looked out, and saw a flashing red light moving through the air. Frightened, she alerted her father, mother, and two women who happened to arrive at the house at that moment. The three women went, with the girl, toward the grounds of a nearby high school to view the object. They reported seeing three lights in the sky—red, green, and white. The center light of the three darted about, and the others "played tag" with it. One woman beckoned to the lights, and the "nearest" one came directly toward her. The light approached, frightening her, and then went back over the high school. Other people and two policemen arrived. The observers were afraid that the police would think the object only a star—but the light brightened and resumed its motion. The police officers drove down to the school parking lot and saw the object at close range—whereupon, reportedly, it sped off, the police in pursuit.

The above paragraph outlines the reported circumstances of this sighting brought to the attention of the Colorado Project by NICAP. A field investigation followed. The three women, the child, and others, including one of the police officers, were interviewed. The officer stated that the object "had a more or less circular motion *but was always over the school.*" Then, he said, the light dimmed and disappeared—*as if going straight away from the observer.*

The investigation revealed that at the time of the sighting the parking lot had been filled with cars because of a basketball game in the school. The observers pointed out the UFO to some youngsters on the school grounds. They watched for a while, then left—apparently unimpressed.

The investigation further revealed that the planet Jupiter was, at the time of the sighting, in a position coincident with that around which the UFO moved.

The conclusion of the Colorado staff in this case is curious. In the brief concluding paragraph of the Condon Report it is first stated that "no explanation is attempted to account for the close UFO encounter reported by three women and a young girl." Then two possible explanations are given for the sighting: Jupiter and the autokinetic effect, a kind of optical illusion in which a stationary light appears to move.[5]

We find that ordinary, rational explanations for this sighting not only exist, but abound. There can be no doubt whatever that the major focus of the evening's activity was Jupiter, then at a magnitude of −1.6, making it eleven times brighter than a first-magnitude star. The reported movement of the object was probably due to the autokinetic effect. That the object would seem to approach when beckoned is not surprising, since the influence of suggestion upon autokinesis is well documented.[6] The multiple nature of the object was probably due to after-images. The color changes can be attributed to both negative after-images, and the ordinary scintillation of a planetary image. And the description of the three lights "playing tag" is perfectly descriptive of the movement of a primary image and accompanying after-images.

In this sighting we find again that the investigators at the time failed to collect certain basic data. What was the emotional state of the young girl when she went to her room that night? What was the nature of her personality? Did she tend normally to be dramatic (as one might expect) or was she unimaginative and phlegmatic? Were personality tests performed? Such important and relevant data are lacking in the record.

This is an instructive case vis-à-vis the accuracy of eye-witness testimony:

1. The girl, in one account, described the object as football-shaped, with flashing red lights. We shall see later how the apperceptive process can transform a proven meteor into a spacecraft with rows of illuminated windows.[7]

2. One woman described the object as a metal disk the size of a large automobile.

3. Two observers described the object as oval-shaped and flashing.

4. One of the police officers described the object as shaped like a half dollar.

These discrepancies provide an excellent illustration of the difficulty the human eye has in determining the size of an object in the sky. This difficulty is increased if the observer has imperfect vision and fails to wear appropriate corrective lenses.

CONDON REPORT, CASE 8

North-Central U.S., Summer 1966

Abstract: Witness was driving in a rural area in late afternoon when, he said, a silvery metallic-looking disk with dome, about thirty feet in diameter, descended with wobbling motion into the adjacent valley, hovered just above the ground about 200 feet from the witness, then took off rapidly with a whooshing sound. Depressions in ground and overturned rocks near landing site were offered as evidence, but may have been caused by animals. The report is unexplained.

We find this case without value from the point of view of scientific inquiry. The Colorado investigators (Hynek and Low, in this case) added nothing to the above account except that the nearby radar station at Minot, North Dakota, AFB had noticed no target corresponding to the sighting. As reported in the Condon Report, we are left with a single-observer anecdote, unsupported by any meaningful evidence.

And here again is a paucity of information about the witness. Was he interested in UFOs? Had he reported previous sightings? What was his personality profile?

After asking ourselves these questions, we examined the Condon file on this case and discovered that the witness was, indeed, a repeater. Why this important datum was not cited in the Condon Report we do not know, but a letter from Hynek to Low may cast some light on the question: "This [the Case 8 sighting] bears some similarities to his recent sighting and might make me feel like dropping a flag on the play . . . But unless a psychologist helps us out on this case, as physical scientists we have no a priori reason for throwing the evidence out of court."[8]

We are unable to accept that point of view, believing that fabrication is a much more rational explanation of this sighting than is the descent into a remote rural area of a spectacular silvery disk, replete with dome and whooshing sounds.

In any case, we must regret that no psychological inquiry, as alluded to by Hynek, was performed. It might have been helpful—as in Case 42 below (pp. 107).

CONDON REPORT, CASE 10

The Haynesville (Louisiana) Sighting

Abstract: A pulsating reddish light seen [by several people] below treetop level from a [Louisiana] highway at night became brilliant white briefly, then resumed its earlier character. Its location was estimated by rough triangulation. By comparison with the car headlights, the white light was estimated to emanate from a source of several hundred megawatts. Inspection of the area ten weeks later revealed no explanation of the light.

The witnesses in this case were a man, a woman, and an unspecified number of children. The man, the principal witness, was a nuclear physicist. He reported the incident, which occurred near Haynesville, Louisiana, in the winter of 1966, to Barksdale AFB, and it shortly came to the attention of the Colorado Project. An investigation was undertaken, the principal conclusion of which was that the physicist's (various) estimations of the power of the light source were extremely dubious.

The Colorado staff, however, found the case interesting *"because of the difficulty in accounting for any kind of light in [the relevant] area."* This is curious, in view of what the Colorado investigatory team (which, for this case, included believer D. R. Saunders), together with the principal witness, found at the site of the pulsating light: they found that the area contained little but trees, underbrush, and—*oil wells!* And if this were not enough, they also found *"a burned area that . . . turned out to be a burned-over oil slick beside a pumping station."* Astonishingly, the report fails to consider this burn as a reasonable source of the pulsating light of varying intensity—perhaps because their investigation revealed that the oil companies operating in the area had no record of any burnoffs or other fires at the relevant time. The fact that records of burnoffs did not exist would not, by a conscientious investigator, be taken for evidence that such burnoff or other fire had not occurred.

It seems to us obvious that in a wooded area dotted with oil wells, and the inevitably accompanying oil slicks, an oil fire or burnoff is a much more reasonable explanation of this light source than is an UFO.

And here again, unfortunately, either the investigation or the reporting thereof is lacking in breadth and discipline. The team found a burned area—did the burn appear old or recent? Why was it not mentioned as at least a possible source of the light of unidentified origin?

CONDON REPORT, CASE 12

Northeastern U.S., Winter 1967

Abstract: Witness reported that while she was driving alone at night a luminous object hovered over her car for several miles, then moved rapidly into the distance, and that several mechanical and electrical functions of her car were found to be impaired afterward. Examination [by the manufacturer] of the car two months later disclosed no faults that were not attributable to ordinary causes, nor any significant magnetic or radioactive anomaly in or on the car body.

Here we have another curious Colorado conclusion: "The case remains interesting but unexplained." We do find explanation in the same Colorado report that produced that conclusion:

1. The witness was a repeater; she had reported several earlier UFO sightings by herself and friends and family in the vicinity of her home. Repeaters are notoriously suspect for all serious UFO investigators, of whatever persuasion.

2. Her account of the sighting was replete with discrepancies.

3. The manufacturer's scrupulous and sophisticated examination of the car found all malfunctions to be the results of gradual wear and deterioration—except for a broken radio antenna. If broken radio antennas were evidence of UFOs, we should indeed have to take notice.

Another case, in short, totally worthless from the point of view of scientific inquiry. Again, a single-witness (suspect, at that) sighting, and no confirmatory evidence whatever.

CONDON REPORT, CASE 13

Northeastern U.S., Winter 1967

Abstract: Two women, joined later by a third, reported three appearances of a disk-shaped object with lights while they were driving in early darkness. Because of elapsed time and other factors, no evaluation was practicable.

We wonder, then, why the case was included. It may be added that one of the two women stated that she frequently saw moving lights.

CONDON REPORT, CASE 14

South-Central U.S., Winter 1967

Abstract: Six UFO reports . . . were investigated . . . Of the six, three were promptly identified . . . The other three remain unidentified as follows:

1. The city police chief and several officers reported sighting an extended object of spherical shape one morning [in the winter of] 1967. It was of whitish or metallic color and showed no surface features as it drifted slowly near the outskirts of the city. The officers watched it for about 1.5 hours before it drifted out of sight.
2. Several town policemen reported a red-and-green light moving irregularly in the western sky in the morning in winter of 1967. The planet Jupiter was low in the western sky also, but according to the witnesses the object displayed movement which would rule out identification as an astronomical object. They also stated that a bright "star" was visible near the object.
3. Three teen-age boys in the city reported to the police that they had just seen a large elongated UFO at the edge of town. Their description closely matched that of a recently publicized set of pictures that have since come under suspicion as a probable hoax. Credibility of these witnesses was considered marginal.

We shall consider these three cases in turn:

1. Jupiter and Venus were both in the early morning sky of the south-central U.S. during the winter of 1967. The sighting of the officers took place during the hour and a half before dawn. The drifting of the object can be attributed to autokinesis and its disappearance to the brightening of the early morning sky.
2. The same considerations apply here. The apparent movement

of the object does not, as stated in the abstract, rule out identification as an astronomical object.

3. This seems a transparent hoax. There was no corroborative evidence whatever for the alleged sighting.

CONDON REPORT, CASE 17

South Mountain, Spring 1967

Abstract: A youth reported that a large, glowing object approached his car and accompanied it more than twenty miles. He described apparent electromagnetic effects on his automobile. Investigation revealed neither a natural explanation to account for the sighting nor sufficient evidence to sustain an unconventional hypothesis.

Here we have yet another case of a single-observer report with no supporting evidence. The magnetization pattern of the automobile was checked and was found to be normal. The engine was found to be badly out of tune, but "no physical evidence could be found that was related to the sighting."

Again we must wonder why the case was deemed worthy of inclusion. And the account of this sighting is defective in that the date is not given; this date would be of interest, since the moon "chasing" a train or auto has been repeatedly misidentified as an UFO.

CONDON REPORT, CASE 21

South Mountain, Spring 1967

Abstract: Operators of two airport radars [in Colorado Springs] reported that a target equivalent to an aircraft had followed a commercial flight in, overtaken it, and passed it on one side, proceeding at about 200 knots until it left the radar field. No corresponding object was visible from the control tower. On the basis of witnesses' reports and weather records, explanations based on anomalous atmospheric propagation or freak reflection from other objects appear inadequate. The case is not adequately explained despite features that suggest a reflection effect.

This is the much-cited case of the Colorado Springs "phantom aircraft." The sighting was, as we show in the next chapter, attributable to radar artifact. Radar artifacts, or ghosts, are numerous and well-known, and spurious "targets" are commonplace. The most interesting question raised here is why, when airport control-tower personnel, plus the crews of two aircraft in the immediate vicinity, failed altogether to make any visual observation of *anything* corresponding to the radar target, anyone found the incident worth reporting, let alone investigating. Moreover, Low sent the basic data to DHM for comments and suggestions. DHM quickly recognized the effects of anomalous propagation and sent his analysis to Low, who commended DHM for his solution of the sighting. Further details are given in the next chapter.

CONDON REPORT, CASE 22

North-Central U.S., Spring 1967

Abstract: A weekend prospector claimed that a "flying saucer" landed near him in the woods and that when he approached the object and touched it with his gloved hand, it soared away, its exhaust blast leaving a patterned burn on his abdomen and making him ill. Events during and subsequent to a field search for the landing site *cast strong doubt upon the authenticity of the report.*

As indeed they might. The Condon Report's conclusion is gentle: ". . . this case does not offer probative information regarding unconventional craft."

Well, it certainly doesn't. First, the project investigator and the prospector together were unable to locate the site of the happening. Second, the "illness" appeared to have been caused by nothing more exotic than insect bites. And third, the project's attempts to establish the reality of the event revealed "many inconsistencies and incongruities . . ." Again, this is a gentle conclusion. We regard the case as a badly executed hoax.

CONDON REPORT, CASE 31

Northeastern U.S., Fall 1967

Abstract: A woman and her children driving on a rural road at night saw a trapezoidal pattern of dim red lights over the road. As the car approached the lights, they moved off the road and disappeared between the trees. The possibility that the lights were on a microwave tower in the vicinity of the sighting is discounted by the witness' familiarity with the road and tower, her accurate account of accessory details, and other factors.

This case illustrates, again, a curious inability of the Colorado staff to come up with an incisive report of a dubious incident. In the brief space devoted to this sighting the presence of a microwave tower at the site is discounted as an explanation of the appearance of the pattern of red lights. Yet in the same brief space it is stated that "the sighting can be explained by the presence of the microwave tower[!]." And nothing whatever is reported about the weather conditions at the time.

In fact, the tower bore a red light on top, plus four red lights halfway down, one on each leg of the tower. The data provided in the report are far from adequate, but our supposition is that the meteorological conditions prevalent at the time, with attendant reflections and refractions, provide the probable rational explanation for this "unexplained" case. Again, the few data available preclude conclusive analysis.

CONDON REPORT, CASE 33

Northeastern U.S., Summer 1967

Abstract: Two teen-aged girls in a rural home reported that in the evening a large glowing object had hovered nearby and that several child-sized figures had been seen running about near the barn. Testimony of others in the area was inconclusive, in some respects supporting and in others weakening their account. No definite explanation was found, but the case is considered weak.

This case is indeed weak. Children, in most times and cultures, are inclined to play pranks—and one of the best is to send aloft a glowing device which will look like an apparition. Even Newton when a child, as we note in Chapter 17, was guilty of this peccadillo. The ufological literature is replete with glowing objects sent skyward by kids—which could be one explanation for this sighting. There is another as well.

Though the Condon Report does not specifically mention the fact, the Condon papers reveal that the two witnesses were given psychological tests; the results of these tests indicated that both girls were more than normally given to fabrication or to exaggeration of anything unusual. One of the girls' test results showed tendencies toward borderline hallucinatory perceptual distortion. The other girl was suggestible and hence might be inclined to make her companion's delusion her own.

Thus there is a plethora of natural explanations for this sighting.

CONDON REPORT, CASE 34

North Atlantic, Fall 1967

Abstract: Information obtained in telephone interviews with officers of Canadian Naval Maritime Command and RCMP indicated that an object bearing several colored lights glided with a whistling noise into the sea. Search by boats and divers found no debris or wreckage.

The original report of this sighting was provided by some Canadian teen-agers—either two or five, according to the differing reports. The incident occurred in Canada, 200–300 yards offshore. There were witnesses other than the teen-agers. The Royal Canadian Mounted Police and the Maritime Command searched the area, but found nothing except a patch of foam. Coast Guard boats and fishing boats were also on the scene. No one actually saw anything enter the water.

The Colorado Project conducted its investigation by telephone, holding the view that, because a search had been made by other agencies at the time of the sighting, further investigation was not justified.

Plate 8. St. Elmo's fire in ships' rigging. The single dread "meteor" Helena hovers over a sinking vessel. The double apparition of Castor and Pollux supposedly brings good fortune; the vessel upon which they are seen rides out the storm. *The Houghton Library, Harvard University*

Plate 9. Marine mirages. Lenses of air produce peculiar inversions, enlargements, and double images. *F. Zürcher and E. Margolié,* Meteors, Aerolites, Storms, and Atmospheric Phenomena, 1876

Plate 10. The Specter of the Brocken. *Photo by J. F. Chappell*

Plate 11. The Specter of the Brocken, showing how the halo is associated only with the beholder—in this case, a camera. *Photo by J. F. Chappell*

Plate 12. *top:* Parhelic phenomena over Nuremberg, 1581. Sundogs and cross, with no halo. *From the Department of Prints and Drawings of the Zentralbibliothek, Zürich*

Plate 13. *bottom:* Sundogs and parts of three halos, as seen in Nuremberg, April 1583. *From the Department of Prints and Drawings of the Zentralbibliothek, Zürich*

All of the alleged facts regarding this sighting are entirely consistent with the identification of the object as a small meteorite.

CONDON REPORT, CASE 39

South Pacific U.S., Fall 1967

Abstract: A businessman reported that his automobile had been stopped by an UFO he observed while driving alone in a rural area. The case was checked as a possible source of information regarding electromagnetic effects of UFOs. Comparison of the magnetic pattern of the automobile body with that of another car of similar make and model showed the businessman's car had not been exposed to a strong magnetic field. The case, therefore, apparently did not offer probative information regarding UFOs.

We agree with the conclusion of the Condon Report. Again, a single-witness sighting, with no substantiating evidence whatever. In addition, the witness's story contained "serious discrepancies." But we question the inclusion of such a pointless case.

CONDON REPORT, CASE 42

North-Central U.S., Fall 1967

Abstract: A state trooper . . . reported a saucer-like object landed on or hovered over the highway 40 feet in front of him. The object departed straight upward at high speed. The trooper could not account for a 20-minute period during which he assumed he must have been near the UFO. No evidence was found that a physical object had been present as claimed. Psychological assessment of the trooper, carried out with his approval and co-operation, also failed to provide evidence that the reported object was physically real.

The trooper "saw" the classic flying saucer, according to the discussion of this case in the Condon Report: proper shape; surface like polished aluminum, brilliantly glowing; siren-like sounds; the inevitable row of oval red-lighted portholes, above a surrounding cat walk; and flame-colored material emitted from below. Of none of this, however, could any trace be found.

A psychological evaluation of the witness left the staff "with no confidence that the trooper's reported UFO experience was physically real." Before studying the psychological test results, we speculated that the most likely explanation of this sighting was either fabrication or hallucination. We found that the test results support either of these explanations; considering all of the data relevant to the sighting, we conclude that fabrication is the more likely explanation.[9]

CONDON REPORT, CASE 43

South-Central U.S., Fall 1967

Abstract: Confused reports by teen-agers of strange lights were attributed to assorted lights on flat countryside and possibly aircraft.

This sighting (which ought not to have been included in the Condon Report) began when a group of six teen-agers, returning home from a basketball game, decided to drive by a cemetery to frighten themselves[!]. They saw a variety of different lights, some of which they attempted to follow. Their descriptions of what they had seen differed widely. The Colorado investigators found that, in the neighborhood of the sightings, lights were visible in *all* directions. These lights were of many kinds—"of various colors and intensities, and degrees of scintillation. Some were in clusters, some alone." One of the boys was a student of UFOs and took them very seriously. The "evidence" in this case consisted of six conflicting stories. The investigators, unable (considering all the lights in the area) to rule out ordinary aircraft, labeled the case "unexplained."

CONDON REPORT, CASE 44

North-Central U.S., Winter 1967

Abstract: Witness driving on highway at night reported having seen a dim shape and a pattern of colored lights above an under-pass. From the farther side of the underpass [the shape] appeared to have moved away opposite to the direction [the witness] was traveling. No field investigation was made.

The witness in this case, the non-field investigation revealed, was a distraught medical student suffering from severe anxiety and possibly "on the verge of a more severe mental disturbance." His mental condition had been evident before the sighting. There were no supporting witnesses to the sighting. The Colorado Project decided not to make a field study.

It would be feckless to speculate on the explanation for this whatever-it-was, but there is certainly no need to invoke visitation by an alien spacecraft. To someone poised on the brink of serious mental illness, every nocturnal stimulus is likely to be misinterpreted.

CONDON REPORT, CASE 46
McMinnville, Oregon, May 11, 1950

Abstract: Witness reportedly saw a metallic-looking disk-shaped UFO. She called her husband, they located their camera, and he took photographs of the object before it disappeared in the distance.

The McMinnville sighting was widely publicized in 1950, and it has remained one of the favorites of the believers. It is another case Hynek thought worthy of further study. The Condon Report's discussion of the case concluded: "This is one of the few UFO reports in which all factors investigated, geometric, psychological, and physical, appear to be consistent with the assertion that an extraordinary flying object, silvery, metallic, disk-shaped, tens of meters in diameter, and evidently artificial [extraterrestrial], flew within sight of two witnesses."

In fact, this is but one more "classic" that took in many people, but was later demonstrated to have been a fabrication. Inde-

pendent investigations by Philip Klass and Robert Sheaffer* have
demonstrated:

1. That there were serious discrepancies in the different accounts of the sighting given by the principal witness, and
2. That the two photographs, said by both witnesses to have
been taken in the late afternoon, themselves revealed that they had
been taken in the early morning.

The conclusion was obvious: the photographs were a hoax. In
addition, as had been known at the time of the Condon investigation, the principal witness and her husband were repeaters.

The clincher, however, were one needed, is that when the Colorado Project photoanalyst, who had previously thought that the
photographs might have been authentic, was presented with
Sheaffer's conclusions, he revised his earlier views.

CONDON REPORT, CASE 47

Great Falls, Montana, August 15, 1950

Abstract: Witnesses I and II observed two white lights moving
slowly across the sky. Witness I made 16-mm motion pictures of
the lights. Both individuals have recently reaffirmed the observation, and there is little reason to question its validity. The case remains unexplained. Analysis indicates that the images on the film
are difficult to reconcile with aircraft or other known phenomena,
although aircraft cannot be entirely ruled out.

This was a widely publicized sighting, a photographic case in
which the question of fabrication did not arise. Something was
photographed; the question is, What?

The sighting was shortly analyzed by the Air Force, and the
case has been repeatedly analyzed since. The basic facts are these:

1. The principal witness—witness I in the foregoing abstract—

---

* Sheaffer, a computer systems programmer currently at NASA's Goddard
Space Flight Center in Greenbelt, Maryland, is a canny student of the UFO
scene. His work is cited in Klass; see note 2, above.

was the manager of a Great Falls baseball team. (Witness II was his secretary.) While at the (empty) ball park he saw two bright objects moving in the sky. He ran for his 16-mm movie camera, and shot a sixteen-second take of the objects sweeping across the sky.

2. The witness at the time of filming was about three miles from the Great Falls AFB (later renamed Malmstrom AFB) where two F-94 jet aircraft landed about two minutes after the sighting. These were the only planes in the air in the area at the time of the sighting.

The first Air Force investigation attributed (correctly, we think) the sighting to reflections of sunlight from the two F-94s. The Colorado investigation did not rule out aircraft as explaining the case, but tagged it with the "unexplained" label because— among other reasons, but this seems to us the main one—the witness said he saw the two aircraft going in for landing *immediately following the filming*. How, then, to account for the two lights?

Besides being the manager of a local baseball team, the witness was a journalism graduate, had been a newspaper editor, and was a radio commentator—clearly publicity-minded and public-relations conscious. We suggest that the witness photographed what were to him at the time unknown moving objects in the sky. When the flight paths were such that the reflections were lost, he recognized the objects for what they were—two jet airplanes. Sensing a story that would bring publicity to his ball club (it did), he withheld the identification.

This is, at least, a rational explanation, certainly far simpler than postulating the presence in Great Falls of extraterrestrial craft, by great coincidence, precisely when two Air Force jets were in the air in the same place at the same time and saw nothing unusual.[10]

CONDON REPORT, CASE 52

Santa Ana, California, August 3, 1965

Abstract: While on duty a [highway] traffic investigator ob-

served that his two-way radio had been cut off just before a
metallic-looking disk allegedly moved across the road in front of
him. He took three photographs of the object before it moved off
into the haze and emitted a ring of smoke. He drove down the
road about a mile and photographed the smoke cloud. The
evidence regarding the object's reality is inconclusive and internally inconsistent.

Though this sighting, to which the Condon Report devoted
nineteen pages of text and six photographs, is listed as unexplained, we believe that it was most likely a hoax. This belief is
based upon the following considerations:

1. The difficulty with the two-way radio occurred before the alleged UFO sighting, not during the encounter.

2. Major Hector Quintanilla, Jr., of Project Blue Book, made a
public statement later to the effect that the Air Force had classified
the case as a photographic hoax.

3. The Colorado investigators decided that the case was without
value. In unpublished correspondence one investigator wrote: "He
[a second investigator, James McDonald, a ufologist who supported the ETH (see p. 83)] and I agree that [this] case now has
little value in establishing UFOs, because of too many discrepancies and the ease of producing a hoax."[11]

4. One of the Colorado investigators easily simulated three of
the four photographs. To represent the UFO he used a Leica lens
cap.

5. The clouds in one of the photographs were inconsistent with
the known weather at the time of the alleged sighting.

6. There were numerous inconsistencies in the various accounts
of the sighting and subsequent events related by the witness.

Why, then, did the report not classify this case as at least a suspected hoax? Because ". . . it is not in general our purpose to
make a judgment on that question. We are concerned only with establishing evidence as to whether or not there exist extraordinary
flying objects."

CONDON REPORT, CASE 56

North Pacific U.S., Winter 1967

Abstract: This case involves two photographs of a disk-shaped UFO. The apparent time interval between the photos is inconsistent with the eight-second reported interval (which was based on careful restaging of the alleged incident). The report must be listed as internally inconsistent and therefore is not satisfying evidence for an unusual phenomenon.

The witnesses in this case were teen-age boys. They said they had seen from their suburban back yard a disk-like object hovering in the sky. They took a Polaroid photo of the object, which then began to move away. As quickly as possible—about eight seconds later—they took a second picture.

The Colorado investigator studied the photographs and found that during the alleged eight-second interval there had been gross changes in cloud structure and position that could not have occurred in that short time. The conclusion, as stated in the Condon Report, was that this inconsistency impaired "the usefulness of these photographs as evidence to establish the existence of 'flying saucers' or other unusual phenomena."

Another hoax.

CONDON REPORT, CASE 57

Highwood Ranger Station, Alberta, Canada, July 3, 1967

Abstract: The witness and two companions reportedly sighted and took two photographs of an object described as shiny and approximately twenty-five feet in diameter. The craft reportedly dropped a small object, which when recovered was reported to be composed of solder, aluminum, and magnesium. A report by the Royal Canadian Air Force implied substantial evidence that the sighting was authentic . . . Although the case was widely described, both in the press and by several investigators, as being exceptionally strong, examination of the original photographs and the circumstances indicates no evidence of probative value for the existence of unusual aircraft. Only the sworn testimony of the witnesses could be described as making this case more impressive than most others.

This sighting, which occurred near Calgary, Alberta, Canada, in 1967, attracted considerable attention. It was investigated by the RCAF who, noting that the photos were consistent with the testimony, concluded that the case was impressive. The Colorado investigator was less impressed:

. . . the rapid panning and blurring of the second photo and the pitch of the disk toward the observer are characteristic of photographs of hand-thrown models. In my opinion, it is basically this problem that makes the Calgary photos of no probative value in establishing the existence of 'flying saucers'; the photographs cannot be distinguished from photographs of a hand-thrown model. . . . Therefore, the case cannot be said to contribute significant evidence in establishing the existence of unusual aircraft.

These, then, are the Condon Report cases left as "unexplained." We cannot agree with that designation. The sightings are explained by chicanery, fabrication, mental illness, radar malfunction, anomalous radar propagation, physiological phenomena such as autokinesis and after-images, and misidentifications of astronomical objects, such as planets and meteorites.

Thus we find, in these "unexplained" sightings, a total lack of support for the extraterrestrial hypothesis. The "inexplicable residue of unknowns" does not exist.

If, among all the smoke of all the UFO sightings everywhere, there should occur the fire of just one sighting "with irreproachable credentials and inescapable significance," the reality and nature of the UFO phenomenon would be established.[12] Such a sighting has not yet been reported.

Astronaut Sightings

We should not leave this array of "unexplained sightings" without discussing the astronaut sightings. The United States space program, virtually from its inception, has produced many reports by astronauts of unidentified objects in space. Because the observers of these objects were skilled and highly trained technicians, many supporters of the extraterrestrial hypothesis have seized upon the astronaut sightings as proof of the validity of that hypothesis. The Condon Report included a chapter on these sightings, but the conclusions presented in that chapter were not incisive; in addition, there have been numerous sightings since the Report was published. We shall now briefly bring the matter of astronaut sightings of UFOs up to date. We are indebted here to the expertise and analyses of James Oberg—a writer, researcher, and historian of aerospace activities.

During the flight of Gemini 4, astronaut James McDivitt saw a cylindrical object with an antennalike protuberance. He said it looked much like the upper stage of a booster rocket. He tried to photograph the object, but when he later examined the films he found nothing resembling his UFO. He reported the sighting to Houston, and the information was relayed on to NORAD (North American Air Defense Command), whose responsibilities include the tracking and cataloguing of objects in space. NORAD provided a list of space hardware in the general vicinity of the Gemini spacecraft. The most likely candidate to explain McDivitt's sighting was Pegasus B, then about twelve hundred miles distant. The object had seemed much nearer to McDivitt. The Condon Report was dissatisfied with the Pegasus B identification and listed the sighting as a "puzzler."

Oberg, in his analysis of this sighting, makes some crucial observations: (1) the NORAD computers had not been asked the whereabouts of Gemini 4's own debris; (2) the Gemini booster had earlier been spotted by McDivitt at the same point in the Gemini orbit where the UFO appeared; (3) McDivitt had on another occasion been unable to recognize his own booster at a range of less than ten miles; and (4) during this phase of the flight he was suffering considerable eye irritation because of an accidental urine spill that contaminated the cabin atmosphere.[13]

In the face of these facts, the McDivitt sighting joins the ranks of previously "unexplained" cases subsequently accounted for when more data were available for analysis. What McDivitt saw was his own Titan booster stage.

Oberg also disposes of a widely distributed Gemini 7 photograph that purports to show two strange hexagonal glowing objects, supported by "force fields." A cloud-covered Earth appears in the background. Oberg shows that the original NASA photo had been doctored by a wily charlatan. The real photo shows the glare of the sun on two roll-control rocket thrusters. In the retouched picture part of the spacecraft has been eliminated, leaving the hexagonal objects glowing in space, suspended by their mysterious force fields. (It should be noted that photographic artifacts are frequently hexagonal, because that is the shape of the camera's iris diaphragm.)

During another Gemini flight Charles Conrad, Jr., saw and photographed an unidentified object. NORAD reported that it must have been a Russian cosmic-ray laboratory, Proton 3. The trouble with this identification, according to the computer, was that Proton 3 would have crossed the Gemini orbit hundreds of miles behind the Gemini spacecraft. Therefore it was an UFO!

Oberg points out that the NORAD identification was, after all, accurate. The computer had not been informed that Proton 3 was in a decaying orbit, soon to make its re-entry into the atmosphere. At the time of the sighting it was traveling well ahead of the schedule programmed into the NORAD computer.

Other examples of UFOs seen from space could be given, but these are sufficient to show that for all cases where the data are adequate and perspicaciously analyzed, there remains no residuum of unsolved sightings. All are attributable to normal unmysterious phenomena.

CHAPTER 9

RADAR—FACT AND FICTION

As I was going up the stair
   I met a man who wasn't there.
He wasn't there again today.
   I wish, I wish he'd stay away.

   Hughes Mearns, The Psychoed

"Radar" is an acronym for "radio detecting and ranging." The basic concepts of radar have been understood since at least 1886, when the German physicist Heinrich Hertz proved that radio waves can be reflected from solid objects. The concept appeared in science fiction as early as 1911 in a novel by Hugo Gernsback, writer of science fiction, and editor of a number of popular journals of science and of science fiction.[1] Though the basic principle is quite simple, radar technology did not approach its present sophistication until the need for it, as a defensive weapon, arose with the advent of World War II.

   In typical radar operation a radio transmitter sends out a sharp pulse of electromagnetic radiation, usually in the UHF (ultrahighfrequency) range. A dish-shaped antenna focuses the pulse in a certain direction. If the transmitted signal encounters something solid—an airplane, rain clouds, a flight of birds, an iceberg—part of the energy is reflected back toward the source, where a receiver measures the time interval between the departure of the pulse and the reception of the echo. Radio waves travel at the speed of 186,000 miles per second. Hence, if the signal returns after an interval of one thousandth of a second, we know that the pulse has traveled 186 miles—ninety-three miles to the target and ninety-three miles back. The phenomenon is indeed a true echo. At the transmitting site a rotating antenna scans the horizon. The return signals are displayed upon an image tube, or screen, similar to that of a television set. The observer is, in effect, at the center of this screen. Bright spots (blips) indicate the presence of targets, or reflecting bodies. If the target is moving, successive rotations of the beam will show a bright spot moving on the screen. There are many other ways of presenting the results, but the fundamental principle is the same.

Though the basic principle of radar is as simple as that of an echo, the military who used the device in World War II soon found that this new technique possessed some remarkable and unexpected peculiarities. One of us (DHM) became extremely familiar with these problems during the war. As a Commander in the U. S. Navy Reserve, he was in charge of the Section of Mathematics and Physics Research for Naval Communications. In addition, he was a member of, and later chairman of, the Wave Propagation Committees of the Joint and Combined Chiefs of Staff.[2] The task of the groups was to study problems of communication, including those associated with radar.

Radar employs electromagnetic radiation of wavelengths much longer than those of light, but far shorter than those used for ordinary radio communication. Preliminary studies had indicated that radar waves behaved much like light waves. Hence they would be limited pretty much to the optical horizon. However, in certain tactical applications, there came to the attention of the Wave Propagation Committees many puzzling cases of what was then called "anomalous propagation."

No one had foreseen that radar waves, like light waves under certain conditions, could be bent to produce mirages. They would sometimes follow the earth's curvature for thousands of miles, producing confusing false images. In the Mediterranean, for example, a cruiser using radar shelled and reported sinking a target that later proved to be a false image of the island of Malta.

And on another occasion a task force in the Pacific witnessed via radar, from a distance of 600 nautical miles, the Japanese evacuation of Kiska—and ignored it because they knew nothing about anomalous propagation. Proper interpretation of the radar record would have enabled the task force to engage and possibly disable the Japanese fleet. Answers to such problems were of vital importance to Naval Operations.

Some frightening and spectacular experiences happened off northern Japan, in the vicinity of the Nansei Shoto (Ryukyu Islands), in 1944, where U.S. submarines were carrying on extensive operations in Japanese waters, sinking ships and otherwise contributing materially to weakening the Japanese war effort.

As far as radar was concerned, our submarines could operate it at a disadvantage and at considerable peril to themselves. A submarine in enemy waters usually surfaced only at night. Then, while its air supply was being replenished and the submarine conditioned, radar reconnaissance was employed to locate possible targets and to check the position of other enemy craft. One of the most puzzling reports came from the Nansei Shoto area and concerned what the Navy observers called "galloping ghosts."

A radar operator, seated before his scope, was checking on possible targets as the submarine cruised slowly on the surface. He at times noticed that one—and sometimes more than one—of the bright points of light on the radar screen was heading directly toward the submarine, on a course apparently designed to intercept it. If, to protect himself, he called for a change in course, the image on the screen would instantaneously follow suit. No matter what the submarine did, the image appeared to be on inevitable collision course with the submarine. Then, just at the moment when impact seemed inevitable, the image would vanish from the screen. Observers on deck reported that they had seen nothing. The galloping ghosts of Nansei Shoto had struck again. This was before the current era of flying saucers or UFOs but, in the middle of a war, it was vital to solve the mystery.

A series of experiments and theoretical studies, under the auspices of the Wave Propagation Committees, in which DHM played an active role, finally did resolve the problem.

The phenomenon proved to be closely akin to that of a "superior optical mirage," which we discuss in the next chapter. A layer of cold air close to the surface of the sea bends the radar waves, trapping them and preventing them from reaching higher levels. In such conditions radar pulses bounce around from ship to shore, and from ship to ship, often over great distances. Sometimes they are reflected more than once by the same moving object, including the submarine that sent out the signal originally. The high velocity of the moving image represented the sums of the speeds of the different reflectors. And the sudden mysterious disappearance of the signal, near apparent collision point, was attributable to the fact that the submarine itself was one of the reflectors. In short, the received echo did not represent, in any sense, the location of the target.

In those days no one suggested that the mysterious radar ghosts might be caused by vehicles from outer space. That could have "explained" the phenomenon, but, for operational purposes, the real explanation was much more important.

The phenomenon of "ducting" or "trapping" of radar waves or other ultrahigh-frequency electromagnetic radiation close to the surface of the earth had various tactical applications during the war. The U. S. Navy had installed, on various Pacific islands, devices known as "transponders"—apparatus that would receive a radio signal from a plane and then send out a signal that would guide it to a landing field on the island. But we were losing far too many of our own planes that had to "ditch." The pilots picked up later in their rubber rafts reported troubles with their transponder equipment. Our studies indicated that the then-recommended tactics for an aircraft lost over the Pacific were entirely wrong: they were supposed to go as high as possible, send out their identification, and then home in on the transponder.

DHM, faced with the need to find an operational solution to the problem, decided that the difficulty probably lay in trapping. The same layer of cold air close to the ocean's surface, which trapped the signal within it, also prevented the plane's signal from reaching the transponder. He recommended, therefore, that lost pilots fly as close as possible to the surface of the sea to send out their signals to the transponder. This program proved to be successful, and losses of American aircraft in this kind of situation were reduced to practically zero.

Many other kinds of false images were experienced in the radar

program. Such images, often referred to as "angels," are frequently associated with clouds of different kinds. The appearance
of cloud-angels occurs most frequently when moist clouds are rising into layers of very dry air. Clouds of flying insects can produce
radar echoes, and birds frequently pose a real problem. Birds are
easily detected by radar at distances up to twenty-five miles, and
large birds at a distance of about ten miles produce an echo very
similar to that of a medium-size aircraft at fifty miles. Astonishingly enough, as few as eight birds per square mile can completely fill a radar screen.³ Sometimes even bubbles of hot air
(clear-air turbulence) produce radar echoes.

In the postwar era one of the most spectacular displays of puzzling radar ghosts occurred in the summer of 1952 in the vicinity
of the National Airport in Washington, D.C. The blips on the
scopes seemed to represent an armada of moving saucers. Commercial planes were grounded, and military jets screamed over the
area in vain attempts to intercept some of these objects. Pilots reported seeing peculiar lights in the direction of their radar targets,
but nothing was definitely identified, except that one of the planes
repeatedly homed in on a yacht floating on the Potomac.

Meteorological data for the interval were unfortunately frag-
mentary, but studies made by the U. S. Weather Bureau (now the
National Weather Service), and by a number of qualified groups
within the military, established beyond doubt that the targets were
spurious, produced by partial trapping. Radar waves were simply
being reflected by bubbles of warm air in the atmosphere. The
reflections came from distant buildings, the aforementioned yacht
on the Potomac, or possibly from moving trains or automobiles.
Regardless of what the flying-saucer enthusiasts have tried to main-
tain, there was absolutely nothing puzzling about these radar
sightings.

At this point we may dispose of another fallacy in the UFO area
—apparent simultaneous sightings of an UFO by radar and by eye.
First of all, the radar, if operating correctly, will indicate the distance and direction of the object that is reflecting the radar pulse.
But if trapping exits, the radar cannot tell how far above the horizon the object is. With multiple reflections, the observer usually
knows how far the signal has traveled, but he cannot be sure of the

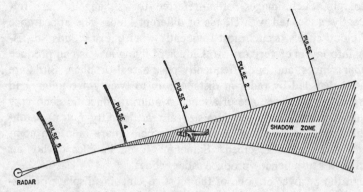

Figure 3. Physicists expected radar pulses to behave much like light waves so that they could not reveal a plane flying within the shadow zone. *Donald H. Menzel,* Elementary Manual of Radio Propagation, © *1948, pp. 147–49. Reprinted by permission of Prentice-Hall, Inc., Englewood Cliffs, New Jersey*

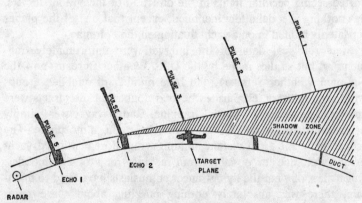

Figure 4. Actually, temperature inversions form a sort of duct, trapping the radar waves. The reflections from even a distant plane can produce strong echoes from pulses other than the nearest reflector. The radar operator will therefore not be able to determine where the plane actually is. *Donald H. Menzel,* Elementary Manual of Radio Propagation, © *1948, pp. 147–49. Reprinted by permission of Prentice-Hall, Inc., Englewood Cliffs, New Jersey*

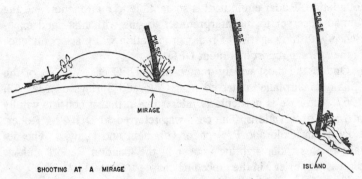

Figure 5. Shooting at a mirage. The ship, observing a strong echo from a distant island, thinks it to be a nearby enemy vessel. *Donald H. Menzel*, Elementary Manual of Radio Propagation, © *1948, pp. 147–49. Reprinted by permission of Prentice-Hall, Inc., Englewood Cliffs, New Jersey*

direction. As indicated previously, the object may simply be a building on the ground.

A visual image, however, at very best, simply tells the direction in which one sees a light. It tells absolutely nothing about the distance of that light. Hence one cannot say with certainty that the source of the radar blip and the visual stimulus are identical. If trapping conditions are present for radar, visual mirage is also likely to be present. Of the hundreds of cases of simultaneous sightings reported in the Air Force files, not one has an unqualified verification that the two targets were identical.

Radar has many other peculiarities. For example, the transmitter sends out pulses at regular intervals—at, let us say, one-thousandth of a second. If we receive an echo after precisely that interval, we infer that the pulse traveled 186 miles during the interval—93 miles to the object and the same in return. However, if trapping conditions exist, the target may be at twice this distance, three times this distance, and so on. Thus, unless the transmitter has capability to vary the signal rate there is always uncertainty about the distance of the target. It was this phenomenon that led to the ambiguities previously mentioned relative to the Malta, Kiska, and Nansei Shoto incidents.

The popular view that radar cannot make an error is without

foundation. Radar equipment is susceptible to malfunction and the human observer to misinterpreting. No one with first-hand experience with the vagaries of radar propagation will place confidence in the average report of a radar UFO.

One of the most widely quoted radar-UFO cases is that of the "phantom airplane" detected near Colorado Springs on May 13, 1967. The case is particularly interesting in that it consists wholly of radar observations. The case was referred to DHM by Robert Low of the Colorado Project for comment and analysis. The details of this radar sighting appear in the Condon Report and we discussed it briefly in the preceding chapter (Case 21).[4]

Two airport radars picked up the image of a Braniff International airplane, a Boeing 720, when it was about four miles from the field. (A second plane, a Continental Airlines Vickers Viscount, also appeared on the radar scope, but does not figure in the case.) Just as the radar operator picked up the Braniff plane on the screen, he detected an extremely faint target about four miles behind the 720. Further observation disclosed that the radar-UFO was following the 720 at approximately twice its distance from the airport radar and was overtaking it. Several alerted observers watched visually for the unknown plane but saw nothing. There was a fear that it might collide with the Braniff aircraft. The 720 came in and landed, whereupon the radar-UFO vanished from the screen; apart from the blip on the scope, nothing had been seen of it. What was this UFO ghost?

Reduced to essentials, the report was one of an UFO moving toward the airport approximately twice as fast as the primary target. The phenomenon has only one explanation: the pulse of radar reflected from the 720 came back to earth within a mile or so of the airport *where something reflected it back to the same aircraft, which again reflected the now-weakened signal.* The second echo, traversing about twice the path length of the first, would always appear on the radar screen to be twice as far away as the primary target. And, of course, as the 720 landed, the UFO vanished from the screen.

The foregoing explanation requires the presence of a reflector of some sort to intercept the downcoming radar pulse and return it almost precisely to the target plane. Such a reflector is well-known both in radar and in optical work as a "corner reflector." It consists of three surfaces at right angles to each other, such as two inside walls and floor of a room. A rubber ball tossed into the general area of such a corner will bounce successively against each of the three surfaces and then return practically along its original path. A light beam reflected from three mirrors so arranged will return precisely to the source. Mirrors made up of multiple corner reflectors have been put in position on the moon to return laser signals sent from Earth. They also circle the earth in orbiting satellites, reflecting back laser pulses. Accurate measures of time intervals permit extremely precise measurements of distances to the corresponding reflectors on the moon or in Earth orbit.

A radar beam, reflected from any corner reflector, will behave in precisely the same way. Many unintended reflectors are available—for example, the inside of a dump truck, the corners of a metal fence or building, or the inside of an empty, open freight car. This simple explanation, based not upon speculation, but on actual radar experience, accounts for the major facts of the phantom UFO of Colorado Springs.

Although Air Force Project Blue Book acknowledged the correctness of this explanation, the Colorado Project, for some reason, failed to accept the explanation and listed the sighting as "unexplained." It is preposterous to postulate the existence of a ghost UFO following the primary plane at exactly twice the speed and twice the distance and then becoming invisible just at the moment it should appear to the observer's vision! Yet this is what the believers attempt to promote.

We have already shown in the preceding chapter how the phenomenon of anomalous propagation accounts for the famous Bentwaters-Lakenheath sighting (Case 2, Condon Report).

Another interesting case, not cited in the Condon Report, is that of the puzzling radar echoes detected at Andersen AFB in Guam in the months following October 1965. Radar operators at this base repeatedly picked up radar returns that had no known or identifiable source. In August 1966 an investigatory team was sent to Guam to determine the cause of the mystifying phenomena.

The investigators discovered that the unidentified echoes indicated targets that appeared to approach Guam from the northeast and to come within about thirty miles of the base and then go off to the northwest. Approach altitude was about 15,000 feet. This altitude diminished to less than 1,000 feet at closest approach, then increased again as the targets moved off.

From the beginning of the investigation the team suspected that the radar blips were caused by multiple-trip echoes. Accordingly, the investigators assumed that the echoes came from aircraft after the radar signals had made two trips to the plane and back. They then plotted the course that an aircraft would have to fly if their hypothesis of second-trip radar return were correct. The flight path proved to be about 250 miles north of Guam, a path flown every day between Wake Island and Clark AFB in the Philippines. The investigating team proved conclusively that the unidentified echoes were from jet transport aircraft flying from Wake to Clark AFB— one more example of anomalous propagation.[5]

Under ducting or trapping conditions, radar pulses are trapped between the earth and a temperature inversion in the atmosphere. The signals are thus confined, are strong (because the energy does not dissipate outward beyond the inversion layer), and may reflect back and forth, from numerous reflectors, many times before returning to the original source. Thus a single pulse can produce multiple images on the screen from targets that, though stationary, may appear to gallop at high speeds. Let us see how such apparitions can occur.

Consider, for a moment, a radar installation whose antenna has stopped rotating. It is transmitting, let us say, 1,000 pulses of electromagnetic energy a second. The pulses follow one another like bullets from a machine gun, spaced precisely 186 miles apart. The pulses strike some solid object: an airborne plane, a distant building, a bridge. The object sprays the impinging energy in all directions. A small amount of the energy of the original pulse returns to the radar antenna, which measures the time elapsed since the pulse was sent out. The interval between the emission of the pulse and the returned echo measures the distance of the reflecting object.

The receiver records this echo as a bright spot on the radar screen. Since successive echoes from the object follow each other at intervals of one one-thousandth of a second, the spot is produced by thousands of pulses. Several targets, at different distances, would produce, of course, bright spots at different distances from the center of the screen.

If the radar antenna is set into rotation, a bright line rotates (turns) on the screen like the second hand of a clock. The "ground return," reflections from a region devoid of targets, shows faintly as a background glow. But the reflection from a target, such as a plane or ship, remains as a bright blip on the radar screen. Hence the operator, watching the scope, can distinguish moving objects from stationary ones. In general, a moving blip signifies a moving object.

Now suppose that intense trapping conditions occur; the pulses are reflected back to earth and may be re-reflected several times before returning to the receiver. Again, imagine that the antenna is not rotating. A pulse, sprayed in all directions by some distant stationary target, is subsequently reflected, let us say, from two other targets still farther away and lying in the trapping zone where the radar signals are concentrated. These two reflected pulses now return to the original reflector, which reflects them to the stationary radar antenna.

The receiver may thus receive many pulses from the same direction, but from different distances. One comes directly from the primary target and the others from multiple reflections from the secondary targets. All will appear as coming from the same direction, for the radar antenna is stationary. Note that radar records the *direction* of the apparent target and measures the *distance* the signal has traveled. In the event of severe trapping, when signals may travel great distance, an image that appears near the center of the screen may actually be that of a target actually lying beyond the boundaries of the screen.

Now cause the antenna to rotate. As it scans the horizon, the images, multiply reflected from different targets, may appear to execute rapid maneuvers, even though none of the targets is moving. Speeds up to twenty miles a minute, or even higher, may be indicated. Fortunately such cases of strong anomalous propagation are rare. Otherwise radar would be much less useful than it actually is. In fact, the rarity of such conditions is one reason why radar operators become confused by them and fail to make proper identifications.

METEOROLOGICAL OPTICS

SOMETIMES WE SEE A CLOUD THAT'S DRAGONISH:
A VAPOUR, SOMETIME, LIKE A BEAR, OR LION,
A TOWER'D CITADEL, A PENDENT ROCK,
A FORKED MOUNTAIN, OR BLUE PROMONTORY
WITH TREES UPON 'T, THAT NOD UNTO THE WORLD
AND MOCK OUR EYES WITH AIR . . .

Shakespeare[1]

According to one dictionary, air is "a colorless, odorless, tasteless, transparent gaseous mixture." Pure air is indeed odorless, but it is far from colorless; in large quantities, illuminated by sunlight, it scatters the blue light to form the characteristic background color of the sky. It is neither odorless nor tasteless when filled with contaminating exhausts of automobiles or by-products of factories. It is not completely transparent. It absorbs, as well as scatters, light. The ozone of the upper atmosphere is completely opaque to far ultraviolet light and to x-rays. Oxygen molecules absorb strongly in the red part of the solar spectrum, and water vapor takes an enormous toll of infrared radiation. Various kinds of clouds form and float in the atmosphere. Fog consists of tiny droplets of water; cumulus clouds contain larger drops that may eventually fall as rain. When the air is cold, the droplets may coalesce, freeze, and fall as hail. In the quieter, colder upper atmosphere, moisture content may form fine ice crystals that comprise wispy cirrus clouds; or the crystals may adhere to each other in characteristic manner to form hexagonal snowflakes.

During a rain storm, ascending columns of warm air and descending columns of cold air may build up powerful electrostatic fields, resulting in lightning discharges. Then, after the discharge has passed, the expanding gases rush out with shock-wave velocities to cause thunderclaps. At times, these electrostatic charges assume the form of roughly spherical masses of glowing gas, sometimes called "ball lightning." These phenomena can produce many startling apparitions. They are, as we shall see, responsible for many reported UFOs throughout history, as well as during recent times.

Under certain circumstances the atmosphere can bend light rays, thus forming unusual and sometimes startling apparitions.

Winds carry many objects into the upper atmosphere. Blown paper, an errant kite, a falling feather of a bird or the bird itself, masses of silken spiderwebs, toy balloons, weather balloons, stratoballoons carrying scientific equipment to high levels, flying seeds of milkweed or dandelion—all of these, shining in the sun, can produce peculiar appearances that only an expert observer will be able to identify. For example, a number of UFOs apparently flying in formation over the New Mexico desert were finally identified by DHM as airborne tumbleweeds, each three or four feet across, carried to great heights in high wind.

Air itself possesses a number of unusual properties. The movement of currents of air of different temperature and density deflect the beams of starlight, causing the stars to twinkle and change color. Many people, unaware of this phenomenon, have argued that a star or planet must be an UFO because of this peculiar optical behavior. A layer of thin, speeding clouds may enhance the illusion of movement of a planet or star. At maximum elongation from the sun, Venus is spectacularly bright and has frequently been misidentified as an UFO—both in broad daylight and at night.

Warm air behaves quite differently from cold air. On a hot day over the desert when the air becomes very hot close to the ground, light from the sky will be refracted upward. A person standing on a slight eminence above the heated surface will often see the blue sky extending from the immediate foreground to the distant horizon. This is the famous mirage, which has so often deceived a hot, thirsty individual into thinking that a lake was near. However, as he tries to reach that lake the water continually recedes into the distance; it is only an image of the sky.

Many individuals traveling along a highway in the daytime have seen a similar phenomenon: a silvery spot of light on the highway, moving rapidly ahead as the car approaches. The silvery appearance against the black macadam and the elliptical shape of the mirage give the illusion that a solid, metallic object is involved. And if the passenger happens to look behind him, he will see that an identical object is chasing him along the same highway. Especially in the early days of the flying-saucer scare, many such sightings were reported and now repose in the Air Force files.

There is nothing to the popular belief that a bright mirage occurs only when a body of water is near. And the fact that the mirage "looks metallic" does in no sense make it so.

This type of mirage, produced by a layer of hot air close to the ground, is known as an "inferior mirage" because the image lies below the source of light, in this case the sky itself. But when a layer of cold air hugs the ground, usually at night when the surface radiation is escaping into space, we encounter the reverse condition of a "superior mirage." Images of objects far away, close to the ground, or even beyond the horizon can be elevated so as to appear above the surface of the earth, projected against the sky. The elevation is usually small, less than one degree above the horizon. (One degree, by way of reference, is about twice the apparent diameter of the moon or sun.)

For either type of mirage, the earth's atmosphere is acting like a lens—an imperfect lens, to be sure, with lots of astigmatism—but the effect can be nonetheless spectacular. On certain occasions one may see several mirages on top of one another, some inverted and some upright. In the deserts of the Middle East a distant camel caravan may appear as a file of upright animals, walking on the feet of their inverted counterparts. Rapidly changing conditions in the atmosphere may cause the images to vary in size, giving the impression of rapid motion toward or away from the observer. Such activity could cause the person unfamiliar with mirages to conclude that the animals were in rapid maneuver.

Mirages of a distant ship at sea led superstitious mariners to believe in the "Flying Dutchman," a ghost ship manned by a ghostly crew whose captain, according to legend, was condemned to sail against the wind until Judgment Day. An inquisitive mariner wishing to explore the mystery further might try to overtake it—whereupon the Flying Dutchman would suddenly vanish into thin air, perpetuating the legend. Flying Dutchman reports have something in common with flying saucer reports—the ship has been seen by many reliable observers who swore to the accuracy of their reports—as have many observers of UFOs. Marine mirage effects are illustrated in Plate 9.

Mirages seen from the air are even more spectacular than those viewed from the ground or from the sea, because the clarity of the atmosphere enhances the apparent reality of the sighting. The distant object may be a bright light hundreds of miles away, or the planet Venus, or a bright star. Anyone who has taken a photograph with an old-fashioned portrait camera can appreciate the optical effect. With such a camera one usually sees the image projected upon a sheet of ground glass. But if the ground glass is removed the image will appear to be hanging in space—and that is precisely what happens with the image formed by a lens of air.

The bright star or planet or light, distorted by imperfections in the atmospheric lens, may appear to be a luminous, solid body only a few hundred feet from the plane. Other atmospheric irregularities may cause the image to twinkle or to produce flashing colors, with red and green predominating, as with the running lights of an airborne vehicle. The apparent nearness of the apparition can be frightening.

Several reports in the Air Force files describe pilots trying to intercept such a mirage, believing it to be a real, material object. There have been a number of dogfights between pilots and images of distant planets. Changing atmospheric conditions or the interposition of mountains or trees on the distant horizon cause the image to change size and shape, so that it seems to maneuver with lightning speed, sometimes disappearing over the far horizon in a matter of seconds. Shortly thereafter it may return, ready to resume the fight. The battle ends only when the object finally sets well beneath the horizon. Accurate time records of several such fantastic encounters enable the astronomer to identify the source beyond all question. Nevertheless, the inner clique of Project Blue

Book often refused to accept such judgments, giving greater weight to the visual conclusion of the "experienced" pilot.

One of us (DHM), while flying in an Air Force plane from Fairbanks, Alaska, to the North Pole and return, on March 3, 1955, via Nome and Bering Strait, had the opportunity to observe such an apparition first hand.

The Air Force had requested DHM to go to Alaska to study the aurora borealis and in particular to evaluate certain problems the Air Force was then encountering concerning radio transmissions on polar flights. The mission, known by the code name of "Ptarmigan," was primarily to study weather conditions within the Arctic Circle. The plane was a battered relic of World War II, a Boeing B-29 Superfortress manned by a crew of ten, plus two airmen trained to make radiosonde* studies and other determinations of atmospheric conditions. DHM was number thirteen, but no one was superstitious.

The flight lasted nineteen hours—a long mission indeed—first over the spectacular Brooks Range, then Point Barrow, and a long flight to the Pole over the frozen Arctic wastes. The flight was mostly at 20,000 feet. The only thing to break the monotony was the occasional activity of the two men who occupied the compartment behind the bomb bay with DHM. The rest of the crew were forward. Every half hour or so these men would place an instrumented parachute into a lock, from which it would be ejected from the plane. Radiosonde apparatus suspended from the parachute would send back coded information about the vertical distribution of pressure, temperature, and water vapor content of the atmosphere below the plane.

DHM had earlier conducted his own experiments on radio communication, using a number of different frequencies according to a schedule set up at Fairbanks prior to departure. He had determined theoretically that the frequencies then in use were too high. On this flight he found that lowering the frequency re-established communication, with the result that the plane maintained contact with the base at Fairbanks throughout the flight.

---

* A radiosonde is an instrument carried or sent aloft to send back information on atmospheric conditions by radio.

The flight was completed in darkness. DHM, while looking over the distant southwestern horizon, in the vicinity of Bering Strait, was startled to see a bright object apparently take off from the horizon, move swiftly toward the plane, and come to a skidding stop just beyond the wingtips, perhaps a hundred feet away. It was flashing red and green lights and seemed to have a tiny propeller on top. It had a silvery, metallic sheen. It was clearly an UFO.

The luminous object, whatever it was, began to follow the plane, even bumping up and down with the motion of the aircraft. DHM observed it from the plastic bubble that served as a window on that side of the B-29. Almost automatically he made a few tests, primarily to determine whether the object was outside the plane or possibly was an internal reflection. Drawing his fur parka over his head and leaning against the internal surface of the blister, he could still see the luminous form with its flashing lights. He took off his glasses and the object was still there. He recognized it, then, as an example of a kind of UFO, the so-called Rotating Lights of Korea, that had been widely reported in the Korean war theater in the early 1950s. It could also be explained as a foo ball, as described in Chapter 5.

Mystified and frightened, DHM suddenly decided he should call the two radiosonde technicians to act as witnesses. But at that very moment the UFO took off and disappeared over the distant horizon within about two seconds. The acceleration of the UFO was instantaneous and enormous. A simple calculation revealed that the distance to the visible horizon was two hundred miles. Thus the object must have traveled at a speed of something like 100 miles a second, reaching that speed instantaneously from a relative dead stop.

DHM's concern heightened when he realized that a flight of 200 miles would have placed the UFO on the western side of Bering Strait, in Russian territory. Was the object, then, some remarkable machine of Soviet manufacture, sent to spy on U.S. planes or at least to inspect them? While these thoughts crossed his mind the UFO suddenly returned, brighter than before, flashing red and green lights. A little propeller was on top, as before. It came to the same short stop and again paced the B-29.

Suddenly DHM recognized the object. Although he had previously identified other people's reported UFOs as mirages of planets or stars, this was his first encounter with the actual phenomenon. The star, it turned out, was Sirius, the brightest star in the sky, which though below the horizon, was raised to visibility because of mirage.

The sudden disappearance? That had a simple explanation: a mountain on the horizon in Siberia had acted like a shutter, momentarily cutting out the light.

Although Sirius was setting in the west, the rapid motion of the plane more than compensated for the setting and, for a short time, the star rose sufficiently above the horizon to meld into the starry background where it belonged. There was absolutely no question about its identification. The clinching evidence, were it needed, came from the records obtained by the two airmen, whose radiosonde studies clearly showed the presence of a temperature inversion—a layer of warm air at higher levels surmounting a layer of very cold air beneath—precisely what is required for the production of a superior mirage.

The flashing lights and the impression of the propeller were caused by scintillation, which makes the image of a bright star or planet twinkle or shimmer. This effect results from inhomogeneities in the refractive index of the atmosphere through which the light from the source passes.

Nevertheless, when the report of this flight became known, certain ufologists, notably the meteorologist James McDonald, of the University of Arizona, a profound believer in the ETH, questioned the identification, implying that DHM did not know a real UFO when he saw one. Other ufologists, all over the country, echoed McDonald's criticism. However, the case went into the Air Force files as solved. Later, when DHM analyzed some of the famous Korean sightings, in every one that provided adequate data it was possible to identify the offending star or planet. Venus was the most frequent culprit.

There are many other sources of mirages. A towering thunderhead, brilliantly illuminated in the sunlight, can be projected over the horizon.

Mirages are just one phenomenon of the general field of meteorological optics. Shadows on clouds or simply on mist or fog can produce some highly spectacular effects. Suppose, for example,

136 THE UFO ENIGMA

that you are standing on a mountaintop at sunrise. The sky is entirely clear to the east, but heavy cloud or fog fills the valley to the west, and rises above the top of the mountain. As you turn to face the west, you see your shadow falling on the fog. But this is no ordinary shadow, because the boundary is not sharp, but extends into the cloud, or fog. Further, the sunlight refracted and reflected by the tiny droplets produces a halo surrounding your shadow. This apparition, not surprisingly, has frightened many people out of their wits. The phenomenon is the Specter of the Brocken, already mentioned, on p. 14. The Brocken is a high peak in the Harz Mountains in East Germany, where the Specter is frequently seen. We show a photograph of this phenomenon in Plate 10.

Under certain circumstances the shadow of the head may be ringed with a miniature rainbow, reflecting many colors. If five people are standing together at the summit, each will see the shadow of his own head ringed by a halo, but, for each observer, those of his companions will not be adorned. Each one notes his own saintliness, but will be too polite to call the attention of the others to his special attribute. Hence each one continues to believe in his own saintliness over that of the others. Plate 11 shows graphically how the halo is associated only with the "eye" of the beholder—in this case the lens of the camera taking the photograph.

This phenomenon can also be seen from an airplane when the plane's shadow falls on a mass of white cloud below. The shadow is usually indistinct, but a brilliant ring of light, usually colored, follows along after the plane. This apparition, known as the "pilot's halo," was frequently observed by pioneer balloonists, who had no idea what it was or what caused it. Any pilot of a plane or balloon wishing to obtain a closer look is doomed to failure, for the apparition moves with the vehicle, always eluding capture or even close inspection.

And there is, of course, the more familiar phenomenon of the rainbow. There was a time when the appearance of this brightly colored bow spanning the heavens frightened observers, and with reason since the rainbow has much in common with the reported behavior of many UFOs.

The primary rainbow, with red on the outside and blue on the inside, forms the arc of a circle 42° in radius. The center of that circle is exactly opposite the sun. Hence we generally see rainbows only in the early morning or late afternoon, because the sun must be less than 42° above the horizon before we can see the primary bow elevated against the sky.

A secondary rainbow also is fairly common. It is somewhat less brilliant, with the colors more spread out and appearing in reverse order, at an angle of 51° for the red and 54° for the blue.

There is no mystery whatever about the rainbow. Sunlight enters a drop of rain, is reflected internally, and exits. The different colors come out at slightly different angles, an effect known as refraction. Every person sees a different rainbow. In fact, it is not impossible for one person to see a rainbow and someone twenty feet away to see none at all. The effect depends on the distribution of raindrops. The center of the rainbow arc is a line drawn from the sun through the eye of the observer. That is why the rainbow appears to move as the observer moves.

We see the rainbow only with our backs to the sun. When the sun is very low and the ground is covered with dew, we can sometimes see the rainbow spread out flat on the lawn, its edges curving away into the distance. This so-called "dew-bow" is rare, being found only where the drops are almost as spherical as they would be when falling through the air—as, for example, when supported by fine cobwebs or feathery plant fibers. Sometimes little droplets of fog or dew may float on the surface of a pond, perhaps deterred from uniting with the main body of water by a thin oil film. Under such circumstances the dew-bow can be very brilliant. The dew-bow, like the fog halo, is a personal apparition. The brilliant halo will surround only the shadow of your head. Meteorologists call this phenomenon *Heiligenschein,* or holy light.

The individual naïve enough to search for the pot of gold at the foot of the rainbow will soon discover, as he sets out to seek it, that the rainbow moves on ahead. When he stops the rainbow stops. If he is frightened and runs backward, the rainbow will chase him. He may even conclude that the rainbow "maneuvers as if under intelligent control"—a statement often heard in respect of UFOs and a conclusion very often drawn by pilots who have been unable to capture an apparition. This reported behavior of the UFO is, actually, the key to its true nature; it is not a material object, but only a visual image centered in the observer's eye.

ICE CRYSTALS

Drops of water in the air are pretty much alike; they are all round (or tear-shaped, if they are falling as rain drops). Ice crystals, on the other hand, present a wide range of possibilities—in shape and in orientation, as well as in size. The simplest ice crystal and probably the most common variety occurring naturally is a tiny needle or prism. Intramolecular forces cause the simple shapes to stick together and form more complex crystals in the characteristic hexagonal pattern of the snowflake.

Light entering an ice crystal is reflected one or more times within it before it finally emerges at an angle very different from the one at which it entered. As a result, we have innumerable patterns of halos and associated phenomena produced by ice crystals. Those that produce the most spectacular effects possess regular forms. A small, flat snow crystal fluttering to earth will fall something like a feather or a fragment of tissue paper; it will tend to lie flat, parallel to the ground. Ice needles behave similarly. The most spectacular effects occur when the atmosphere is extremely calm, so that the longer axis of the crystal tends to be quite horizontal.

Such crystals produce one of the simplest of all the solar apparitions: a vertical pillar of white light. One can see a somewhat similar column by looking sunward through a window covered with a venetian blind whose slats are horizontal. The reflected sunlight will form a column. If the sun is very low, the column will manifest a reddish sunset color.

When snowflakes are falling in air that is slightly turbulent, especially when needles rather than flat plates are involved, one may see a horizontal as well as a vertical band of light. The two bands meet at the sun, producing a startling apparition in the form of a cross, sometimes of a fiery hue, suspended in the air. When the crystals are distant, the cross appears to hang against the far sky, but if the flakes are concentrated in a narrow curtain close to the observer, with the sun shining through from the opposite side, the cross may appear to be only a few hundred feet away. However, like the rainbow, the cross moves with the observer and is stationary when he stands still.

It was probably such a celestial apparition that caused Constantine the Great to embrace Christianity in A.D. 312.

We should mention that ice crystals are not always densely packed, as in a snowstorm. Sometimes they occur in light cirrus clouds—or they may be so thinly spaced that the atmosphere appears to be transparent except where the "pillar of fire" appears.

Floating ice crystals can cause another interesting phenomenon: a pair of halos, one whose radius is about 22° and the other about 45°, both centered around the sun. These halos, which are not at all uncommon, are sometimes wrongly called rainbows. As we have seen, one has to turn his back to the sun to see a rainbow. Halos formed by ice crystals appear relatively close to the sun, and their coloring is very different from that of the ordinary rainbow. Inner edges of both of these halos have a warm, ruddy tint. The outer edges, instead of being blue or violet, possess a pearly iridescence, glowing almost as if the halo were self-luminous. The halos and the cross are essentially independent phenomena. We can have either one without the other. Their simultaneous occurrence is rare. Plate 12 depicts parhelic phenomena, with cross and sundogs, but no halo. This apparition appeared over Nuremberg in 1581.

When the upper atmosphere is extremely tranquil, so that the minute ice crystals tend to lie flat, the portion of the inner halo whose altitude equals that of the sun displays an increased luminosity, which on some occasions almost approaches the brilliance of the sun itself. Thus the sun appears to possess on either side brilliant, glowing mock suns, commonly referred to as sundogs, and known technically as parhelia. These images are colored like the halos, red toward the sun, and white or amber away from the sun. These phenomena are shown in Plate 13. This display was also seen over Nuremberg, in April 1583.

The halos may also show a bright spot above and one below, so that the complete apparition of a cross centered in two beautifully colored circles, with the mock suns glowing like burnished brass, is one of the most stupendous sights in all of nature. Add to it a few of the other arcs and horns that sometimes appear in a selection of other mock suns, shining like eyes on the rim of the outer circle, and you indeed have an apparition that would frighten the ignorant and alarm the superstitious.

A short arc that curves upward, like horns, from where it touches the uppermost edge of the outer circle, possesses a special characteristic that distinguishes it from all the other circles, because it is the only one that resembles a rainbow. It is red on the side toward the sun and sapphire blue on the upper edge. On rare occasions, especially in a very clear sky at a high altitude, the uppermost portion is a rich violet. The correspondence between this phenomenon and the vision of Ezekiel was discussed in Chapter 3.

Various sizes, shapes, and orientations of ice crystals produce a very wide variety of associated phenomena; seldom are two exactly alike.

From a plane, balloon, or mountaintop another apparition is sometimes visible: a brilliant reflection of the sun in a mirrorlike layer of flat ice crystals. The image, called a "subsun," lies just as far below the horizon as the sun is above the horizon. The mirror is usually imperfect, and the reflection tends to form a vertical ellipse, which may undergo even further distortion to form the elliptical shape of an alleged UFO. The subsun itself can develop subsundogs and halos, producing a still greater complication of pattern.

Like the rainbow, these reflections of the sun are also centered in the eye of the observer. To be visible they require a light source. In the daytime the source is usually the sun and at night the moon —in which case, we refer to moondogs, or paraselenae. Although sundogs, especially near sunset, are by no means rare, fully developed ones are quite rare, though *portions* of such apparitions may appear without casual observers becoming aware of them.

These phenomena were regarded, especially during the Middle Ages, as omens of propending evil. A remarkable collection of old engravings and woodcuts of sundogs and other frightening meteorological phenomena lies in the Zentralbibliothek in Zürich, Switzerland.

Sundogs and subsuns are "attached" to the observer in exactly the same way as rainbows or other sun-induced halos. If seen from an airplane, the very brilliant reflection of the sun from a nearby cloud or from ice crystals stays in the same relative position as long as the plane maintains a straight course. But if the pilot believes he is chasing a bright metallic object and tries to intercept it, he can no more do so than the person trying to find the foot of the rainbow. And if the ability of the image to maneuver to avoid interception leads the pilot to the conclusion of "intelligent guidance," he would no doubt find it difficult to accept the fact that the only intelligence present was his own.

One of the most widely publicized UFO cases was a sighting from the airport in Salt Lake City, Utah, on October 3, 1961. A civilian pilot, taking off from the airport, saw a bright silvery disk ahead of him in the air. He supposed it to be another aircraft. When he was airborne, however, the object was there in the same place, though now having the shape of a silvery pencil. Deciding the object could not be an airplane, the pilot tried to intercept it, meanwhile having alerted the control tower to the presence of the UFO. During the attempted interception the object began to move. With a sudden burst of speed it faded away into the distance. Observers on the ground, alerted by the pilot, easily found the object, a bright spot in the sky directly below the sun. One group on the ground reported that the object, before disappearing, showed no motion; other observers claimed to have seen the object take off at high speed.

This sighting was clearly one of a parhelion. Yet the meteorologist McDonald rejected DHM's explanation on the basis that the reported altitude of the object did not conform to that of the characteristic sundog. This was nonsense, as the apparition was precisely where one would expect to see that portion of this parhelic disturbance, known as the "lower tangential arc." McDonald was apparently entirely unfamiliar with meteorological optics and did not know that fragments of parhelia can appear without the full display. Similarly, as the distribution of ice crystals changes, one observer may report motion while another sees the object as stationary. There is no need even to invoke the autokinetic effect (see Chapter 13).

Most people are familiar with contrails—visible condensations of water droplets or ice crystals behind an airborne plane, usually a high-flying jet. When ice crystals are present, as is often the case, a portion of this trail can also exhibit a partial sundog phenomenon to an observer in the right place. To a person in another plane, the bright concentration of light from one location may appear like a solid, metallic object. A moment later, however, as the plane's course changes, the contrail will vanish, appearing to take off into the distance.

Such apparent motions are absolutely characteristic of ice-crystal phenomena. The Salt Lake sighting was no exception. Like many other pilots before and since, the pilot tried to catch the UFO, only to see it vanish, at tremendous speed, into the distance; he did not realize that the disappearance occurred because he had flown out of the cloud of ice crystals.

We could multiply such instances by the dozens. No doubt our conclusions would be questioned by the die-hard ufologists, who are unable to accept obvious scientific explanations because of their near-religious need to believe in the ETH.

Finally, there is a rare and little-understood phenomenon which may be called an "inverse contrail." A plane flying through a thin layer of cloud or ice crystals can cause the condensations to disperse, leaving oddly spaced gaps or holes in the surrounding medium. Occasionally these gaps look like black balloons, projected against a gray cloud background.

The field of meteorological optics, then, provides a multiplicity of apparitions that can readily mystify even the experienced observer. And, as noted, these apparitions account for many UFO sightings.

In 1955, when DHM made a visit to the Air Matériel Command at Offutt Air Force Base, in Fort Crook, Nebraska, he had an opportunity to discuss the question of the competence of the average pilot to recognize the basic phenomena we have described in this chapter. General Curtis LeMay, then commander of the base, readily conceded that Air Force pilots had no training in the field of meteorological optics. The general agreed that such training would be invaluable, but said that the Air Force did not have time to include such studies as part of the educational experience of a pilot. He further agreed that the common tendency of analysts in and out of Project Blue Book to give exceptional weight to observations of UFOs by airline or military pilots was completely unjustified.

"METEORS" AND THE UPPER ATMOSPHERE

Misled by fancy's meteor ray,
   By passion driven;
But yet the light that led astray
   Was light from heaven.

Robert Burns[1]

The term "meteor" originally referred to any unusual phenomenon or apparition in the atmosphere. Most of the sightings discussed in the preceding chapter, such as rainbows and sundogs, would once have been so classified. Today, however, the meaning of the word is more restricted, except for its broad use in the field of "meteorology," the general study of the weather.

Scientifically, a meteor is a material body, large or small, that enters the earth's atmosphere from outer space. Swift passage through the atmosphere heats the body to incandescence. A meteor displays a fiery trail and often shoots off what appear to be sparks. The fainter bodies in this category are generally called "shooting stars"; the brighter ones are known as bolides, or fireballs. They strike the earth's atmosphere with a speed of from ten to twenty miles a second.

Shooting stars are common. If you stand outdoors on a clear, moonless night and look upward, you will rarely have to wait more than five or ten minutes before you see a tiny flash of fire dart across the sky. The term "shooting stars" is, of course, a misnomer, because they are not stars.

Plate 14 depicts a number of fiery "meteors." In addition, this fearsome sky contains a halo around the moon, stars, a comet, and a flying dragon.

Most of the fainter shooting-star flashes are caused by particles no larger than a grain of sand. One as large as the eraser in a lead pencil would shine so brilliantly that we would term it a bolide, or fireball. Still larger masses, ranging in weight from a few pounds up to a number of tons, occasionally strike the earth. When these heavy masses crash down they cause big explosions, sometimes devastating large areas. Such an event happened in 1908 when a large meteorite or other object crashed into the bleak Siberian tundra near one of the Tunguska rivers. We say "or other object" because at the site of the Tunguska explosion no large meteoritic crater was found, nor were any meteorites, though the devastation of the forest into which the object fell was extensive, covering some 1,600 square kilometers.

According to Dr. Fred L. Whipple of the Harvard College Observatory, later Director of the Smithsonian Astrophysical Observatory, this object could not have been an iron meteorite, but could have been a friable stony meteorite or a small cometary mass.[2] Consensus favors the latter, according to Whipple.*

There are a number of large craters, undoubtedly meteoric, here and there on the surface of the earth; perhaps the best known, though by no means the largest, is the Canyon Diablo Crater in Arizona, near the town of Winslow. This crater is shown in Plate 15.

Meteors large enough to reach the earth without being consumed entirely in the atmosphere are called "meteorites" and of these there are two major classes: rocklike masses called "aerolites," and chunks of iron-nickel steel called "siderites." There are other varieties, such as carbonaceous chondrites.

Although the aerolites are probably far more abundant, it is easier to identify siderites because of their metallic composition. It

---

* As this book goes to press, the authors of another book, just published, propose that the Tunguska explosion was atomic. Nuclear explosions in 1908? The authors suggest that a crippled alien spacecraft with an over-heated nuclear power plant blew up while trying to make an emergency landing.[3]

is much more difficult to distinguish between an aerolite and common earth rock.

Stony meteorites reveal nothing extraordinary; with minor exceptions, their chemical composition is the same as that of the average sample of rock we find on the surface of the earth. They contain an abundance of silica, magnesium, and calcium. They show traces of many other elements, including copper.

Plate 16 shows a cross section of a nickel-iron meteorite fragment from the Canyon Diablo crater. The lines are Widmanstaetten figures, which show the crystalline pattern of the metal. The dark inclusions are chondrules—masses of olivine or pyroxene.

Bright meteors, which are not uncommon, are particularly spectacular when seen from an airplane. Since human eyes have no stereoscopic vision for objects more than about a quarter of a mile away, the pilot may conclude that the object is very near, possibly about to strike his plane. He may then swiftly take evasive action, even imagining that the shock normally accompanying that action is the result of the wake of a bright fireball that may actually be 100 miles or more away.

The Air Force files are also filled with cases of bright fireballs identified as UFOs by pilots. One of the classic sightings falling into this category was that by two Eastern Airlines pilots, Captain Clarence S. Chiles and his co-pilot John B. Whitted, near Montgomery, Alabama, in July 1948. (See Chapter 13.) They saw what appeared to be a huge, cigar-shaped, wingless aircraft, with two rows of illuminated windows. A brilliant blue glow accompanied the object and red-orange flames shot from the rear. Hynek identified this UFO as a bright meteor—an identification with which we concur.

Man-made Spacecraft

Another sighting the ufologists would like to forget was one of the most breathtaking ever. The event occurred during the evening of March 3, 1968. Bright UFOs were reported from at least nine states: Indiana, Kentucky, Massachusetts, New York, Ohio, Pennsylvania, Tennessee, Virginia, and West Virginia. Hundreds of people observed one or more fiery objects streaking across the sky, sending out showers of sparks, and leaving bright trails behind them. The Air Force files burgeoned with the detailed reports; we have examined a complete copy, which runs to more than four hundred pages.

By far the most detailed and graphic report came from a woman, named Marie, in Tennessee.[4] She, her husband, and the mayor of their town were the observers. Her complete report follows, edited only to remove identifying names:

Sunday, 3 March 1968. A number of us had enjoyed dinner at the mayor's home in ———. About 8:43 P.M., C.S.T., the mayor, John, and I left the house and walked through the parking lot where the three of us stood talking. I saw a light traveling in the sky a little above the southwest horizon. This light seemed only a bit larger and brighter than a star and it seemed about the same color as a star.

As I yelled to the mayor and John to look, the light became brighter and larger. While I was observing this "traveling light" from a great distance, it did not look to me that it was traveling in a flat trajectory. Rather, it seemed to travel in a slight arc and, at this point of flight, I began to note the "orangish-colored" trail of light behind the "star-colored" light. John asked, "You do know what we're seeing, don't you, Mayor?" John's talking was an annoying distraction to me while I was trying to listen for some sound, so I bossed loudly, "Hush your mouth!"

The three of us stood silent, almost motionless, and very much in awe as we realized that the "thing" was headed our way and was coming surprisingly near us! There were some leafless trees in the yard that partially obstructed our view for a moment. Then—IMPACT!!!—the impact referring to is the impact on my emotions, for with breathtaking suddenness, the "thing" was nearly overhead and seemed to be quite large and close! To be more explicit, the "thing" looked like it was headed directly over the far corner of the mayor's house!

It was shaped like a fat cigar, in my estimation. I was impressed that it seemed of considerable size, the size of one of our largest airplane fuselages, or larger. (The mayor thought it was smaller than my estimation.)

It appeared to have square-shaped windows along the side that was facing us. I remember the urge to count the windows, but other details flashed in view and my curiosity made me jump to other observations. For an instant, I thought I caught a glimpse of a metallic look about the fuselage, and this really made me feel that the "thing" was close! (Later, John said that he saw this "metallic look" too.) It seemed as though a faint light reflected on the fuselage. (Perhaps the faint light came from the lights of the city or from the lights of the "thing.")

It appeared to me that the fuselage was constructed of many pieces of flat sheets of metal-like material with a "riveted together look." It occurred to me that the fuselage was not of smooth contour. The many "windows" seemed to be lit up from the inside of the fuselage with light that was quite bright. This light seemed to be about the same color as light coming from the windows of our homes. I did not observe anything other than the light in the windows. (It occurred to me that I might see objects or persons, but there was little time for a *good* look.)

My rough estimate is that two-thirds or three-quarters of the fuselage near the front end had windows that were lit up. About one-third or one-quarter of the fuselage toward the rear end was dark or without lights. I did not observe any blinking lights on the "thing" like we have on our planes. From out of the back end of the fuselage came a wide (roughly about the width of the fuselage) long, reddish-orangish-yellowish stream of dusty fire. It seemed as though particles of dust were on fire. These tiny sparkles seemed to make up the tail and the light from it seemed of quite low intensity when compared to the light emitted from the "windows."

I listened intently for some sound from the "thing," but I didn't hear a whisper of a sound! This was the most eerie part of my whole experience! Certainly, there should be some sound from an aircraft that looks so near! It flashed in my mind that perhaps the sound was yet to follow.

I was impressed with what looked to me like low altitude of the craft at this point of my sighting—I thought, around 1,000 feet or less. Also, when the craft was flying near us, it did seem to travel in a flat trajectory. I toyed with the idea that it even slowed down somewhat, for how else could we observe so much detail in a mere flash across the sky? (John doesn't think it slowed down.)

The craft was headed away from us now. I concentrated on the "trail of fiery particles" that seemed to come from the end of the fuselage. I was expecting to see a bright ball of fire close to the fuselage end, but I saw no bright ball of fire. However, I noticed that the trail's light intensity did increase somewhat. Mayor noticed this increase in tail brightness too, but this was understandable, since we were looking at a denser view of "fiery particles." In other words, along the length of the trail instead of the previous width of the trail. Because this light pattern of the craft was at a slight angle from where we were standing, it was possible for a brief moment to see near the "fiery trail's end" one or a few lit-up "windows" simultaneously.

Upon this observation, I concluded that there must be an outward bulge in the fuselage, especially after taking into account that there were no windows toward the rear end. Also, the simultaneous view of nearly full "trail light" and one or a few window lights gave me the opportunity to compare light intensities again. The light from the window or windows seemed brighter than the trail's light.

All too soon, the "thing" was flying away, low over the treetops toward the Northeast. I could see only the "orangish-colored" light of the trail now. Certainly, SOUND would come from this craft!!! The three of us remained quiet while looking and listening. I was still expecting to hear noise, but, instead, there remained only silence! The three of us remained quiet for awhile, even after the craft was well out of sight. We were all baffled by that.

Then—HULLABALOO!!—we all started talking at the

same time! In the course of our expression, the conversation went something like this.

SOMEONE: "It didn't make any sound!"
MAYOR: "That wasn't a meteor, because a meteor doesn't have windows, but I'll be damned if I'll report it!"
MARIE: "I'm not going to report it either!"
JOHN: "I'm not going to report it!"
(*Laughter.*)
SOMEONE: "Tremendous speed!"
MARIE: "What time is it?"
MAYOR (*looking at his watch*): "Quarter to nine."
MARIE: "How high would you guess it was?"
MAYOR: "Not more than 2,000 or 5,000 feet, or maybe lower. That thing was really low!"
MARIE: "What direction?"
MAYOR: "Southeast to Northeast."
JOHN: "Whatever it was, it will be in the papers tomorrow."

As we excitedly compared notes, we agreed with each other on most of our observations. This "agreement" seemed to comfort me, for I certainly didn't want to think that I had just experienced my first hallucination while I was wide awake! All three of us agreed that we had seen something other than any planes we had seen or read about from our Earth. We thought we had seen a "craft of top-secret category from our Earth," or that we had seen a "craft from Outer Space."

It was chilly outside and mayor wasn't wearing a coat. Besides, our short discussion of the event seemed to suffice. It didn't seem strange that, so soon after, all three of us went back to our routine of daily living, for, after all, can anything really surprise us in these days in this scientific era?!

A sketch of a Zeppelinlike craft, containing ten windows, accompanied this report, with the comment:

I was more interested in looking *into* these windows than I was in studying window shapes. However, I feel strongly that

the windows had definite symmetrical shapes, were clearly
outlined as the craft passed by, and were lined up in a row,
horizontally. I feel safe to stress that the windows did not
look blurred or fuzzy, but had clear, definite shapes. I observed, also, that the windows looked quite large. I would say
larger than the windows we have in our planes.

A letter from Marie accompanied the foregoing report and referred to the newspaper accounts of the event, dated some sixteen
days after the sighting. This letter contained the information that
Marie had had two predinner drinks of bourbon, ice, and water.
She had had two glasses of wine at dinner, an after-dinner drink of
Irish Mist, and a final after-dinner drink of some other liqueur that
"was tasty, not potent, and definitely was not absinthe." Marie
attested: "I felt mentally and physically alert by 8:45 P.M.!!!" The
letter continues for more than two pages, indicating her varied activities and giving character references accompanied by various
printed records indicating the high regard the community held for
the mayor and for her husband John.

Marie was not the only one who gave a vivid report. Elizabeth,
a Ph.D. from Ohio and a teacher of general science, also made a
report to the Air Force. She had served in the U. S. Navy during
World War II. She claimed that she was very much interested in
UFOs. Her report begins by stating: "This is no natural phenomenon. It's really a UFO."

Elizabeth made sketches of the object, which she viewed
through field glasses as well as with the naked eye. At first it appeared to her like a meteor or comet. She concluded, however,
that it could not have been a "falling star" because of its peculiar
behavior and the colors. The object slowed down as it approached
the horizon, then suddenly became three objects. The colors
"ranged orange-white-red-orange, similar to the color of the sun."
The objects flew in perfect military formation. Each object was flat
and the bottom part had a protrusion; it moved very slowly in the
north-northeast direction.

Elizabeth flashed S O S in Morse code four times with a flashlight. There was no visible response. No noise was audible to the
human ear. However her dog, a Boston terrier bitch, aged one

year five months, who hated the cold, crawled between two trash cans beside the garage and whimpered, lying on the drive between the cans as though she were frightened to death.

Elizabeth reported an effect upon herself, as well:

After I came into the house I had an overpowering drive to sleep and since I was expecting a phone call at 10:20–10:25 I had to force myself to stay awake. I opened the windows wide in hopes the cold room would help, but even then I dropped off several times. This is extremely unusual behavior for me. I had slept ten hours the night before and had an hour's nap in the afternoon. I had been outside in the cold and should have been wide awake. I felt physically depleted and just had to sleep. This gradually wore off until by 11:00 P.M. [I] was wide awake again. My friend recalled that this had happened to me in 1966 when I saw a UFO then. I had forgotten until she remarked that it had happened to me previously. I did not know others had seen this until I heard about it on the news.

Another report, this time from Indiana, was equally graphic.

About 9:45 P.M. I looked out the window and saw some kind of fire-colored object fly across the valley. About two or three minutes later my cousin, aunt, and my uncle came running into the house yelling and trying to tell me about the UFO they saw. They and some neighbors all observed it from horizon to horizon, which took a very short time.

The object flew at about tree-top level and was seen very clearly since it was just a few yards away. All of the observers saw a long jet airplane, looking like a vehicle without wings. It was on fire both in front and behind. All the observers observed many windows in the UFO. My cousin said, "If there had been anybody in the UFO near the windows, I would have seen them."

The next morning we heard it was supposed to have been a meteor. But the other observers and myself know the UFO could not have been a meteor because meteors don't have

windows and turn corners like IT did. And it didn't make any
noise whatsoever. I believe what we saw was a Flying
Saucer . . .

One observer called attention to the large number of grass fires
in the neighboring county on March 4, 1968. He wrote: "I do not
know if this is true, but I heard there were 72 grass fires in this
area on the day following the sighting. I would think there might
be a possible connection."

He concluded: "Please send me information on what to do in
the event of future sightings. I have often wondered about reports
of landings and why people did not shoot it or attempt to capture
it or something. I think some effort should be made on the part of
the sighter to obtain proof and identification, since he is the only
one on hand."

Hundreds of people called in to local airports, local police stations, and other places where authorities might be able to furnish
information about the unusual sighting. Most of these descriptions,
reports, and conclusions are no doubt lost forever. But the foregoing selection from the Air Force files clearly demonstrates that
something unusual occurred on the night of March 3, 1968, and
that it was observed over a wide area ranging from Tennessee and
Kentucky in the south to Massachusetts in the north.

What, indeed, caused this remarkable apparition? Earlier that
day Moscow announced that a Soviet spacecraft, Zond IV, had
been placed in a parking orbit around the earth. Presumably the
rocket engines would be reignited later, to send the experimental
vehicle into space, for various scientific purposes. Something went
wrong with the experiment, however, and Zond IV did not achieve
as great an altitude in space as had been planned. In consequence, Zond IV re-entered the earth's upper atmosphere, where
friction heated it to incandescence and broke it up into several
fragments, giving a spectacular display. When it disintegrated the
spacecraft was at least seventy-five miles above the earth's surface
—not, as various American observers of the UFO of March 3 had
reported, just over the treetops or at altitudes of a thousand feet or
so. Irregularities and the illumination undoubtedly gave the illusion of windows, but the spacecraft did not contain windows. And

thus the mystery was solved, promptly and conclusively. The UFO turned out to be a phenomenon that is becoming quite familiar in the space age—the fiery re-entry of a piece of space hardware.

Of significance is the tremendous variance of the American reports. Most people are simply not good observers or good reporters of what they see. Hence, when the UFO is a report by only one or two observers how can we reassure ourselves about the reliability of the reporting? Observer Marie had an impeccable reputation. She, John, and the mayor were certainly not making things up: what she reported was what they thought they saw. And if the mystery had not been solved, no amount of reinterviewing these witnesses could possibly have gotten them to change their conclusions about the character of the UFO. This story carries its own warning. No matter how reliable the observer may seem to be, his estimates of size, shape, appearance, brightness, and other physical characteristics of what he observes are often very far from the truth.

UFOs attributable to the re-entry of all kinds of space hardware are relatively new phenomena, but the meteors are indeed ancient visitors. Our atmosphere and our oceans have almost eradicated some of the large scars left by prehistoric meteors, but we have only to look at the surface of Mercury, the moon, Mars, or Venus to see clearly the results of meteoric impact. In fact, astronomers now think that accretion of meteoric material by the planets may account for a substantial amount of their present masses.

COMETS

In passing, we should also mention comets, or "hairy stars," which were generally regarded by the ancients as the most terrible of portents. Even very recently, for example, during the 1973 approach of the comet Kohoutek astrological charlatans tried to frighten us with wild predictions of potential disaster.

Telescopes have shown that comets are by no means the rare objects that naked-eye observation would lead us to believe. For every bright comet we see there exist literally dozens of smaller, fainter ones whose cometary character we deduce only from the shapes of their orbits or from a minute trace of haze surrounding them. Only the brightest comets, the ones that come fairly close to the sun, develop appreciable tails.

What men do not understand, they usually fear, and these "blazing stars," with tails stretching sometimes halfway across the heavens and looking like a curved sword or scimitar, would astound the person who had never seen one before or who had no knowledge about the nature of comets.

The ancients generally regarded comets as being exhalations of the earth, and with good logic, according to their mode of reasoning. The great Greco-Egyptian astronomer Ptolemy, in explaining in the second century A.D. the motions of the planets and stars, imbedded each of the seven recognized astronomical bodies—the moon, Mercury, Venus, the sun, Mars, Jupiter, and Saturn—in a crystal sphere, each turning on a special axis according to a particular rule. The spheres, supposed to be of the finest crystal, were thus perfectly transparent. Outside these seven spheres was an eighth, which carried the background of stars in the sky.

Men believed that these crystal spheres really existed. Hence a comet could not possibly come in close to the earth, say, from a distant region of space, simply because it would have to break through the crystal spheres to do so. Since there was no evidence of crystal breakage, the comets would have to be found only between the earth and the nearest sphere, that is, between the earth and the moon. And that is why Ptolemy and others concluded that they were exhalations of the earth, perhaps akin to "seeing one's breath" on a cold day.

Exhalations were of various sorts. Some of them carried pestilence, some the seeds of war, and others death—especially to persons in high places. Shakespeare has Calpurnia say to Caesar: "When beggers die, there are no comets seen. The heavens themselves blaze forth the death of princes."

There were some who held that the great comet of 43 B.C. was the soul of Julius Caesar, enroute to its heavenly abode.

One of the earliest records we have of a comet occurred during the boyhood of Aristotle, in 371 B.C.—a comet described by contemporaries as "a blazing torch."

As for the disastrous effect of a cometary apparition, Jean Bodin, a sixteenth-century French lawyer, asserted that the "appearance of a comet is followed by plague, pestilence, and civil war; for the nations are deprived of the guidance of their worthy rulers, who, while they were alive, gave all their efforts to prevent internecine disorders."

Not every person believed in the effectiveness of comets in bringing catastrophe and death to himself. Vespasian, in A.D. 79, is credited with having said to his associates who were worried about possible disaster: "That hairy star does not portend evil to me. It menaces rather the King of the Parthians. For he is hairy, and I am bald."

Johannes Kepler, the great seventeenth-century German astronomer, established the fact that the orbits of the planets around the sun are elliptical, not circular. The orbits of comets, also around the sun, are much longer ellipses. Comets spend by far the greater portion of their lives in the distant realms of interplanetary space, perhaps beyond the orbits of Neptune and Pluto, where the gravitational force is so weak that many hundreds or thousands of years are necessary for a comet to complete a circuit. By contrast, a comet usually spends only a few days, or at most a few weeks, in the vicinity of the earth and the sun, during which time it is moving very fast.

Scientific researches have established that a comet is a celestial body in its own right, quite closely related to a meteor. The cometary model now generally accepted was proposed and developed by Fred Whipple. The head of a comet, he believes, consists of a conglomerate of ices of different kinds, ranging from ordinary water ice to solid methane and ammonia. The head also contains an amount of "dirty" particles, such as dust or rock fragments; it is like a great plum pudding, with the rock and perhaps some metallic granules for the plums and the great bulk of the comet's ices for the pudding.

At great distances, the heat from the sun is negligible, and the cometary ices remain frozen; in this state the comet has little if any aura surrounding it. When it nears the sun, however, some of the ice melts and evaporates. This action produces an atmosphere, which grades into the long, luminous tail that stretches into space in a direction away from the sun. Thus, as comets come in toward the sun, their tails follow behind. But as the comets move away from the sun, their tails precede them on the return trip. The tails are composed of extremely rarefied gas, glowing, when near the sun, because of ultraviolet light absorbed from the sun.

Two forces drive the tail of a comet away from its head. The more important is the solar wind, a stream of atoms and electrons coming from the sun. These particles strike the comet's atmospheric envelope, thrusting its component atoms and molecules against the gravitational pull of the comet's head, in the direction away from the sun. A smaller force, acting in somewhat the same way, is that of solar radiation—the force of sunlight itself. (Sunlight falling upon a medium-sized automobile when the sun is directly overhead presses the car to the road with a force slightly smaller than one one-hundredth of a gram, less than the weight of a gnat.)

The concentrated solid matter forming the nucleus of a comet is generally small, probably not more than a few miles in diameter, but the hazy mist comprising the entire head can be very large indeed. Some comets have had gaseous heads larger than Jupiter, and a few even larger than the sun.

To our knowledge, no one since 1947 has misidentified a comet as an UFO. Writers of fiction, however, have transformed comets into spaceships, inhabited by beings who are observing us.

Comets are untidy celestial objects, filling interplanetary space with debris. When the ices melt and evaporate they leave behind dust and rock, which disperses throughout almost the entire elliptical orbit of the comet. Even though we do not see this matter moving through space we know that it exists; when the earth intersects an old cometary path the heavens become lighted with meteor showers. These displays have frequently spread a considerable fear among the ignorant and the superstitious. Indeed, in 1866 a meteor shower observed in the southern United States caused large segments of the populace to believe that the end of the world was near.

In Plate 17 we show Halley's comet, photographed in 1910. It is easy to understand how such a sight could strike terror into the hearts of the superstitious and the ignorant.

Aurora Borealis

Another spectacular phenomenon of the earth's upper atmosphere, which has now and then produced startling UFO reports, is the aurora borealis. Few apparitions in the sky are more beautiful or have caused more wonder than the aurora. We show in Plates 18 and 19 two spectacular auroral displays, photographed in Alaska.[5] About the only people who seem to have taken this phenomenon for granted are the Eskimos and the inhabitants of Scandinavia. As the name implies, the "northern lights" are indeed most common in the far north. We usually associate them with intense cold and arctic snow fields, but occasional displays appear in temperate latitudes. In past centuries these auroral apparitions have taken their turn in frightening people. The association of the aurora with the great UFO of 1882, to be discussed shortly, justifies our consideration of the phenomenon here. Even though we have no direct evidence to connect aurorae with modern UFO reports, some persons did believe that the green color of the New Mexico fireballs, described in Chapter 2, indicated an auroral phenomenon.

The northern lights, by virtue of the higher number of inhabited places in the northern hemisphere, have had wider publicity than their southern counterpart, the aurora australis. The southern lights furnished a natural illumination to the famous Byrd expeditions of the 1920s and 1930s and to other Antarctic expeditions.

Primitive ideas about the aurora borealis in general have been extremely far from the truth. The Eskimos, for example, have regarded the glow as light reflected from arctic snow fields still illuminated by the sun, as certain gods intercepted the sun at the western horizon and carried it around under the northern sky, so it would be ready to rise again the following day. A rather ingenious theory—but wrong.

A much more common view, apparently widely held by the ancients, was that aurora borealis depicted events on the surface of the earth. The superstitious and imaginative could see kings, armies, beasts, great processions, battles, and funerals—in addition to other apparitions like angels, devils, and dragonlike monsters the like of which never walked the earth.

Franz Reinzer, the Jesuit astronomer, in his *Meteorologia Philosophico-politica,* writes:

One should remember the year 1568 when on one bright night, as Fomianus Strada testifies, two armies in the sky met in real order of battle, encountered with shining spears; now retreating, then advancing. With shields colliding, and fighting, as when a new race of giants had risen up to storm the heavens. This strange apparition caused no unreasonable fear and terror to the Duke of Alba; thereafter it came to light that this work was heaven's charity—a warning given to rouse the Duke's foresight. The portent prognosticated, as the historian has observed, the approach of the armies of the Prince of Orange, the horrid pillaging and massacring, and a long, miserable war.[6]

The earth is a magnetized sphere. It is this magnetism that makes the compass needle point north. But the north and south magnetic poles do not coincide with the geographic ones. Instead, they lie roughly 12° from the poles of rotation. The earth's north magnetic pole, which we should really refer to as a "south-seeking" pole because it attracts the "north-seeking" end of a compass needle, lies near Baffin Island, north of Hudson Bay, on the continent of North America. The south magnetic pole lies on the Antarctic continent. These poles, however, are not precisely fixed; they wander slowly and with some regularity in roughly circular paths in the northern and southern polar regions.

Study has shown that the aurora borealis occurs most frequently not at the poles, but in zones about 23° away from the magnetic poles. From this zone of the auroral maximum, the numbers of visible aurorae decrease both toward the magnetic pole and away from it, toward the equator. At the present time we in the temperate zone of North America are much more favorably located for observing the aurora borealis than the people of Central Europe, for instance.

Although the forms and patterns of the auroral lights vary as widely as those of summer clouds, we nevertheless can recognize certain definite types. The aurorae fall into one or the other of three classes, those with and those without appreciable ray structure, and those that pulsate. One of the most common forms assumed by the aurora is that of the arc—a circular belt of light girding the northern sky. Some of the arcs merely glow and show no marked internal features, whereas others display a series of rays, like the teeth of a comb. Usually the patterns of light shift slowly, but occasionally the brightness flickers and flashes like flames from a bonfire. Thus there are three important classes of auroral forms: homogeneous arcs, ray arcs, and pulsating arcs. When the arcs are so far away from the observer that their brightest portions lie below the horizon, only a faint glow indicates the presence of an aurora. Occasionally the rays themselves appear individually or in bundles, sometimes steady, at other times flickering. Not infrequently the auroral light assumes the form of drapery hanging in graceful sweeping folds that may move back and forth like a curtain or a long skirt swaying in the breeze.

When the arcs are not well defined, the northern sky may be traversed by homogeneous or rayed bands. Occasionally we see only a uniform, diffuse, pulsating surface.

In very intense displays, the auroral glow will sometimes reach to the zenith or beyond and form the beautiful crown, or corona. The corona usually appears as a series of streaks radiating from a dark center, which lies in the direction toward which a compass needle would point if it were free to move vertically as well as horizontally. This point is known as the magnetic zenith.

The auroral glow arises from various atoms and molecules that occur in the earth's upper atmosphere. The characteristic green glow comes mainly from oxygen. The oxygen atom, however, under certain circumstances can also contribute a reddish hue. Nitrogen, the most abundant constituent of the earth's atmosphere, also can produce a deep red glow. Auroral displays occasionally show radiations from the very light atom of hydrogen. Observations indicate that the hydrogen gas, instead of being stationary in the earth's atmosphere, is rushing at us from space with a speed of from 200 to perhaps a couple of thousand miles a second.

The development of commercial fluorescent lighting has made

us all familiar with glowing gas. Many advertising signs, like the red neon ones, shine because electrons, driven through the gas, smash into the neon atoms with sufficient force to make them radiate.*

Explosions on the sun and other types of solar activity are responsible for the aurora borealis. We now have evidence of the clouds of gas coming in to the earth from the sun, the fast-moving hydrogen referred to above. But, for a long time, the evidence for a solar cause was indirect.

A compass needle points toward the north magnetic pole. If the compass is very sensitive we soon discover that the needle is never really still. It swings first to the east and then to the west, making a fairly regular progression in the course of twenty-four hours. But the total amount of the swing and the smaller fluctuations associated with it change markedly, sometimes from just one day to the next. Days when the needle shows a big fluctuation we call "magnetically disturbed." Intense auroral displays often accompany these big disturbances.

THE GREAT UFO OF 1882

Auroral phenomena have, in the past, caused considerable consternation. This was notably the case in 1882. On the night of November 17 of that year one of the greatest UFOs of modern times sped swiftly and silently across the heavens over England and northern Europe, exhibiting the characteristic cigar-shaped form when it attained maximum altitude.

The object was remarkable in other ways. By all odds, it was the best-observed "flying saucer" in history, and it is one of the most difficult to explain. The observers included a number of respected scientists skilled in the art of observation. E. Walter Maunder, a Greenwich Royal Observatory astronomer and a foremost student of the sun, and J. Rand Capron, a well-known spectroscopist, saw the event from England. Observers on the Continent

---

* Perhaps it should be noted, in a time when there is some concern about accidents at nuclear power plants, that the kind of radiation referred to here is harmless.

included the Dutch scientists Audemans and Pieter Zeeman—of whom the latter eventually received a Nobel prize for his researches on magnetism.

For a description of this phenomenon let us turn to the account given by Maunder, not the original report he gave at the time of the event, but one he wrote almost thirty-four years later. We have checked the two versions and find that they are consistent with one another. Professor Maunder entitled his 1916 paper "A Strange Celestial Visitor."[7]

In response to the invitation of the Editors of *The Observatory* to furnish some reminiscences to the 500th number of this Magazine, I tried to recall my most striking experiences during the past 43 years, and my memory has gone back to one that stands out from its unlikeness to any other.

It was a quiet and fairly clear evening in the late autumn, and the time was nearly two hours after sunset. The Moon was near her first quarter, and had crossed the meridian a little more than half an hour before. There was, therefore, a fair amount of light in the sky, and the principal stars were clearly seen.

I was at the Royal Observatory, Greenwich, and, as a violent magnetic storm had broken out at about $10^h 15^m$ in the forenoon, was expecting an auroral display. I had therefore taken up my position close to the "Sheepshanks Dome," on the "Library Leads," as the flat roof over the smaller library was then called, whence I had a view uninterrupted in all directions except for the great dome towards the S.E. Nor was my expectation disappointed, for as the sunset tints faded away in the W.S.W. quarter, a rosy glow, at first hardly to be distinguished from them, spread itself all over the N.W. and gradually strengthened, until about 5.30 P.M. a brilliant ray, mainly of the same red or rosy colour, but with a greenish vein in it, shot up from the horizon in the north and reached the zenith. Other less conspicuous glows and rays showed themselves, but presented no features of special interest.

Then, when the display seemed to be quieting down, a great circular disc of greenish light suddenly appeared low

down in the E.N.E., as though it had just risen, and moved
across the sky, as smoothly and steadily as the Sun, Moon,
stars, and planets move, but nearly a thousand times as
quickly. The circularity of its shape when first seen was evidently merely the effect of foreshortening, for as it moved it
lengthened out, and when it crossed the meridian and passed
just above the Moon its form was that almost of a very elongated ellipse, and various observers spoke of it as "cigar-
shaped," "like a torpedo," or "a spindle" or "shuttle." Had
the incident occurred in the next century, beyond doubt everyone would have selected the same simile—it would have
been "just like a Zeppelin." After crossing the meridian its
length seemed to contract, and it disappeared somewhat to
the south of the west point. Its entire passage from rising to
setting took less than two minutes to complete, and it disappeared at $6^h5^m59^s$ G.M.T.

The "torpedo," on the other hand, was many times
brighter than this northern glow, much brighter even than the
Great Comet (of 1882) then visible in the early morning sky,
and it had a clearly defined outline, but a plain and uniform
surface. The greatest length which it presented was about
$30°$; its breadth was from $2°$ to $3°$. But in colour the light of
the "torpedo" was evidently the same as that of the auroral
glow in the north, and this showed me in the spectroscope the
familiar auroral line in the "citron-green," to which, indeed,
its colour was plainly due, a line now considered to be coincident with a prominent line in the spectrum of krypton.*

This "torpedo-shaped" beam of light was unlike any other
celestial object that I have ever seen. The quality of its light,
and its occurrence while a great magnetic storm and a bright
aurora were in progress, seem to establish its auroral origin.
But it differed very widely in appearance from any other
aurora that I have ever seen. It was unlike auroral shafts and
rays, with their glancing, flickering movements so generally
radiating from the magnetic north, since its motion was a
steady uniform progress from (magnetic) east to west. It was

* We now know that the green auroral line comes from oxygen.

equally unlike auroral "arches" or the auroral "crown," and its clearly defined outline and restricted size differentiated it as distinctly from the ordinary diffused auroral glows.

It appeared to be a definite body, and the inference which some observers drew from this was that it was a "meteor," not in the old vague sense of some object high in the Earth's atmosphere, but in the sense of a solid cosmical substance the orbit of which has brought it within the terrestrial atmosphere. But nothing could well be more unlike the rush of a great meteor or fire-ball, with its intense radiance and fiery train, than the steady—though fairly swift—advance of the "torpedo." There was no sign of the compression of the atmosphere before it, no hint that the matter composing its front part was in any way more strongly heated than the rest of its substance—if substance, indeed, it possessed. The gleam of a search-light, focused on a cloud and steadily swept along it, is a more accurate simile for the impression which the appearance produced upon my own mind.

The late Mr. Rand Capron, of Guildford, who made the study of aurorae one of his chief specialties, communicated an interesting discussion[8] of the observations of this singular phenomenon to the *Philosophical Magazine* for 1883 May, pp. 318–339, a paper I briefly summarized in *The Observatory* for 1883 (vol. vi, pp. 192, 193). For myself, the "torpedo beam" stands out in my memory, not only as a celestial object unique in my experience, but as associated with the great magnetic storm of 1882 Nov. 17–21, and as synchronizing with the great sunspot group, No. 885 of the Greenwich Photoheliographic Results, the largest I had then observed. From that date onward I had no doubt that in some way or other magnetic disturbances on the Earth were connected with disturbances in the Sun, though it was not until more than twenty years later that the nature of the connection became clear.

J. Rand Capron, F.R.A.S., F.R.S., gave a detailed analysis of all available observations shortly after the event of 1882.[9] He points out many interesting features of "the auroral beam," as he terms the phenomenon. And indeed, several independent arguments suggest that the apparition was of the character of or at least associated with the auroral display that Maunder reported.

First, the month of November 1882 was remarkable for its high degree of magnetic activity, that is, disturbances of the magnetic compass, and for the associated series of auroral storms that appeared over a wide geographic area.

The sun, which we now know to be the source of both auroral and magnetic activity on the earth, was intensely spotted. In fact, one of the largest spots ever recorded up to that time was then visible on the surface of the sun.

As Maunder reported, the expectation of seeing a brilliant auroral display had brought out many observers, who were certainly well repaid for their effort by the sight of the remarkable light.

Another fortunate circumstance resulted from the expected auroral display. Five students of auroral spectra, including Capron, quickly and independently swung their spectrographs around to get some data regarding the colors of light radiated by this object. All seemed to agree that the light was auroral and showed the characteristic green line—"citron," as some of the observers graphically described the precise tint. In addition, Capron reported a "faint greenish-white continuous spectrum." By that expression he meant that some radiation seemed to be present other than that from a glowing gas. And indeed the range of colors reported by many observers placed as much emphasis on the white as they did on the green shade.

Of course, it is difficult for anyone to describe the precise color of faint illumination. At night we are all more or less color-blind. Even in brightest moonlight it is difficult to separate flowers according to their hue. A bright aurora, however, will usually appear distinctly green, sometimes with red fringes. However, many observers emphasized the "brilliant white" color of the 1882 light.

But there is another reason for associating the 1882 light with auroral activity. A number of observers independently noted that it did not move exactly from east to west along a path parallel to the rising and setting of the stars. The motion, somewhat askew with respect to the geographic north and south, corresponded closely to magnetic co-ordinates. Since the aurora is a magnetic phenomenon, with the positions of the auroral rays, curtains, and arcs dictated by magnetic rather than geographic directions, this triple coincidence of a light associated with an auroral display, apparently also containing auroral radiation, and conforming to the geometry of the aurora, is indeed compelling.

As for the shape of the light, the descriptions and similes varied, though they leave little doubt as to the general outline. Near the horizon, it appeared to be nearly circular, but as it rose higher in the sky it lengthened as previously described. Then, on setting, it reverted to the original circular form. It gave the impression of being a roughly cylindrical light something like an enormous baseball bat hurled directly toward one, parallel to the ground, and overhead. While still at some distance away, the bat would look nearly circular. Then it would lengthen out as it swung overhead and contract again as it sailed away.

The actual words used to describe the shape of the beam varied: "spindle-shaped," "like a torpedo or weaver's shuttle," "cigar-ship," "lenticular," "like a comet's tail," or "like a discus seen on edge"—yes, almost the very words we hear sometimes used today: "a flying disk."

The colors named were "white," "pearly white," "greenish white," and "yellow white." Various observers described the texture as "glowing." The reports of the detailed structure of the object varied, perhaps, more than any other reported feature. Some of the observers noted no structure at all. Others regarded the outline as clear-cut, with well-defined boundaries. One of the observers from Holland used the adjective "feathery" to indicate that the outline was not quite sharp.

Descriptions of the internal structure also varied, from structureless uniformity to an actual internal "boiling." One report called attention to an apparent "rough, splintered appearance" of the ends. Many observers, however, saw an internal shadow ranging from "central dullness" to a "dark nucleus" parallel to the long axis of the spindle.

Capron used the observations of his fellow scientists to determine the height of the phenomenon above the surface of the earth. This study placed the torpedo-shaped object at an altitude

of about 130 miles—a value not inconsistent with the observed
heights of other auroral forms. If we accept this measured distance,
we then can calculate that the body was roughly seventy miles long
by ten miles in width and that its speed was about ten miles per
second. This speed, incidentally, is not inconsistent with values observed for some meteors.

Although some of the persons watching this phenomenon
thought they were seeing a material body, the figures given above
show that this could not have been either a single large body or a
swarm of small ones. It could not even have consisted of a cloud
of "cosmic dust," as a few persons suggested.

A solid body of this size, moving at this speed through the
upper air, would have produced a very different type of phenomenon. Its leading edge would have seemed to be on fire, and sparks
would have showered behind to form a long, luminous trail that
would probably have persisted for hours.

The swift, silent motion, performed without any changes of
shape ascribable to the motion itself, makes it imperative for us to
discard the hypothesis that the body was solid. Similar arguments
apply perhaps even more forcefully to liquid objects, which could
scarcely persist for any time in interstellar space, without either
solidifying or evaporating. Hence we are left with just one possibility: namely, that the luminous region was gaseous—that is, if we
are to consider it as being material at all.

We generally accept the idea that great clouds or filaments of
gas shot from the sun cause the aurora borealis. We have occasionally seen the sun spewing intense clouds of gas into space, and
many scientists believe that the aurora occurs when one of these
clouds strikes the earth, causing the upper air to glow. For the moment, we see no better alternative than to describe the great UFO
of 1882 as an unusual form of auroral activity.

When a cloud of hot hydrogen gas encounters the earth, the
earth's magnetic field tends to concentrate the gas and focus it, by
a sort of funnel action, along a parallel of magnetic latitude. The
more common form of the aurora consists of a curtain hanging
nearly vertically over such a parallel rather than a cigar-shaped
beam tunneling its way through. But the light of 1882 certainly
followed a parallel, and the new science of "magnetohydro-

dynamics" indicates that such tunneling can occur. The studies further show that the magnetic fields themselves would probably serve to bind together a cloud of gas and temporarily keep it from dispersing or diffusing away, as gas would ordinarily do if no magnetic field were present.

There is no doubt that the 1882 UFO was very different from the average modern variety, but it was nonetheless a flying saucer, which term we use to include a multitude of odd atmospheric apparitions. Condensations and bright auroral beams have appeared with sufficient frequency to warrant this comment.

UFOs AND SUNSPOTS

It has been suggested that a positive correlation exists between frequency of modern UFO sightings and sunspot number. Accordingly, we present in Figure 6 a scatter diagram comparing UFO sightings with sunspot numbers for the years 1947 through 1969. The sighting frequencies were provided by the United States Air Force, and the sunspot numbers were provided by the Fraunhofer Institut in Zürich, Switzerland, official headquarters for such records.

Inspection of the scatter diagram does not suggest a positive correlation—nor any significant correlation—an impression confirmed by a correlation coefficient of −.21.† A correlation coefficient is a statistical measure of the degree to which two (in this case) variables are related to each other. There would be a high correlation, for example, between sunspot activity and the degree of ionization of the ionosphere. A correlation coefficient of 1.00 would indicate that the two variables were totally correlated; .00 would mean that only a chance, or random, relation existed between the variables. Different researchers might interpret r somewhat differently, but *generally* a value in excess of about .95 is considered significant. Thus, in this case, there is no significant

---

† $r = \dfrac{n \sum xy - \sum x \sum y}{\sqrt{[n \sum x^2 - (\sum x)^2]\ [n \sum y^2 - (\sum y)^2]}} = -.21$

correlation between sunspot activity and frequency of UFO sightings. The insignificant negative correlation is caused by a very large number (1,501) of UFO sightings in 1952, a year of relatively few sunspots (31.5).

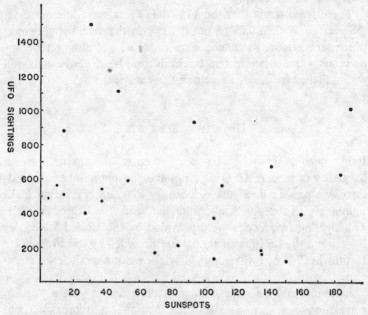

Figure 6. Scatter diagram showing absence of significant correlation between frequency of UFO sightings and sunspot activity, 1947–69. *Ernest H. Taves*

CHAPTER 12

UFOs AND PHYSIOLOGICAL OPTICS

SEEING IS BELIEVING.

Proverb

Yes, and all too frequently. There can be no doubt that countless UFO sightings are attributable to normal phenomena that are misinterpreted because of faulty visual perception, and apperception. Other sightings are based upon misinterpretations of things seen by normal, healthy eyes. Remarkable though the human eye is, it is an imperfect instrument. Further, it functions in concert with another imperfect instrument, the human brain behind it.

The hazards of accepting, at face value, eyewitness testimony to *any* event are enormous. Though eyewitness testimony is generally assumed (by the uninformed) to be the best kind, it is frequently the worst. Thucydides, in discussing the problems involved in producing an accurate history of the Peloponnesian War, said, "My conclusions have cost me some labor from the want of coincidence between accounts of the same occurrences by different eyewitnesses."

This was an early statement of the unreliability of eyewitness evidence, but the tradition did not stop with Thucydides. It has been established beyond question that when a number of observers witness an unexpected, startling, or dramatic event there are usually as many differing reports of the event as there are observers. This has been demonstrated endlessly in staged happenings in psychology classrooms in colleges and universities, in law schools, and in the laboratory.

Thucydides attributed discrepancies in reports of his observers to emotional bias and to failure of memory. Today we have a more sophisticated grasp of the magnitude of the problem. As Cornell psychologist G. M. Whipple has said,

> [The accuracy of any verbal report] involves the whole psychology of sensation, attention, and apperception; it hinges upon attention and recall, and thereby involves the whole psychology of memory; it issues in verbal statements, and thereby involves the psychology of language and expression; it is conditioned by numerous subjective factors, such as ideational type, emotional reaction, temperamental tendencies, sentiment, susceptibility to suggestion, etc.[1]

Thus eyewitness accounts of any event should be considered with caution, and skepticism, and we suggest that in the controversial realm of ufology caution and skepticism should be maximal.

Consider the Chiles-Whitted case mentioned in Chapter 11, a "classic" sighting much cited by the ufologists and still defended by some of them. Clarence S. Chiles and John B. Whitted were, respectively, captain and copilot of an Eastern Airlines DC-3 flight early in the morning of July 24, 1948. Flying over Alabama, near Montgomery, that morning they had, they said, had a frightening encounter with a giant cigar-shaped object. The alien aircraft, or spacecraft (for such it appeared to be), had, both men agreed, two rows of brightly illuminated windows, or portholes. One passenger of the DC-3 also sighted the terrifying object, but described it only as a streak of light. The crew of another commercial aircraft in the same general vicinity at about the same time reported having seen on the far horizon a jet or rocket trail moving at "terrific speed."

It seemed to Captain Chiles that the spacecraft was intelligently controlled; when the DC-3 veered, the exotic object appeared to veer. So convincing was this apparent movement of the alien craft

that both pilots dismissed any possibility that they might have encountered a meteor—which would immediately occur to many as a
likely cause of their unusual experience. But it is almost certain
that the Chiles-Whitted object was just that—a fireball, or bolide.[2,3]

As we have seen in Chapter 11, observers of the re-entry of
Zond IV provided *that* fireball also with windows, or portholes,
that it did not, of course, have. The fact is that any observer of an
unexpected, startling, or dramatic event is likely to misinterpret it
in a way that brings the stimulus into the realm of the familiar and
the understood.

In a staged happening in a psychology class, for example, it has
been shown that a banana may be identified as a handgun—surely
a startling misidentification of a very familiar object. Since it
doesn't make sense to pull a banana on an intended victim, while
drawing a handgun on a victim does make familiar sense, the banana was seen as a weapon.

To an airline pilot, another aircraft in the sky is a much more
familiar object than a bolide. The Chiles-Whitted UFO sighting
occurred during the annual Delta Aquarid meteor shower, which
produced numbers of other UFO sightings that year, as it does
every year. Unexpectedly confronted with a brilliant light flashing
through the sky, Chiles and Whitted interpreted the stimulus as
something familiar. They recognized that it wasn't a familiar type
of aircraft, so they "saw" it as a strange vehicle—with portholes.
Aircraft, with rare exceptions, do have windows, or portholes. So
the pilots provided the streaking light with these, as at a later time
did some observers of the re-entry of Zond IV.

Seeing may indeed be believing, but the interpretation of the seeing is all too often at variance with what the stimulus actually is. A
common example may be cited. Where two lights are alternately
flashing—as in a highway school-crossing sign—if the size of the
lights, the distance between them, and the flashing rate are just
right, the lights will be seen as moving from one location to the
other as a single light, smoothly crossing the intervening space.
Motion is perceived where none is present. This is known as the
"phi phenomenon" by the experimental psychologist.

Another important phenomenon in physiological optics has
been described by C. Pulfrich, who discovered that nerve impulses

generated by a bright stimulus apparently reach the brain more quickly than those caused by a darker object.[4] If a suspended bright ball is caused to swing back and forth, from left to right and right to left, against a darker background, a viewer's two eyes will perceive this motion as it really is—a pendulum swinging in a plane perpendicular to the line of sight. If the observer places a dark glass over the right eye, because of the reduced illumination the image of the swinging pendulum seen by the right eye lags behind that seen by the left.

When the pendulum is swinging to the right, the observer will therefore see two images unless he converges his eyes to make the images coalesce. (The effort to merge the images is precisely that required to focus the eyes on a single, nearby object.) The observer has the impression that the pendulum, instead of swinging in a plane, is moving in an elliptical path centered directly under the point of suspension. It seems first to approach the observer and then to recede into the distance as the direction of its swing changes.

This almost-forgotten effect was recently dramatized by Edwin H. Land, inventor of the Polaroid-Land camera, in a lecture at a meeting at Johns Hopkins University in Baltimore commemorating the centenary of the birth of Robert W. Wood, distinguished American physicist and authority on physical optics (see p. 230). Members of the audience, holding dark filters over their right eyes, became so convinced by the illusion that many automatically extended their free arms to fend off what appeared to be imminent collision of the moving sphere with their heads.

To illustrate the same phenomenon, instead of using dark glass to reduce the illumination received by one eye, the observer may simply squint an eye or view the swinging object through a tiny hole in a piece of cardboard. The effect is essentially the same. When the observer refocuses his eyes, a bright object moving from side to side appears to approach the observer and then recede into the distance.

This phenomenon may shed further light upon the Chiles-Whitted case. The two pilots evidently saw a bright meteor flash across their path, but so convinced were they that the object was pursuing a collision course, they executed evasive action. They refused to believe that what they saw could have been only a distant fireball. But, in terms of the Pulfrich phenomenon, the incident becomes understandable—together with hundreds of similar cases in the Air Force files.

There is great need, as Land has pointed out, for further research in this area of physiological optics. How well balanced, for example, are the two eyes of the average person? Can ocular disbalance cause the illusion described above? It seems reasonable to suggest that military and airline pilots should be subjected to specific visual tests, based on Pulfrich's swinging-pendulum demonstration.

VISUAL DEFECTS

Many misinterpretations of visual stimuli are based upon defective vision. Accurate visual observations can be made only by people with unimpaired eyesight, or by people whose visual defects have been adequately corrected. Rare indeed, however, is the report of an UFO sighting in which the visual acuity of the sighter or sighters is discussed. In many sightings, such as that of Chiles and Whitted, we probably have no cause to raise the question of faulty vision, but in many other cases the question would arise.

An investigator should ask the following: What was the visual acuity of the sighter at the time of the sighting? Does the sighter normally wear eyeglasses? If so, were these worn at the time of the sighting? Regardless of possible visual defects involved, what were the seeing conditions at the time of the sighting?

In a court case recently reported by Dr. Robert Buckhout, an associate professor of psychology, and director of the Center for Responsive Psychology at Brooklyn College in New York, a police officer testified that he had seen a black defendant shoot a victim while both victim and shooter stood in a doorway 120 feet distant.[5] Buckhout, for the defense, checked on the seeing conditions at the site and found that these were poor; the area was very dimly lit. The jury was taken to the place where the shooting had occurred. One black juror stood in the doorway while the others gathered where the policeman had stood while making his obser-

vation. The jurors were unable to identify their fellow juror, and
the defendant was acquitted. The accuracy of any visual observation is suspect unless (among other data) the seeing conditions are
specified. In most reports of UFO sightings, questions relating to
seeing conditions or to the visual acuity of the observer are generally ignored.

A common visual defect is myopia, or near-sightedness, the
prevalence of which is wide in all industrialized societies. One
study has shown that myopes comprise up to 26.8 per cent of certain European populations; another study found an astonishing 67
per cent of Japanese to be myopic.[6] In the United States, as elsewhere, the statistics vary according to the population under investigation—school children, factory workers, college students, and so
on—but the prevalence of myopes in all segments of our population is extensive.

Thus we deduce that many UFO sightings have been made by
myopes. Some of these individuals undoubtedly wore corrective
lenses; some, no doubt, did not. Statistics are not available, because investigative techniques have been inadequate. Yet the importance of considering the visual acuity of the UFO sighter is obvious, since the uncorrected myope has difficulty seeing *any* object
distinctly unless it is relatively close to his eyes. Further, it has
been clearly demonstrated that an individual with normal vision in
daylight may become myopic at night. Also, there is recent evidence that transient myopia may be caused by emotional stress.[7]

And myopia is, of course, but one of the many defects to which
the visual apparatus is subject. Another is hyperopia, or far-sight-
edness. This condition is also of interest in respect of UFO sightings because of a frequently associated complication bearing the
imposing label of "accommodative asthenopia." This condition occurs when the eye is strained beyond its capacity, that is, when the
ciliary muscle—the muscle of accommodation that adjusts the eye
to focus upon an external object at whatever distance—is called
upon to do more than it is capable of doing. Vision becomes
blurred and objects seem to waver to and fro. Stationary objects
are then perceived as moving—and the literature of UFO sightings
is replete with instances that may reasonably (though we can't
prove it) be attributed to accommodative asthenopia. The mov-

ing object may be anything the observer is looking at, but the most deceptive phantom movements in the UFO literature have been those of stars and planets. Weakness of the ciliary muscle through overuse is but one cause of the perception of motion where motion does not exist.

THE AUTOKINETIC EFFECT

It is impossible to perceive a visual stimulus accurately unless it can be fitted into a framework containing other visual stimuli. If a subject is placed in a dark room and presented with a stationary pin-point light source, the light will shortly seem to move—usually within five seconds. The nature of the motion varies from moment to moment and from subject to subject, but for almost everyone the light will seem to move. It may slowly swing through large arcs, it may more rapidly zoom and twist, or it may move rhythmically to and fro. Studies have shown that the apparent motion may be, to a degree, subjected to voluntary control. It has also been shown that the apparent movements may be partly controlled by external suggestion.[8]

This phenomenon, first discovered by astronomers, is known to psychologists as the "autokinetic effect." Here, again, motion is perceived where nothing moves. The implications of the autokinetic effect for the student of UFO sightings are clear—particularly when we note that the phenomenon was first described by astronomers.

It should be said that the apparent movement perceived by the subject is not merely suggested or uncertain; it is very real. Many subjects flatly refuse to believe that the light is indeed stationary. Some, aware that the light's position is fixed yet clearly appears to move, become uneasy and apprehensive. Most people find the autokinetic effect interesting, and the reader is urged to try it himself. Simply provide a pin-point light source, such as a light in an opaque box containing a pinhole, and sit before it, at a distance of four or five yards, in a dark room.

THE DANCING MOON

Even so massive a body as the moon has been seen to appear to
dance in the sky. In 1888 there appeared in the correspondence
columns of the British scientific journal *Nature* an account of a
strange occurrence experienced jointly by a group of three people
in Australia:[9]

> We noticed the moon apparently dancing up and down
> . . . The motion was visible only when she was behind a nar-
> row stream of cloud, and continued at intervals for thirty
> minutes. I felt quite seasick watching it, and Miss H. was so
> frightened; she thought there might be an earthquake coming,
> so went to bed in her clothes to be ready for an emergency.

Since the dancing moon was seen simultaneously by three observers we conclude that the cause was quite likely meteorological,
though physiological or psychological causes can by no means be
summarily dismissed.

Nature's correspondent, incidentally, suggested that a possible
cause for this exotic visual experience was varying refrangibility of
the atmosphere caused by a mixture of hot and cold air; he said he
would be glad of further information, but a search of ensuing correspondence reveals no response.

AFTER-IMAGES

When a ray of light enters the human eye and is focused upon the
retina, a train of events is initiated, a series of responses too complex to discuss here. The important point, for our purpose, is that
the processes taking place in the retina do not cease when the initiating stimulus ceases—as anyone who has ever whirled a Fourth-
of-July sparkler around his head knows. The glowing path is continuous because of "persistence of vision." The retinal image of an
object persists after the object has ceased to exist (as with a flash

of lightning) or has changed in position. It is persistence of vision that makes the moving picture on film or the moving image on the television screen real to us; without persistence of vision the flowing motions of these media would be perceived as series of frozen scenes in rapid succession, which would make for difficult, if not impossible, viewing.

When the retina is stimulated by light, a retinal image forms, and the image that persists after the removal of the original stimulus is the after-image. After-images may be either positive or negative. If one stares for a few moments at a brightly illuminated black spot upon a white background, and then shifts his gaze from that stimulus to a blank gray screen, he will see a light spot upon a dark background. If the spot is colored, the negative after-image will be of the complementary color. Close observation, particularly with practice, may reveal a series of after-images, alternately positive and negative. When the stimuli are colored, very beautiful effects may be obtained, as were described by Helmholtz, an eminent German physicist and biologist (d. 1894).[10]

The after-image is not a product of the imagination; it is an entirely normal physiological phenomenon. Since the image of the seen object persists on the retina after the actual object is no longer seen, the relevance of the after-image to the study of unidentified flying objects is clear. The human eye is seldom stationary, and when the eye moves the after-image moves—so we have yet one more normal situation in which movement is perceived where no movement exists. Or, to be more accurate, where external movement is seen when in fact only the eye in the head of the observer is moving.

An after-image of the sun, to cite a common example, can perform very strange tricks indeed. When the sun is low in the sky or partly obscured by haze or cloud and not so bright as to be dangerous to look at directly, an after-image will persist after a brief glance at it. If the observer looks away from the sun, there is a dark orb in the sky, moving as he moves his eyes. If one looks toward, but not directly at, the sun, he will see an after-image just off the center of vision. As the sun is a very bright object, solar after-images can persist for several minutes, as many people know from having accidentally glanced at a too-bright sun. Thus a single

observer can populate quite an area of the sky with flying objects
which exist only upon his retina. (The reader is warned against
trying this experiment when the sun is bright; permanent retinal
damage could result.)

Conditions for the formation of solar after-images must have
been particularly favorable one day in the seventeenth century, as
evidenced by the woodcut reproduced in Plate 20. Here the sky is
filled with flying objects—positive and negative after-images of the
sun—to the astonishment of the beholders. Note that the sun is
near the horizon, the location most conducive to the production of
solar after-images.

Thus we see that seeing should not always be believing. How
many UFO sightings can be attributed to the visual phenomena
discussed here we do not know, but we suggest that the vagaries of
physiological optics account for many otherwise puzzling ufological occurrences.

Plate 14. Meteors and other lights in the sky, including a comet, stars, and a flying dragon. *The Houghton Library, Harvard University*

Plate 15. *facing page, top:* Canyon Diablo meteor crater, Arizona. *Photo courtesy of the Harvard College Observatory*

Plate 16. *facing page, bottom:* Cross section of a nickel-iron meteorite fragment from the Canyon Diablo crater, Arizona. The lines are Widmanstaetten figures, showing the crystalline pattern of iron-nickel. The inclusions are chondrules—masses of olivine or pyroxene. *Photo courtesy of the Harvard College Observatory*

Plate 17. *above:* Halley's comet, 1910. *Lick Observatory photo*

Plate 18. *top:* The auroral curtain. Characteristic ray structure sometimes suggests the presence of a huge curtain hanging in the sky. Rapid changes in the brightness have led superstitious persons to see huge armies in battle. Silhouetted in the left foreground is the antenna of a radio telescope. *Vic Hessler, University of Alaska*

Plate 19. *bottom:* The auroral corona. The beautiful corona, converging toward the magnetic zenith, often appears to be a doorway into heaven. One of the most striking of auroral forms. *Vic Hessler, University of Alaska*

CHAPTER 13

UFOs AND THE MEDIA

"THEY'RE JUST COVERING IT UP."

> Comment by a member of the public quoted in
> a newspaper account of a recent UFO hoax.[1]

During 1974 a wave of reports appeared throughout the United States on many radio and television shows and interviews to the effect that the Air Force was then harboring (top-secretly, of course) at Wright-Patterson Air Force Base, in Dayton, Ohio, not only a captured spacecraft from an alien world, but a crew of frozen little green men as well. This report was broadcast from coast to coast, the media—particularly radio, in this case—giving it full exposure. In these broadcasts, which were usually interviews of self-styled authorities, it was set forth that President Ford would shortly make an announcement of importance with respect to this secret business—within two weeks, it was usually stated. Such announcement has yet to be made, though expectations were high amongst the believers at the time.

We addressed ourselves to Wright-Patterson AFB for the official word about these high-flying rumors. We received the following response: "There are no craft or creatures from space at Wright-Patterson now. There never have been. The report is without foundation."[2]

The believers will, of course, view this as but the most recent extension of the ubiquitous "cover-up."

The broad exposure of the public to this particular manifestation of the UFO mythos is a good example of the remarkable enthusiasm with which the media embrace the outer fringes of ufology.

Another example of media pro-believer bias was a television special, "UFOs: Do You Believe?" This program was televised nationally on the NBC network on December 15, 1974. Our response on viewing the program was that it was heavily biased toward the believer side. It devoted much time, for example, to the Pascagoula case, discussed in Chapter 17, which seems to us a pathetically obvious hoax. We obtained a transcript of the full text of the program, and analysis of the content confirms our initial subjective impression of pro-ETH bias.

Perhaps this is not surprising, in view of DHM's exclusion from the program.[3] It should be stated that when the program was in its formative stages, DHM was approached by the producers and was asked if he would participate in a consultative or advisory role in the preparation of the scenario. He was told that all the roads they had been following seemed to lead directly to his office at the Harvard College Observatory. DHM responded that he would be glad to act in any useful way in preparing the script, provided that the presentation would be balanced and would attempt a scientific approach. DHM, whose reputation as a scientific student of the ufological field was by then well-known to the producers of the program, heard no more from them.

Further, though Philip Klass was indeed interviewed on the program, his time was cut to less than a minute—a fraction of the time allotted to J. Allen Hynek.[4]

What is now called an "UFO flap" would not, it is obvious, be a flap were it not fed by the media. Indeed, the 1897 airship, described in Chapter 6, would scarcely have left the hangar but for the flood of newspaper dispatches that kept it alive—until another newspaper story, an interview with Thomas Edison, punctured the balloon. We've come a long way from 1897 (media-wise, one is tempted to say), and now we have phone-in radio programs that

give us opportunity to address ourselves directly to experts and authorities; we have national television, upon whose screen "con-
tactees" are (often to their profit) interviewed; and we have books,
lots and lots of books, wherein we may read of little green men
and chariots of the gods. The media have done a lot for UFOs.
And vice versa. A pleasant symbiosis.

Many young people are interested in, if not addicted to, the
media, and they are also interested in UFOs. Some of them, it is
true, perpetrate amusing hoaxes, but some have a more serious interest—as recently demonstrated by the sociology class of a mid-
western high school. We found the report of an experiment performed by this class in the Condon papers, and we do not
understand why the results were not presented in the Condon Report. We remedy that defect here. The research was done by John
Forkenbrock's students in the West Central Community School, in
Westgate, Iowa.

Forkenbrock's class had been studying collective human behavior—the Orson Welles-inspired Martian panic in the United States
in 1938, Adolf Hitler's rise to power in the 1930s and 1940s, and
so on—and were in search of a climactic experiment to perform
upon the society around them. They decided, accurately, that the
fabrication of an UFO incident might produce interesting results.

On the night of the "sighting" three members of the class—
somewhat to Forkenbrock's surprise, one gathers, for he had apparently been encouraging his students merely to discuss what
might happen—ignited gasoline in a pasture. They burned a circular area about ten feet in diameter, to indicate the purported landing site of an UFO, together with the added nice touch of four
smaller circles, meant to suggest some kind of ancillary gear on
each landing leg.

Except for a neighbor who had been informed of the plot, no
one except the perpetrators knew the truth. The students activated
the scheme the next morning by reporting the "sighting" to fellow
students and to a local radio station. Before nine o'clock one of
the student-perpetrators had been interviewed by someone from
the radio station, and by ten o'clock an UFO expert had arrived at
the school. Public reaction to the experiment escalated rapidly,
possibly to the students' surprise. They noted in their report:

"Within a few hours a relatively small burned patch near a little country church and a statement by a few high-school boys had gained state-wide and finally nation-wide attention."

The media do not come out well under the inquiring scrutiny of this high-school sociology class. Apparently some photographs were taken, but the report is not altogether clear about this. It is steely-clear, however, about the report appearing in the local newspaper saying that "the boys have pictures to prove some sort of 'unidentified flying object' really did touch down . . ." "Please take note," the students' report sternly demands, "of the words which say that the pictures 'prove' that something 'really did' land."

This rather remarkable report makes other trenchant observations. The media, the students note, embellished the story. The original "ball of reddish-orange flame" became "an oblong object, reddish-orange on one end and metallic-grey on the other." The students came (quite properly) to the conclusion that the mere fact of media coverage convinced some people "that the incident was true."

They also discovered that repetition alone tends to make things believable. "One girl in our class who didn't know the UFO was a hoax later stated that she shrugged off the first report but the more she heard, the more she believed it."

The class was obviously impressed, and perhaps a little frightened, at what it had wrought, as its report indicates:

Of critical importance in this situation is the actuality that the national wire services were handling unsupported word only . . . All of that extensive coverage was the result of a phone call by a high-school boy and a burned place on the ground. None of the information released was actually verified by any experts or officials. Apparently, however, this didn't cause any real slowdown or hesitancy because within two hours of the initial phone call people of the press were on the scene and representatives from local radio and television stations were en route. The big, but unverified, story caught on quickly. Twenty-four hours after that one phone call the story was aired on WLS radio station, Chicago, and WCCO

station of Minneapolis . . . So much important—but unverified—news about something that never happened!

The . . . most serious and frightening aspect of this experiment is that the results imply that one may use the media for
his own purposes. The mass media can be manipulated to
serve one person's intention. This is implicit in the fact that we
did just that. We used the media to serve our purpose. We
saw and revealed to others a wide scope of human emotional
behavior. The mass media was used to convey the emotional
contagion. In this case, manipulating of the media served an
educational purpose. However it is just as possible that the
same could be done to serve a very bad purpose.

Shortly after their experiment, having learned more, perhaps,
than they had hoped to about the irresponsibility of the media
and about human suggestibility, the students confessed openly that the
sighting had been a hoax. Not, however, before other observers in
nearby towns stated that they, too, had seen the UFO!

After their confession, the students observed some more reactions they had not anticipated. The local school board received an
anonymous letter: "Sure glad you've got [the teacher] in your
school system, *then he won't be in ours* . . . I hope [his] class can
help him grow up and avoid such a child-like affair in the future."
In a preconfession poll, the students found that about 90 per cent
of those polled "felt that it was true and they believed it." In the
postconfession inquiry, they found that the same percentage questioned now stated that they had had doubts all along and that they
didn't believe in UFOs at all.

People thought that "the local radio station had been made to
look like a fool." As, indeed, it had. One hopes that the news staff
of the station was chastened, and educated, by their feckless participation in the affair. And the mayor of the town, having fenced
off the landing area and made plans for its preservation, was (un-
derstandably) angry and embarrassed.

It is to hoodwinked WCCO's credit that they later said of the
hoax that it had been "a good educational experiment . . . this
represents real student involvement in learning." One hopes that

the station, a major radio voice in the Midwest, also learned from the experience.

We leave this heartening study with a summary of the students' conclusions as presented in their report:

1. Emotions increase suggestibility.
2. Emotions ruin perspective.
3. Interaction with other people fans emotions.
4. The media give reality to unreality.
5. People tend to blame what they distrust, and believe what they fear.
6. The media are not always reliable and can be used.
7. The public can be manipulated.
8. People welcome even negative experiences as a release from boredom and tension if they offer excitement.
9. Excitement grows with [the number of] people who are involved.
10. People are not prepared for a surprise.

It's been a long time since *The New York Times* ran an UFO story, and people who read only the large metropolitan dailies would probably be astonished at the number of UFO and related sightings reported every week in the United States and in other countries. The quality of reportage varies greatly but the coverage is there, and it is essentially continuous. A clipping service we subscribed to averages about fifty items each month.[5] There is a seemingly unending flow of headlines:

RUSSELL WOMEN BLINDED BY UFO

PILOT CHASED UFO

MAN, SON SEE UFO ABOVE CORN FIELD

EXPERT: UFO WAS NO PHONY

SAUCER SEEN IN CARSON

The list could be extended to any desired length. Occasionally the voice of reason is heard:

STRANGE FLYING OBJECT REPORTED
NEAR FINDLAY
WRITTEN OFF AS MIRAGE

LIGHTS IN SKY WERE SATELLITES—EXPERT

but many of the accounts manifest a total and uncritical acceptance of the sighting, regardless of the improbability of the object sighted. Some articles are accompanied by drawings or photographs.

One cannot—at least, we cannot—examine the tremendous amount of newspaper space given in so many papers, week after week, month after month, to so many sightings in so many parts of the world, without asking this question: How is it that, among all these events, not one sighting has shown up that would convince a panel of objective scientists of the validity of the extraterrestrial hypothesis?

Regarding the reported sightings, we ask other questions: If beings from space *are* visiting us, why don't they wish to establish contact? Why do they appear so often? Why do they land so often in corn fields, pastures, tobacco fields, athletic fields? If they land without wishing to, they land because, presumably, they are in trouble, and if alien spacecraft with problems are landing, why haven't we found one? Rich reward, monetary and otherwise, is waiting for the first person to produce solid evidence that an alien spacecraft has visited Earth. But that reward remains unclaimed.

We believe that the rational answer to these questions is that we have not been visited by spacecraft from outer space.

The media, however, continue to mislead some of the public. Quite recently, on October 20, 1975, the NBC network televised a two-hour special, "The UFO Incident." This movie was based on the 1961 "abduction" of Mr. and Mrs. Barney Hill, which we discuss later, in Chapter 19. Though the Hill case has, we think, been thoroughly discredited, "The UFO Incident" opened with the statement that the movie about to be shown was based upon documented fact. There was no clarification whatever of what was meant by "documented fact," and the statement certainly misled many of the credulous before the film had started.

In one scene the inevitable Air Force officer made the inevitable allusion to the "five-per cent residuum" of unexplained cases. We have shown in Chapter 8 that where the sighting data are adequate, there are no unexplained cases. At the end of the movie, the so-called Zeta Reticuli star map (p. 246) was brought in to furnish astronomical "proof" of the reality of the Hill incident. As we shall show, the Zeta Reticuli map does not withstand critical scrutiny. But it is a certainty that many gullible people were taken in by the pseudoscience of "The UFO Incident."

That TV special was followed only a few days later by the appearance on another network of a one-hour show on UFOs. This one made not the slightest pretense toward balance, but instead offered, as fact, a tired parade of many hoary and discredited cases in the literature, including the Chiles-Whitted (p. 145) and Great Falls (p. 110) cases already discussed, and the Tremonton case, discussed later (p. 192).

We submit that the media in general, and television in particular, have been, in their relation to the UFO question, enormously irresponsible.

UFOs AND PHOTOGRAPHY

ONE PICTURE IS WORTH MORE THAN TEN THOUSAND WORDS—
BUT DOESN'T NECESSARILY PROVE ANYTHING.

Ancient Chinese proverb, amended.

The current interest in UFOs began in 1947, and the art and craft of photography became a part of the ufological scene shortly thereafter. There have been two kinds of photographic participation in this field: many hoax photographs have been fabricated; and innumerable photographs, honestly taken, have been erroneously interpreted. We shall consider the second category first.

MISINTERPRETED PHOTOGRAPHS

We usually take for granted the excellence of the photographic film we buy in rolls, in film packs, or on glass plates. We tend to forget that the processes involved in film manufacture are intricate and complex and that crucial stages of these processes must be carried out in darkness. The basic operation is the deposition upon plastic film or glass plates of a thin layer of gelatin which contains the photo-sensitive material, usually a solution of silver salts, chiefly silver bromide.

The process of film manufacture, though highly mechanized, is still something of an art. Despite every effort to achieve extreme cleanliness in factories, occasional specks of dust become embedded in the emulsion and appear in the final product. Since the film cannot be scanned for such defects—the light required for scanning would expose the film—their occasional occurrence cannot be prevented. Such defects, appearing later in the sky of a printed photograph or of a slide, have often been interpreted as UFOs. (One of us—DHM—once found in a photographic emulsion the remains of a thoroughly squashed housefly that had managed to work its way into the inner sanctum of Kodak Park in Rochester, New York. Sometimes a few flakes of exposed silver grains may become embedded in the emulsion, to produce a peculiar object in the finished picture.

Despite stringent rules against workers carrying matches or smoking material into photographic plants, it is not impossible for an occasional packet to be smuggled in. The absent-minded smoker, lighting a cigarette in the darkened rooms of the manufacturing area, can seriously damage film. Again, the final developed photo taken with damaged film may be strange and difficult to interpret.

Strenuous efforts are made to keep foreign substances from getting into the film, but when that does happen it is not always detrimental. In one instance of such contamination, film handled by one particular individual was found to be appreciably more sensitive than the run-of-the-mill product. The plant technicians tried unsuccessfully to reproduce this highly desirable quality in regular manufacture. It was finally discovered that this particular employee, a long-time worker in the plant, was addicted to chewing tobacco. Forbidden to smoke, he had adopted the practice of chewing—and occasionally expectorating into a convenient open vat of photosensitive material. For some reason that the chemists were unable to find, this small amount of tobacco juice increased the sensitivity of the film.

The foregoing story was related by C. E. Kenneth Mees, head of the Research Department at Eastman Kodak. Whatever method they may have later adopted to duplicate this increased film sensitivity on a commercial scale was no doubt regarded as an industrial secret.

Since many thousands of miles of film are manufactured every year, it is not at all surprising that occasional defects occur. And even the most perfect film has peculiarities that the average photographer is unaware of. There is, for example, the phenomenon of solarization, which can be confusing and upsetting to the amateur photographer. Perform this simple experiment: In a darkroom, cover a piece of unexposed film with opaque, black paper in which is a small round hole about an eighth of an inch in diameter. Now expose the film through the hole in the paper, moving the hole between exposures whose duration increases geometrically—one second, two seconds, four seconds, eight seconds, and so on, until the longest exposure of, let us say, 1,024 seconds. Each exposure except the first is twice as long as the one immediately preceding. Then develop the film.

Offhand, one would expect that the photographic negative would show the tiny spots increasing in density throughout the set of exposures. But that is not the way photography works. The film will attain a certain maximum density, and thereafter the blackness will begin to *decrease* for the longer exposures. This is the phenomenon of solarization. It can cause a very bright object to appear dark, or even black, on a positive print.

Ansel Adams, the famous nature photographer, in one of his recent sets of published photographs shows a picture entitled "The Black Sun, Owens Valley, California."[1] The sun, distinctly black, is an example of solarization. An amateur, seeing the photograph for the first time, might erroneously conclude that the sun had temporarily ceased to shine and had hung like a black sphere in the otherwise luminous sky.

Other aberrant things can happen to the film during the process of picture taking. The camera may be defective. Old-fashioned cameras, with the lenses held in the middle of a protruding leather bellows, often allowed light to fall on the film through cracks or pinholes in the leather. Dirt on the lens will rarely cause any serious problem, since it is not in focus on the film, but a photographer wearing a diamond ring that glints in the sunlight can produce some extremely weird images if the ring happens to be in such a position that some of the light reflected from it falls on the

surface of the lens. One photograph of an UFO in the Air Force
files proved to have been caused in this way.

Most amateur photographers understand that they should not
take pictures directly into the sun, but if light from the sun does
happen to fall on the lens, internal camera reflections can produce
mystifying effects.

We have recently been sent, for comment, a series of stellar
photographs taken by an amateur astronomer. He had been photographing the constellation Perseus and other constellations, and
the photographic session seemed normal in all respects. When the
film was developed, the photographer was puzzled to find that in
four slides taken of Perseus an inexplicable glow was present, as if
there had been some adventitious light source in the constellation
or somewhere in the space between the camera and the stars. The
mysterious object was ovoid in shape, and cruciform rays extended
from it. In the first three pictures the object was in essentially the
same place in the sky. In the fourth picture the object was larger,
had moved considerably, and did not display rays.

This object had not been visible to the photographer during the
picture taking, and he wondered if this might be some celestial object radiating energy in the ultraviolet. DHM replied that this was
not likely, since it is difficult to generate ultraviolet radiation without producing radiation also in the visual spectrum. Further, glass
lenses are almost opaque to ultraviolet radiation. Our view was
that the glow was produced by reflection of ordinary (in the visual
spectrum) light from an unnoticed street light or house light or
other source. The moon was, in fact, in the sky at the time the pictures were taken, though it was not in direct view, being behind a
house. We suggested that experiments be undertaken at the site to
see if our analysis could be substantiated. We have not yet heard
that this has been done, but we believe that these photographs are
excellent examples of inadvertent "UFO" pictures caused by internal reflections. We reproduce one of the pictures in Plate 21.

And lenses themselves have unavoidable defects. An image of a
sharp point of light, such as a distant lamp or star, for example,
will rarely show as a point on the film. Lens distortions create an
optical image in the form of a comet. Or, in many cases, the image
may be that of a tiny cross. A photograph reproduced in one of

George Adamski's early works (with D. Leslie) on flying saucers showed a factory over which, the author claimed, UFOs were flying. The peculiar "vehicles" were, however, only secondary images from bright lights surrounding the building.

This sort of phenomenon frequently appears in a television picture when the cameraman "pans" a scene. Reflection from the sun or from a bright light will cause extraneous images to appear, some closely resembling UFOs.

Accidents to a film can occur during the loading of a camera, causing unwanted exposure of a part of it. Inadvertent pressure on a portion of the film may cause an image to develop, though no light actually fell on that part of the film. This is another source for images resembling UFOs.

The iris diaphragm of a camera, which governs the size of the aperture, or F number, of the lens can also produce image defects. A six-sided diaphragm will produce rays that extend from any bright object in a distinctive hexagonal pattern. The shutter of a camera can cause a similar phenomenon.

Although most of the newer hand cameras have fail-safe devices to prevent double exposures, there are many ways in which double exposures can occur. A film can, for example, be loaded and run through the camera twice; this may produce some extremely bizarre effects.

A film must be developed in a darkroom to bring out the image, and this process is in itself somewhat complicated. The film is first placed in the developer, which must be held at some optimum temperature for the best results. The film is then partially washed and placed in hypo, or fixer, which dissolves the unexposed and undeveloped silver compound, leaving the image in the form of metallic silver deposited upon the transparent film or plate, held in position by the gelatin emulsion. Many accidents can and do occur during the development process. The darkroom may not be completely dark. The solutions may not be as clean as they should be.

It is well known in the photographic field that a darkroom must be immaculate. Yet, even with the greatest care, accidents happen. Their occurrence is, of course, facilitated by the darkness. One of the worst accidents that can occur—and no one knows this better than an astronomer—is for a bottle of hypo to fall on the floor, breaking into pieces, with the liquid splashing over the walls and even to the ceiling. When such a catastrophe occurs, it is imperative to flush out the darkroom completely. Even so, tiny flakes of hypo will remain attached to the walls or ceiling. These can become detached and, later on, during developing, attach themselves to a film before it is put into the developer. An undeveloped spot will appear on the photographic negative as a dark area on the positive print.

A somewhat less catastrophic event is the spilling of a drop of the fixing bath on an undeveloped film. Such accidents happen in commercial developing plants even though they use various forms of automated processing.

The sky ordinarily contains many objects, especially in the daytime, that can be photographed. A number of these have raised the hopes of the ufologists that, at last, they have evidence of extraterrestrial vehicles. Consider, for example, the bright, silvery spots of light that cavorted against the deep blue sky at Tremonton, Utah, on July 2, 1952. A naval officer who took motion pictures of this display could not tell what the objects were, but many took them for flying saucers. A thorough examination of the photographic record, together with pictures taken under similar conditions, proved conclusively that the mysterious objects were flying gulls. Tremonton lies about fifteen miles north of Great Salt Lake; gulls are plentiful in the area.

There exist many other photographs of objects in the sky, both by day and night, where the best interpretation is that the objects photographed were birds, moving either individually or in flocks. These include the well-known Coast Guard pictures, taken on July 16, 1952, in Salem, Massachusetts, and also the once-famous pictures of nighttime UFOs recorded in Lubbock, Texas, on August 30, 1951. Although we believe that some of the Lubbock photographs may have been hoaxes, they are in no way inconsistent with the conclusion reached by some of the Lubbock viewers themselves, that flying flocks of birds illuminated by city lights produced the apparitions.

There are, in short, many ways in which adventitious happenings throughout the photographic process, from film manufacture to the preparation of the final product, can result in images on prints or slides that may be falsely interpreted as evidence for extraterrestrial vehicles. The fabrication of such photographs with intent to deceive is a different matter.

HOAX UFO PHOTOGRAPHY

One need not be an expert in trick photography to produce realistic but phony pictures of UFOs. This has been accomplished repeatedly in recent years by wily young children, aided by the fact that many natural objects closely resemble the conventional concept of an UFO: a garbage-can lid, the top of a cigar humidifier, a lens cap, a Frisbee, and even a straw hat. One of the earliest fake UFO photographs appeared in Adamski's *Flying Saucers Have Landed*.[2] The alleged UFO in the photograph is clearly identifiable as the top of an ordinary chicken brooder. What Adamski alleged to be the landing gear of the craft are clearly identifiable as three infrared bulbs, meant to supply heat to chicks in the brooder. The photograph was not in sharp focus, so the string or wire used to suspend the object in midair could not be seen.

A single UFO hoax photograph cannot always be easily identified as such, but a series of photographs, purporting to have been taken at about the same time, may quickly reveal the presence of a hoax. Unless the hoaxer is very knowledgeable and careful, sophisticated photogrammetric analysis will inevitably reveal discrepancies between what really happened and what the photographer said happened. The Roseville, Ohio, photographs, described in Chapter 16, are a good example of this (page 215). Case 56 of the Condon Report, discussed in Chapter 8, is somewhat similar.

In the case of the McMinnville, Oregon, pictures, in Condon Case 46 discussed in Chapter 8, long-overlooked shadows clearly showed that the photographs had been taken at times far different from those reported by the photographer (Chapter 16).

A hoax notorious in UFO annals was launched in February 1958, when a professional photographer aboard the Brazilian training ship, the *Almirante Saldanha,* took a series of photographs of an alleged UFO flying over the island of Trindade, in the South Atlantic Ocean east of Brazil. Acclaimed by the flying-saucer clan as the most convincing UFO pictures yet available, the photographs were published internationally. The apparent endorsement by the Brazilian Navy and later by the Brazilian government itself quickly collapsed when it was established that the photographer was well known for his trick photography and that no one else, except a friend (and presumed accomplice), had seen the disk flying overhead. It also came to light that the same photographer had, a short time before, attempted to sell a number of fabricated photographs of UFOs.

The method used in this instance was extremely simple, especially for anyone possessing a Rolleiflex camera. In the privacy of his home the photographer had snapped a series of pictures of a model UFO against a black background. He then reloaded the camera with the same film and took pictures of the scenery in the ordinary fashion. When the film was then developed, there was the saucer hanging in the sky. The photograph in Plate 22 was taken by Robert Sheaffer. It demonstrates this method.

A simpler method is to draw a convincing UFO, eight or ten inches across, on paper or cardboard; color it with paints or a crayon, adding windows and some little green men; and then cut out the UFO and paste or tape it to a large picture window. Now take some photographs through the window, showing the saucer silhouetted against the scenery beyond. By stopping the lens down you can get a photograph with both background and saucer in reasonably good focus. A little fuzziness may be desirable. Take care to avoid reflections in the glass of the window.

Another simple method, the one probably used by the photographer in Condon Case 52, discussed in Chapter 8, is to suspend a lens cap or other disk-shaped object in front of an automobile windshield and photograph it from the inside. We present such a picture, taken by us, in Plate 23. The total time required to produce this picture was less than five minutes. The object is a lens cap, and the camera was a Polaroid Model 250.

We have previously mentioned internal reflections within the camera as one inadvertent cause of producing UFO photographs.

Such photographs can be produced deliberately also. When the sun is fairly low, in the late afternoon or early morning, hold the camera so sunlight falls on the lens, though the image of the sun does not lie in the field of view of the picture. As you aim the camera in this manner, you will almost certainly see in the finder a bright, out-of-focus image, easy to interpret as an UFO. Reflections of the sun in the upper windows of a house will produce much the same effect.

There are, then, a very large number of ways in which photographs of UFOs may be produced, a few of which we have considered here. Some of these ways are without guile, some are intended to deceive. All may be explained rationally. The convincing UFO photograph has yet to be taken.

THE QUESTION OF EXTRATERRESTRIAL LIFE

THE UNIVERSE THAT LIES ABOUT US . . . IS
INCOMPREHENSIBLY VAST. YET THE CONCLUSION
THAT LIFE EXISTS ACROSS THIS VASTNESS SEEMS
INESCAPABLE. WE CANNOT YET BE SURE WHETHER
OR NOT IT LIES WITHIN REACH, BUT IN ANY CASE
WE ARE A PART OF IT ALL; WE ARE NOT ALONE!

Walter Sullivan[1]

A few hundred years ago men generally believed that the earth was the center of the universe, that the sun, moon, planets, and stars whirled about it as a center and that man was a unique being for whom the universe had been specially created.

Today few would subscribe to this anthropocentric view. The earth has shrunk from its dominance as the center of the universe to a speck the size of a minute grain of sand. Earth and others in our family of planets orbit around a minor star in the galaxy that we call the Milky Way. Our telescopes have resolved the Milky Way into about one hundred billion (100,000,000,000) stars, whose pattern of distribution forms a flat spiral, something like a pinwheel. Light, traveling at 186,000 miles per second, takes about 100,000 years to traverse the major diameter of the Milky Way and about a fourth of that time to travel through the thickness of the system.

Beyond our galaxy, as far as giant telescopes can penetrate, are other spiral objects similar to the Milky Way system. The total number of these other systems is also estimated at about one hundred billion. Thus the total number of stars in the part of the universe now accessible to our telescopes may be as many as ten sex-tillion—1 followed by twenty-two zeros. Light from the most distant of these galaxies takes something like ten billion years to reach us. And we are not sure that this figure represents the boundary of the universe or whether the universe may continue outward into infinity.

The magnitude of our universe defies human comprehension, but it certainly encourages us to speculate that, among these myr-iads of stars, so many of them resembling our own sun, other planets may exist and that some of them may, like our earth, have become afflicted with that organic mold, life, which appears to in-fect matter in its old age. In other words, we may expect that life exists in many worlds scattered through the vast universe.

Many people, having reached this conclusion, quickly launch into the following argument: Today we are putting man into space, landing on the moon, and our probes explore the solar sys-tem. Why should not some of these other planets have creatures upon them, perhaps far more advanced than we, who have solved the problems of interstellar travel? And are not the reports of UFOs evidence of such interstellar travel?

We are sympathetic to the view that life may exist on many planets scattered throughout the universe. But it does not follow that our earth is being visited by extraterrestrial spacecraft. Two basic facts must be kept in mind: the enormous number of stars and potential planets and the tremendous distances between them.

If each star in our universe were reduced to the size of a grain of fine sand just visible to the eye, ten sextillion such grains, placed into a pile, would form a mountain more than a mile in height, and covering an area of some four square miles. If now we spread these ten sextillion tiny grains to form a model of our universe on a comparable scale, we find that the nearest star in our galaxy is a tiny sand grain about sixteen miles away. Our entire galaxy in this model, a flattened spiral of such grains, is just about encompassed by the orbit of the moon. The most distant observed galaxy other than ours lies in the depths of space more than ten times the dis-tance of Pluto, the outermost planet in our solar system.

If, then, every one of the stars in this galaxy possessed a planetary system, why should their hypothetical inhabitants pick out the earth as an object of intensive surveillance? The distances involved are too enormous to be visualized. Interstellar travel is impractical unless we can travel faster than the speed of light. But, science fiction notwithstanding, there is no evidence that material objects can travel at such speeds. One may argue that, after all, man certainly doesn't know everything about the universe and that perhaps there are ways to circumvent this limitation. We believe that the limitation is real and that it will stand. We must take account of this limitation, for example, in the construction of atom accelerators, in which material particles do approach the speed of light.

We shall presently return to this point, but first let us leave speculation behind and examine some of the scientific evidence supporting the existence of life forms elsewhere in the universe.

Life, as we understand it, requires the presence of complex molecules, and these are not generally found in stars because of the high stellar temperatures. Even so, in our own sun we do find, through spectroscopy, a number of diatomic molecules, including cyanogen (CN) and carbon hydride (CH). More complex molecules are found in the atmospheres of the other planets of the solar system. Carbon dioxide (CO_2) is plentiful on Venus. Methane (CH_4) and ammonia (NH_3) are found on Jupiter. More importantly, more than a hundred complex molecules have been discovered in the depths of interstellar space itself.

There is, in fact, a great deal of grain alcohol (C_2H_5OH) in outer space. A. E. Lilley, a Harvard astronomer, has studied the presence of alcohol in B2 Sagittarii, a gaseous nebula in Sagittarius. He estimates that the nebula contains ten billion billion billion (10^{28}) fifths of 200-proof ethyl alcohol. If this vaporized alcohol were condensed to liquid form, it would require more than a thousand vats, each of the volume of our earth, to contain it— enough for a binge of truly cosmic proportions.

Carbon plays a unique role in the chemical processes involved in life. Chemists have long recognized that this element has a remarkable property distinguishing it from other atoms. It can "glue" other atoms together in long chains, principally those of hydrogen, oxygen, nitrogen, and phosphorus. These chains form organic molecules, which chemists once thought could be produced only as the result of some kind of life process. Some scientists once believed that organic molecules contained "vital force" or "living spirit."

This view collapsed in 1828 when an enterprising German chemist, Friedrich Wöhler, discovered that if he heated ammonium cyanate (NH_3CNOH), its atoms rearranged themselves into urea ($CO[NH_2]_2$), then well known to be a product of protein metabolism. Since then chemists have synthesized innumerable other complex organic molecules. Hence we surmise that if life processes are not necessary to produce organic molecules, perhaps life itself is nothing more than a chemical process. A great deal of evidence now supports that conclusion. How, then, did the development of life on the earth begin?

We now believe that the earth was formed about five billion years ago. In the steamy atmosphere of primeval earth there were no living organisms whatever. Great jets of different gases spouted from the hot interior of the newly formed planet. Many of these gases we would now term "lethal"; the word would then have had no relevance, since there were no forms of life on earth for the gases to kill.

As the earth gradually cooled, great clouds formed in the humid atmosphere, which then consisted largely of marsh gas (methane), ammonia, nitrogen, cyanogen, and water vapor. This was a stormy atmosphere, in which occurred innumerable bolts of intense lightning. In the presence of these electrical discharges the relatively simple components of the earth's atmosphere combined to form new molecules of much greater complexity, molecules that would lead eventually to the appearance of living organisms.

The knowledge that such processes are possible and presumably *had* to take place on the primeval earth is relatively new. Perhaps the clinching work in support of this view is an experiment performed by S. L. Miller. He passed electrical discharges through a mixture of methane, hydrogen, ammonia, and water vapor—and found that he had synthesized amino acids, the basic components of protein, molecules necessary for the existence of life. Such synthesization depends upon the aforementioned ability of carbon to string atoms together by the hundreds to form molecules of the highest complexity.

Over millions of years, then, lightning bolts, aided by ultraviolet light from the sun, formed large numbers of reasonably complex organic molecules which gradually contaminated the warm seas until they came to have the consistency of weak bouillon. The oceans had, in fact, been transformed into an enormous nutrient broth.

Among the substances in this broth were four of crucial importance: adenine (H), thymine (T), guanine (G), and cytosine (C). These are called "nucleotides," because they are vital components of the nuclei of living cells. Now, time can accomplish much that the scientist cannot in his laboratory, and nature is a patient experimenter. She is willing to wait millions of years, if necessary, for an experiment to be successful. After some millions of years the conditions in the warm-broth oceans of the earth became just right for this experiment. The organic molecules began to cling together, to polymerize, forming longer and longer chains and more and more complex molecules.

The four nucleotides mentioned above, A, T, G, and C, began to develop into a very complex substance indeed—deoxyribonucleic acid, or DNA, a tremendously labyrinthine substance now known to be the bearer of the genetic code. This complex molecular structure embodies a ladderlike configuration, in which the two uprights are composed of sugars and phosphates. Affixed to the uprights are long chains of nucleotides. The form of these chains of DNA is not linear, but helical.

The order of nucleotides along one upright determines the order along the other upright; A is always opposite to T, and G is opposite to C. Thus, if the order along one chain were ATGC, the other chain would contain the molecules in the order TACG. These chains, or uprights in our ladder analogy, are complex. In a relatively simple bacterial virus each DNA chain will be composed of about 200,000 nucleotide pairs. Within the nuclei of human cells each of these two chains will contain about *two billion* such pairs.

A complex of DNA molecules lies within every living cell. The length of the chain and the ordering of the nucleotides differs from species to species and, within a species, from individual to individual, except in identical twins. In every cell of the body of a living organism the DNA is the same. This remarkable substance contains the blueprint that distinguishes people from monkeys, and monkeys from amoebae.

Identical twins are as similar as they are because they come from the same ovum and have the same DNA. Events happening after conception will shape them differently—one, for example, may have the lion's share of the placenta—but their DNA chains will be identical.

When a cell reproduces, one of these spiral DNA molecules splits neatly in two, as if each rung were sawed down the middle. The half-ladders separate, and each begins to pick up nucleotides, following the plan of matching pairs we have mentioned. After the reconstruction, two helical ladders exist where there was but one before. Both are identical to the original.

In the simplest organisms—unicellular forms—the cell itself then divides into two parts, each with a DNA nucleus. During this process the organism absorbs various other molecules of nourishment from the environment, and thus grows.

The splitting process occurs again and again, producing four cells, then eight, sixteen, and so on. This may not seem a rapid means of reproduction, especially if we assume that a primitive organism might reproduce rarely, say once a year. However, such is the power of compound interest, or exponential growth, that in only 160 years one such organism would multiply into a mass far exceeding that of the earth, if sufficient food and space were available.

DNA contains the blueprint, not only for a specific cell, but for the entire organism. But if DNA is the blueprint, a similar substance, ribonucleic acid, or RNA, is the contractor, carrying the necessary information to places in the cell where proteins are synthesized. The RNA reads the genetic code and builds the cells appropriate to various locations in the body: an eye, the brain, a muscle, and so on.

Species tend to breed true. Bacteria generate bacteria; spiders produce spiders; and humans give birth to humans. But nature occasionally seems to make a mistake. A T molecule, for example, may slip in where a C molecule should be in the DNA. This introduces a change into the blueprint, which causes a change in the product, producing a mutation.

Mutations are generally harmful, and the mutated offspring tend to die out after a few generations. Some mutations, however, result in a better product, a flourishing new strain. This is a fact of the greatest importance, since in this way complex forms of life gradually evolve from simpler organisms.

One of the most important early mutations, which must have occurred in the primitive seas, changed the instructions that ordered the daughter cell to separate from its parent. When the organism failed to subdivide, a new creature began to develop—the first multicellular organism.

By the time this new animal grew to contain, say, a thousand cells it would no doubt encounter some difficulties. When separate, these cells had derived their nourishment directly through their membranes. Now the organism, if spherical in form, though larger in volume by a thousand times would have a surface area only a hundred times greater. The cells on the inside would die from malnutrition unless the organism could alter its shape, as by stretching itself into the form of a thin pancake or taking on the shape of a hollow tube. Thus a primitive worm might develop.

This worm could then further increase its food intake by sucking or propelling water through its prototypical digestive tract. Presumably it would thusly assimilate other, smaller, organisms. Creatures that developed sensory organs near the mouth, feelers or claws to aid in the capture of larger prey, and a means of propulsion would have a much better chance of survival than would those less well equipped.

Primitive worms still exist, and we learn much from studying them. Some species can reproduce either asexually or sexually. In the first case, the offspring grow from cells having the DNA of one parent. They will thus develop into a duplicate of that parent. If, however, the reproduction is sexual, the fertilized ovum will contain two sets of DNA, not necessarily exactly alike, one from each parent.

In time, then, creeping and crawling things emerged from the watery slime to attempt survival under the more difficult environment of dry land. Some of these grew wings to become progenitors of modern insects. Others came to be reptiles and birds. Lastly came the mammals. There are now millions of species of life, comprising a very great number of genera. The evidence is compelling that all of these sprang from common ancestry in the primitive life forms of the warm primeval ocean. Mutations led to the differentiation of species. Natural selection kept the number under some control, weeding out the weaker forms.

The mutations themselves—changes in the order of molecules in the DNA ladder—arise in a number of ways. A primary cause is radiation. X-rays and cosmic rays can produce such changes. So also can radioactive atoms, such as strontium-90, a product of atom-bomb explosions. This is why radioactive fallout is dangerous. Chemicals—mustard gas, for example—can also alter the DNA structure.

The development of living organisms may be thought of as a sort of cosmic game of cards. The game, which requires the matching of the molecules A, T, G, and C, more nearly resembles rummy than bridge. Nature shuffles the decks through energy acquired from the sun. The cards come in contact with one another as do autumn leaves swirling in a breeze. At what stage, then, does the complex supermolecule come alive? Mere growth and change are not sufficient indicators of life. Crystals can grow, but they are not alive. The answer to the question is that life begins when the game starts to play itself, when a given pattern of cards splits in two and then reproduces itself by rebuilding the lost half by drawing cards from the surrounding deck.

The line of descent from the first living form to a contemporary human is incredibly long, covering several billion years. During this time the earth has undergone profound changes, to which life has had to adapt. The atmosphere of the planet has also suffered major changes, some of them caused by the presence of life.

We have only to look to the earth to see how varied creatures, from single-celled animals to man, have existed over the ages. Fossils of organisms no longer living, such as dinosaurs, giant butterflies, and many varieties of marine life, show that natural processes have not always followed the same paths. We find fossil remains of many life forms that are not related in any way to those now alive.

One of the surprising features of the evolutionary chain, in view of the general slowness of the development of species, is the rapidity with which primitive man became *Homo sapiens*. This happened within a very few million years, a twinkling of an eye in the cosmic time scheme. One almost concludes that man himself unconsciously greatly accelerated the natural processes of his own evolution.

We must postulate a series of genetic changes that led to the development of the highly organized central nervous system of man. His enhanced intelligence gave him an enormous advantage over his erstwhile fellows. Breeding within the newly arisen intelligent type produced, in a relatively short time, a race quite different from its primitive ancestors.

In all probability, man is not the acme of intelligent life in the universe. Indeed, man's ignorance often seems a positive deterrent to his further advance. We readily concede, therefore, that there may well exist elsewhere in the universe other beings more intelligent, perhaps far more intelligent, than we. We are reminded of the graffito on a wall in London which asked the cogent question, "Is there intelligent life on Earth?" Someone had added, "Yes, but we're only visiting."

What will these superbeings be like? We speculate that they will probably live on land or perhaps be amphibious. They will probably have limbs for locomotion. They will possess a mouth and digestive tract resembling those of some terrestrial organism. Their eyes and ears will occur in pairs near the mouth, where they served their primitive ancestors in the detection and capture of food. They will probably stand upright, though they may be quite different from terrestrial primates. We speculate that their brains will be, relative to ours, large.

We do not believe that the fundamental molecules A, T, G, and C will differ much from those we have on Earth, no matter where they are found in the universe. The complex organic molecules our radio telescopes have been detecting in space are, without exception, familiar to terrestrial chemists. In brief, we believe that life will come into existence wherever there are Earthlike planets, wherever the atmosphere has a suitable composition, and wherever there is plenty of water of the right temperature.

Our surveys of our own solar system have pretty much disposed of any possibility that we might find advanced forms of life on any of the other planets in orbit around the sun. Mars, the most likely possibility, exhibits a desolate surface. Our Viking space mission, en route as this is written, will explore the soil of Mars; perhaps simple biological forms may be found. The other planets are too hot or too cold. The moon has neither water nor atmosphere, and there is no evidence whatever that life has ever existed there.[2]

If there is intelligent life elsewhere in the universe, why do we believe that their spacecraft have not, are not, and probably shall not visit Earth? There are many answers to this question; the most cogent of these involve probability theory and very large numbers. For our present purposes we shall limit discussion to our own galaxy, the Milky Way. The difficulties posed by interstellar space flight are quite sufficient without going into the much larger problems of intergalactic travel.

Limiting things to our own galaxy, then, we have, as noted earlier, more than a hundred billion stars to contend with, arranged somewhat in the shape of a spiral disk with a central thickening, the galactic nucleus. The distance across our galaxy, as we have seen, is in the order of 100,000 light-years—a figure not easily grasped, being in miles approximately 6 followed by 18 zeros. Thus, though we limit ourselves here to but one galaxy out of the universe of galaxies, the number of stars is large, and the distances between them are truly enormous.

These stars are of different kinds, including white dwarfs, red giants, and variable stars. Some of these stars will likely have planets, some will not. Some of the planets will be reasonably suitable for the development of life. Let us assume, with Ronald Bracewell, a Stanford University astronomer, that there are in the galaxy some ten billion "likely stars."*[3] It follows, from the known

---

* Stars whose conditions are likely to favor the evolution of complex life forms on their planets.

distribution of stars in the galaxy, that within 100 light-years of Earth there will be 1,000 "likely stars."

If we are to be visited by interstellar travelers within our galaxy, there must be on some planetary system or systems in the galaxy what Bracewell calls a "superior community"—a community technologically more advanced than ours. We willingly concede that such communities may exist, but their existence by no means ensures interstellar communication even by radio, let alone starship, and one of the reasons for this is that communities have lifetimes.

It is in the nature of life to be born, to grow, to mature, to become old, and to die. This is true for worms, for humans, for societies and cultures, and for stars. Thus many of the presumed planetary systems in our vicinity are in a prebiological evolutionary phase, with no life at all yet. Some may be pretty much where Earth is in the evolutionary scale. It is possible that some planets in other systems have produced superior communities; if so, many of these will have come and gone. Thus communication among different galactic communities requires that they be in the right place—reasonably near to each other—*at the right evolutionary time*.

This would be statistically more feasible near the galactic center, where stellar distribution is more dense, but it must be remembered that Earth is off at the edge of things in a sparsely populated part of the galaxy. Bracewell argues persuasively that if a community reasonably near Earth sent us a radio message as soon as they were capable of doing so and that if we replied as soon as we received it, our reply would arrive just as that community was going under! "A certain threshold density of superior communities has to be reached if the members are to be able to converse," he writes, "otherwise their average lifetime will generally not be sufficiently long for a message to traverse the vast depth of space to the nearest neighbor and return."[4]

The problems, difficult enough for radio communication, multiply if we think of actual interstellar travel. The question of time arises, of course. The distances involved are measured in light-years. How do we get there and back? These problems are easily solved by writers of science fiction (which, by the way, both of us are), but reality is a different matter. Until Einsteinian relativity is refuted, there is no reason to believe that a spaceship, or any other material thing, can travel at speeds faster than that of light. If we assume, however, that man can eventually travel at speeds approaching that of light—"relativistic speeds"—the temporal problem is somewhat simplified.

It is a consequence of the special theory of relativity that when an object travels at relativistic speeds the time dimension is drastically altered. The passage of time aboard a spacecraft traveling at relativistic speed would be retarded. Clocks would run slower than those left behind. Hearts would beat slower, and the aging process would decelerate. Traveling at 99 per cent of the speed of light, to a star 100 light-years away, the crew of the ship would age 28 years. Elapsed time back home, however, would be 202 years.[5] An interstellar traveler making a lengthy voyage at such speed would return to a world vastly different from the one he left.

Travel at relativistic speeds raises other problems as well. Interstellar space contains particles of many kinds, including dust grains, protons, electrons, atoms, and complex molecules. These are intrinsically not dangerous, but a spaceship sent through this mix at relativistic speed would "see" these particles as radiation of very high intensity. In Carl Sagan's term, the crew would be "fried," even on a short flight, unless careful and extensive precautions were taken.[6]

There is, of course, the possibility that we, or other life forms, may be unable to achieve relativistic speed. In this case, there are other approaches to dealing with the time required to traverse the depths of space. One is the multigeneration spaceship, in which the voyage is completed by the descendants of the original crew. Many good science-fiction stories have centered on this theme. Another approach is that of metabolic slowdown—through cryogenic or pharmacological means, the body processes of the crew would be slowed to the extent that a trip could be completed before the crew died of old age. This method was used in the widely distributed and well-received science-fiction film *2001: A Space Odyssey*.

Another grave problem of interstellar travel is that of the stupendous amount of energy required to propel the craft of the size necessary for such a voyage. The ratio of the takeoff mass of the vehicle to the payload mass (the "mass ratio") will be very large indeed, even if we assume that controlled nuclear fusion will be available.

Edward Purcell, a physicist at Harvard University, has calculated that if this nuclear process were available (the reaction, for example, in which two deuterons combine to yield a helium nucleus and a neutron), and if *all* of its energy were efficiently used, the mass ratio required to send a ship to Proxima Centauri and back, with acceleration to 99 per cent of the speed of light, would be *one billion!* A modest spacecraft of, say, a mere hundred tons payload would require one hundred *billion* tons of fuel.

If we assume that the ultimate source of energy, the annihilation of matter, could be harnessed, the mass ratio drops to something like 40,000, still a forbidding figure.

These large mass ratios are dictated by acceleration required for space vehicles to attain relativistic speed. If we (or they) are content to go slower, the mass ratio is drastically reduced—and the time required to make the trip is equally drastically extended.

If interstellar travel already exists in our galaxy, it is almost certain that it began and/or is now to be found in the galactic center, where stars are relatively close together. Perhaps the ultimate—and unanswerable, at least now—question is, Why would advanced members of a flourishing galactic society wish to spend the enormous (even for them) amounts of energy involved to visit us, retarded cousins in the backwoods?

Interstellar travel, it seems to us, will be enormously difficult for any community, no matter how advanced. The probability of its occurrence in sparsely populated parts of the galaxy is remote. The idea that Earth is under more or less constant, or even sporadic, surveillance by interstellar spacecraft, whose crews have gone to very great lengths to get here and who do not then reveal themselves to us, is, simply, preposterous.[7]

CHAPTER 16

UFOs AND HOAXES

EVEN NEWTON, IT IS RECORDED, CAUSED TROUBLE IN
HIS LINCOLNSHIRE VILLAGE AS A BOY BY FLYING
AT NIGHT A KITE CARRYING A SMALL LANTERN.

R. V. Jones[1]

Since many perpetrators of UFO events have confessed that their works were hoaxes, we need not belabor the point, but we state with emphasis that a definite, though not precisely determinable, percentage of UFO sightings and happenings are firmly established within this category. The hoax cases fall into four groups: (1) those in which the hoaxer has confessed; (2) those in which hoax is strongly suspected but has not been conclusively established; (3) those in which the hoax is unconfessed, but established beyond reasonable doubt; and (4) those attributable to juvenile pranks. We shall, briefly, give examples of each of these.

CONFESSED HOAXES

The current interest in flying saucers began June 24, 1947, with the Arnold sighting in Washington state (Chapter 1). The Maury Island case followed exactly one week after.

You will look in vain for Maury Island in most atlases; it is a small body of land in Puget Sound, about three miles from Ta-

coma, Washington. On June 31, 1947 two men identifying themselves as harbor patrolmen, Harold A. Dahl and Fred L. Crisman,
claimed to have seen from their boat near this island a group of six
disk-shaped objects flying overhead. They had, they said, photographed these strange craft. One of the objects seemed to be in
trouble, and before they all disappeared into the blue this object
showered metallic fragments upon the boat of the patrolmen.
(They weren't patrolmen, as it turned out, but salvagers of floating
lumber—impostors as well as hoaxers.) They mailed some of the
metallic fragments, together with their story, to Ray Palmer, then
editor of *Amazing Stories,* a publication familiar to Crisman and
one which had been running a series of eye-popping fantasies as
fact.

The details of the ensuing happenings are complex and will not
be gone into here, but the major consequence emerging from the
bizarre pattern was the appearance in Tacoma of two Air Force
investigators who flew in from Hamilton Air Force Base in California. The strange metallic fragments turned out to be slag from a
local smelter, there were no photographs, and the investigators
recognized a flagrant and unskillful hoax. On the return trip to
Hamilton AFB their aircraft crashed, and the investigators were
killed.

Dahl and Crisman later admitted that their "sighting" had been
a hoax that had gotten out of hand—a modest enough statement in
view of the fact that two men had died in consequence. The motivation of the hoaxers was not obscure; they wanted money, publication, and publicity.

HOAX SUSPECTED BUT NOT PROVEN

Certainly the most conclusive case for the extraterrestrial origin of
UFOs, if just one could be established beyond doubt, would be
one in which one or more earth people went aboard an alien
spacecraft and engaged in some kind of contact or communication.
Though many such cases have been reported, unfortunately there
is not a shred of proof or evidence anywhere that any of these
events happened as reported. Anyone providing such evidence can

collect $10,000 from Philip Klass, if he meets the terms of Klass's offer.

And he won't have to provide the evidence himself. Klass offers to pay anyone entering into an agreement with him $10,000 within thirty days after *any one* of these three conditions are met:

1. The U. S. National Academy of Sciences expresses the opinion that a crashed spacecraft, or a major part of one, is clearly identifiable as being of extraterrestrial origin.

2. The same body announces its opinion that other evidence conclusively proves that Earth has been visited in the twentieth century by extraterrestrial spacecraft.

3. The first extraterrestrial visitor, born on a celestial body other than Earth, appears live before the General Assembly of the United Nations or on national television.

In exchange, the person entering into the agreement is to pay Klass $100 a year until one of the three events listed above happens, or until total payments amount to $1,000.

Thus far Klass's bank balance has not been threatened.

We place almost all contactee reports in the "Hoax Suspected" category. *Almost* all, because we must leave room for psychiatric illness, manipulation by magazine writers and editors, autosuggestion, and the like, under which influences an individual may indeed come to believe, with no intent to defraud or to perpetrate a hoax, that he has been taken aboard an alien spacecraft. We believe, however, that most contactee cases lie within the "Hoax Suspected" group.

Consider the Pascagoula, Mississippi, incident of 1973. This was no doubt the most publicized UFO happening of that busy year. Two shipyard workers, Charles Hickson, aged forty-two, and young Calvin Parker, nineteen, in the night of October 11 were fishing in the Pascagoula River, not far from the center of the town of the same name. While doing so they saw flashing lights and heard strange sounds. These emanated, they said, from a roundish object hovering over them, from which three creatures emerged and floated down, proceeding then to float the two men upward and into the strange vessel.

It was dark outside, and inside the spacecraft the illumination was so bright it hurt, but these conditions didn't prevent Hickson from providing a very detailed description of his captors.

The creatures were about five feet tall, had elephantlike skin, and lobster-claw hands. Cone-shaped organs took the place of ears and nose. They did not walk, but floated. Hickson and Parker were levitated or floated separately into different rooms aboard the craft. After what seemed to Hickson like a physical examination—a large round object passed to and fro over his body—both men were floated to the ground and the spaceship took off. The site of this alleged occurrence was within a few hundred feet of a traveled highway.

Hickson's memory of this striking event was detailed; Parker fainted at the beginning of it and remembered almost nothing of his experience. Both men were soon celebrities. Hickson took a polygraph (lie-detection) test and passed with good marks. He gave up his job and made appearances on national television; Parker went back to the farm.

Philip Klass, a serious and skillful investigator in this field, is persuaded that the Pascagoula case is a hoax.[2] He notes multiple discrepancies in Hickson's various accounts of his experience. Klass's investigation revealed that the administrator of the polygraph test was not fully qualified, though qualified technicians were available in the area. He notes the failure of passing motorists to witness the flashing lights of the hovering spacecraft.

Another point, not mentioned by Klass: on a program televised nationally in 1974, "UFOs: Do You Believe?", considerable time was given to the Pascagoula case. (The slant of this program, as we have noted, was favorable to the extraterrestrial hypothesis; see Chapter 13.) In the program a Pascagoula bridge attendant was interviewed. He had been on duty at the time of the alleged occurrence. From his post on the bridge the site of the "abduction" was clearly visible. Yet this attendant, whose business it was to keep his attention on the river, stated that he had seen nothing out of the ordinary.

Finally, let us examine the demeanor of Hickson and Parker in the time immediately following their report of the incident to the Jackson County sheriff's office. They were "scared to death and on the verge of a heart attack." This has been considered by some to lend credence to their tale. But there is another point of view. If they were hoaxing, they had just created a real whopper and were about to see what would happen in consequence of trying it out. We suggest that their visible anxiety and apprehension were entirely understandable and were consistent with their awareness of what they were doing—putting on the authorities with a monumentally tall tale.

We believe that the Pascagoula case rests comfortably in the "Hoax Suspected But Not Proven" category.

UNCONFESSED BUT ESTABLISHED HOAX

In 1966 a barber exhibited in his shop in Zanesville, Ohio, a pair of photographs showing an object in the sky over his home, which was in the suburb of Roseville. He said he had taken the photographs himself. For a time the pictures were of local interest only, but in due course they came to the attention of a Columbus, Ohio, journalist and were soon sold to the Associated Press. They were distributed to the press early in 1967 and achieved a considerable notoriety and were widely reproduced. We reproduce them here in Plates 24 and 25.

In the course of the University of Colorado inquiry, a contract had been given to the Autometrics division of the Raytheon Company for the purpose of obtaining complex analyses of photographs like those of the Roseville sighting. For such a study it is highly desirable to have two photographs of the sighting taken at different times from different places, which was just what the Roseville photographs were. Had the photographer taken but one picture, the task of the analyst would have been much more difficult, but with the two the analysis was conclusive.

The alleged provenance of the photographs is given in the Condon Report: "The photographer says that he was leaving home with a camera when he chanced to look back and see the saucer flying over his home. He says he quickly snapped what we call picture A. Thinking the UFO was about to disappear behind a tree, he ran to the left about 30 feet and snapped picture B . . . He estimated that there was less than a two-minute interval between the two pictures, with A followed by B."[3]

The photogrammetric analysis was intricate and complex, involving measurements of the lengths of shadows in the photographs, trigonometric determinations, and a survey of the grounds around the Roseville house, as a geographical check upon the accuracy of the strictly photogrammetric results.[4] The analysis showed conclusively (1) that photograph A had been taken seventy-eight minutes *after* photograph B, (2) that the distance of the object had been no more than five feet from the photographer (compared with his stated estimates of forty-eight feet in one picture and 150 feet in the other), and (3) that the object (whatever it was) was no more than two feet in diameter.

The Colorado investigators wrote to the photographer asking for clarification of the discrepancies, but their letters were unanswered.

Many other examples of unconfessed but proven hoaxes could be cited; we shall mention but one other, the McMinnville, Oregon, sighting of 1950—an important case in the history of ufology and already discussed (Case 46) in Chapter 8.

In May of that year a couple living outside McMinnville stated they had seen a giant silvery object flying through the late evening sky near their farmhouse. Furthermore, they had two photographs to prove it. The sighting received much publicity and stood for more than two decades as a "classic." Even the Condon Report left it as "unexplained." We are indebted to Philip Klass and Robert Sheaffer for exposing the pictures as hoaxes almost a quarter of a century after they were taken.[5]

JUVENILE PRANKS

Many of the young people in the United States seem to be drawn, as if by magnet, to the faking of UFOs, an art in which they find much pleasure. There is a rich history of such hoaxes, and they continue, as demonstrated by a case recently brought to our attention.

On Saturday night, November 9, 1974, three teen-aged boys reported that they had seen a whirling object fall into a pond in Carbondale, Pennsylvania. The object, they said, had emitted sparks during its descent. Subsequent investigation revealed that on the bottom of the pond lay a glowing object. Police shot at this object and crowds collected. An investigator arrived, claiming to have been sent to the scene under the aegis of the Center for UFO Studies, in Evanston, Illinois; he forbade scuba divers from entering the water, fearing radioactivity, though there was no evidence of untoward radioactivity at the site.

Considerable effort was expended both to pump out the pond and to open a channel to drain it. Before these objectives could be accomplished, however, Carbondale Police Chief Francis Dottle allowed a scuba diver, Mark Stamey of Auburn, New York, to search the pond. Stamey went down and shortly came up with a Sears, Roebuck waterproof flashlight, one bulb of which was still glowing dimly.

A good testimonial to the quality of the flashlight, but no artifact from outer space.

The Carbondale case is, in itself, perhaps trivial, but it is of considerable importance in one respect. In the last paragraph of one newspaper account of the incident it is stated that at least one person said, when the flashlight was brought up, "They're just covering it up."[6] One more indication, in the face of a transparent hoax, of the tenacity with which the public cling to the concept of the cover-up.

Whether the statement quoted was imagined or misquoted by the journalist or whether it was an accurate report is not relevant; what is relevant is that the newspaper account suggested once more to thousands of readers that the cover-up is still on, that the little green men with pointed ears are here, all right, but that *they* won't let us know about it.

We conclude our discussion of juvenile pranks in the UFO field with a note that hot-air flying-saucer kits are now readily available from several suppliers. The catalog of a well-known science, optics, and hobby supply organization exhorts the reader to "Make and fly your own UFO." The finished product, complete with portholes, is shown in Plate 26.

A more elaborate model is advertised elsewhere:[7]

FOR SALE: SIMULATED SAUCER. Be the first in your block to create a real scare. Breaks down quickly and packs in ordinary station wagon for fast getaway. Glows in many colors and provides simulated radiation effect. Built-in static generator creates radio and TV interference in one-mile radius. Will not fly and is not to be confused with CIA models. Set up saucer beside a road and watch for fast results! Then be the first on the scene to "investigate" the sighting and get fat interviews with newspapers and big-time UFO researchers.

THE HOAX SYNDROME

*We cannot speak of deception and say that
one age knew more of it than any other, only
that each succeeding era discovers refinements
on the accomplishments of the older.*

Ralph Hancock[8]

We must now put the UFO hoaxes into a proper perspective. The position is that since hoaxes and hoaxers are everywhere, it is entirely predictable that they will be found in quantity in such a fringe world as that of the flying saucer.

Hoaxes for amusement and hoaxes for fraudulent gain have been found in such disparate fields as science (all of them), literature, religion, music, publishing, TV and radio and automobile repairing, sexual behavior, real estate promotion, quiz shows, pharmaceutical manufacture, stock brokering—and onward as far as one might wish to go. The list could be extended for pages. To help put the UFO hoaxes into a proper perspective in the larger world of the omnipresent hoax, we shall discuss a few examples of non-UFO frauds and fakeries.

The case of the Piltdown skull is of surpassing interest, as a classic scientific hoax, and we shall begin there. Briefly, the facts are as follows:

One Charles Dawson, at the turn of the century, lived near Piltdown, in East Sussex, England. He was an amateur archaeologist and, as a student of fossils, he became interested in 1908 in a gravel pit in Piltdown from which workmen were extracting material for road repair. He asked the workmen to save for him anything that looked interesting. Sometime in 1908 (the exact dates of most of the crucial events of the Piltdown case are unclear) a workman presented Dawson with a piece of bone, which Dawson identified as a part of the cranium of an ancient human skull. Dawson continued to search for bone fragments, and in 1911 found four more, together with other fossils.

Now, Dawson was a longtime friend of Dr. (later Sir) Arthur Smith Woodward, a distinguished scientist and then Keeper of the Geological Department of the British Museum. In 1912 Dawson took his five skull fragments to Smith Woodward, whose interest was immediately aroused. The two men organized further digging, in the course of which, in that same year, Smith Woodward himself found four more cranial fragments in the same gravel. All of these fragments, now numbering nine, were demonstrably parts of the same cranium.

During 1912 Dawson also unearthed at the same site a half mandible, which bore two molar teeth. There were other finds later, but these will suffice. (The interested reader is referred to the work of Francis Vere, from which this account is largely drawn.[9])

The half mandible was clearly simian, but the two molar teeth were equally clearly human. This anomalous finding, in conjunction with the upper skull, caused Dawson and Smith Woodward to think they had found the so-called Missing Link between man and the anthropoid apes, for which so many had been searching for so long. They announced their find publicly in December 1912 at a meeting of the Geological Society in London, at which they both read papers. Their discoveries and conclusions unleashed a furor that continued unabated for decades. Some scholars did accept the conglomerate skull as the Missing Link—*Eoanthropus dawsoni*—but many were unconvinced, skeptical from the beginning, unable to reconcile the simian jaw and its human teeth with the human cranium.

Casts of the fragments were made and were distributed to scholars far and wide, but the specimens themselves were held most closely within the British Museum; otherwise it is likely that the hoax would have been discovered long before 1953, when the facts finally came to light.

Anthropologists studied the casts and found it difficult to make sense of them. For one thing, the skull suggested that man had existed on earth for some 500,000 years—a then disconcerting time span, inconsistent with the main body of anthropological theory.* Also, it was impossible to fit the skull into an acceptable evolutionary tree. And there were other troublesome aspects. Confusion and acrimony reigned until 1953 when the skull was demonstrated, beyond any doubt, to be a hoax.

The story of the unraveling of the hoax is an engrossing narrative of scientific detection. For the first time the fragments were subjected to rigorous anatomic, chemical, and radiological scrutiny. Crystallographic studies were made. X-ray analyses were undertaken. Chemical examination included determinations of fluorine, iron, nitrogen, collagen, and organic carbon content. All of these analyses separated the cranium from the jaw and the jaw from the teeth. The teeth were demonstrated to have been fraudulently machined and shaped prior to their insertion into the ape's jaw. The stains on many of the fragments were shown to have been fraudulently applied. The jaw, the teeth, and the cranium were from three different entities. The Dawn Man of Piltdown, *Eoanthropus dawsoni,* stood revealed as a colossal hoax.

Though there remained no question about the fakery of the Piltdown skull, the evidence was not clear as to who had perpetrated the hoax. J. S. Weiner is persuasive in his suspicion of Dawson—who died long before the exposure of the hoax.[11]

As scientific hoaxes mark our wayward past, they similarly confront us in our uncertain present. In 1973 Dr. William Summerlin, a researcher at the Sloan-Kettering Institute for Cancer

---

* Recent (1974) findings suggest that a recognizably *Homo* species existed in central Ethiopia three or four *million* years ago.[10]

Research, in New York City, was found to have falsified some of his experimental data. And in 1974 Dr. Jay Levy, director of the Institute for Parapsychology, in Durham, North Carolina, was detected in fraud.

Dr. Summerlin had applied paint to mice used in his experiments in such a way as to make it appear that a new skin-graft procedure had been successful when, in fact, it had been a failure. Dr. Summerlin was given a leave of absence in which to seek psychotherapy.

Dr. Levy had manipulated automated equipment in his experiments in such a manner as to cause the results to suggest that rats have psychokinetic powers. Dr. Levy resigned.

Cancer research, or oncology, is an entirely respectable area of scientific inquiry. Parapsychology has been trying for decades, with scant success, to achieve academic acceptance and respectability. The study of UFOs, as Robert Low noted in his later widely publicized memorandum to the Dean of the University of Colorado (Chapter 7), lies on the very fringe of academic respectability; at least, it lay there for the one-shot Condon inquiry.

In mentioning in the same paragraph—and in the context of hoax—oncology, parapsychology, and ufology, we do not, of course, imply that oncological research is generally suspect, that parapsychological research is broadly suspect, or that the majority of UFO sightings are based upon hoaxes (we have already shown that many sightings are misidentifications of a broad array of natural phenomena). What we do suggest is that the hoaxer is active everywhere, and particularly so in fringe areas such as those of ufology and parapsychology. It behooves the investigator of unidentified flying objects to be particularly wary of the hoaxer. Trained and experienced investigators, themselves scientists, have been led astray repeatedly by practitioners of deceit; the uneducated, the untrained, and those who need to believe are far more susceptible prey. Until cautious and healthy skepticism replaces human naïveté and gullibility, the hoaxer will have no difficulty finding willing victims.

We conclude this chapter with an account of an amusing hoax that never got, so to speak, off the ground.[12] The hero of this tale is one Harold Murphy. In 1938 he was an editor of a northern

New York newspaper. The story was related many years later by a fellow journalist who worked for the same newspaper, whose account we quote from here.

Murphy, in the late summer of 1938, picked up a wire-service report giving the results of a survey of newspaper editors concerning what they thought would be the ten greatest news stories of all time. Among these was "news of communication with another planet."

This wire-service item, together with the fact that he had been told that on October 30 the planet Mars would be in favorable relation to the earth for possible Earth-Mars communication, set Murphy into action. He proposed fashioning some metal plates, upon which he would carve or etch a variety of strange symbols.

"Now here's the way we do it. I got to go to a Grange meeting on this night, see? I got a farmer friend near the Grange Hall, and at a pre-arranged time he's going to set off a whopper of a dynamite explosion in his back lot. I'll be drivin' home from the Grange, see, and I'll see and hear the explosion and I'll say I saw what looked like a meteor or something shooting through the sky just before."

The strange metal plates, carefully placed there by Murphy, would later be found at the explosion site. It would be big news. Murphy had access to the wire services, and would spread the story. Scientists would come from all over. A fence would be put around the site, and admission would be charged. Later, Murphy and his colleague would exhibit the plates at the World's Fair in New York City. They would make a fortune.

"Well," Murphy's fellow worker asked, "what happens if we get caught?"

"Great!" shouted Murphy. "Then we'll have the greatest hoax of them all. People will spend even more to see a famous hoax than the real thing!"

So the great evening came. Murphy's co-worker was at his desk in the newspaper office. There was a sound of running feet. Murphy appeared.

"Ruined!" he shouted. "Ruined! Dammit! We got beaten by Mars itself! They've landed rockets and Martians and every damned thing in New Jersey! Damn! Damn!!"

Murphy turned and ran out.

October 30, 1938. Sitting at home, waiting to put his show on the road, Murphy had been derailed by the Orson Welles "War of the Worlds" broadcast! The Murphy hoax was never executed.

The Welles radio broadcast was a major Halloween stunt, of course, and it was not intended to be believed. The alert listener was never in any doubt that this radio version of H. G. Wells's novel *The War of the Worlds* was anything but a dramatic presentation, but the gullible and credulous were taken in by the hundreds of thousands. Some six million people heard the broadcast, and of these at least a million were frightened. Many in New Jersey fled their homes to escape the invading monsters. Telephone lines and some highways were clogged for hours. The broadcast provided one more instance of the truth of Barnum's dictum that there's a sucker born every minute—a grossly conservative estimate.

CHAPTER 17

THE LIAR, THE BELIEVER, AND THE NEW NONSENSE

THUS, DECEPTION IS UNIVERSAL. SO IS CREDULITY,
THE NECESSARY GROUND FOR THE SUCCESS OF DECEPTION.

Alexander Klein[1]

There is no doubt that a great number of alleged UFO sightings
are attributable to liars telling lies and that large numbers of people believe the liars and the lies, often in the face of overwhelming
evidence of falsehood and hoax. This leads us to two questions:
Why does the liar lie, and why does the believer believe?

Of these questions the second is of the greater importance, and
we shall address ourselves to that question shortly. First we briefly
consider the question of why people lie.

As the epigraph to this chapter suggests, deceit has always been
with us. We are all guilty. God himself, in the Old Testament, is
not above the use of ruse. He forbids Adam to eat of the fruit of
the tree of the knowledge of good and evil, adding the ominous
threat that "in the day that thou eatest thereof thou shalt surely
die." Adam does eat the forbidden fruit, but he doesn't die, not for
a long time. In the ancient text that relates this history no particular point is made of the lie, the empty threat. Thus, early on in
human affairs, lying seems to be taken for granted.

Arnold Ludwig, in *The Importance of Lying,* asks:

Who has not falsified, misstated, misquoted, misinterpreted, glossed over, disguised, colored, varnished, dressed up, embroidered, exaggerated, invented, trumped up, fudged, or doctored the truth? Who has not equivocated, quibbled, fenced, beat about the bush, dissembled, dissimulated, feigned, simulated, deceived, or malingered? Who has not been hypocritical, mendacious, artful, political, tricky, cunning, wily, sly, or faithless? Show me a man who denies all of this behavior, and you show me a liar![2]

Quite so.

Leaving UFOs aside for the moment, the point we wish to make here is that hoaxes, fraud, and deceit are everywhere and everytime: in science, in literature, in religion, in crime, in journalism, in politics, in sports, in almost everything, almost everywhere, almost any time.

Still the planet rotates upon its axis and modern society has not yet collapsed. Not yet. How is this possible if truth is so hard to come by? The answer is that though truth is often enough a commodity in short supply, the ways in which we depart from truth are many, ranging from the presumably harmless "white lie" and the practical joke to, say, the monumental deceptions practiced by national governments upon their gullible citizens.

Because lying is so frequently encountered in the world of the UFO, we shall consider here a simplified taxonomy of lying. Our classification begins at the least nocuous end of the scale and progresses onward. Or downward.

1. Many lies are creative, benign, or simply social. These lies are useful tools, instruments used for the most part to attempt to achieve some desirable social or interpersonal result. The benign lie is harmless—often, indeed, humanitarian. Though contemporary thinking along these lines is undergoing some change now, many would still wish, for example, to lie to their spouse or other close person to shield the one lied to from the knowledge of incurable disease and impending death.

Many benign lies are simply social lubricants. We all resort to these so frequently that it would be redundant to give examples. Lies about Santa Claus, the Easter Bunny, and the Tooth Fairy fall within this category. No doubt these lies are used less frequently now than in other times, but they're still told often enough.

2. The defensive lie, the lie to keep the liar out of trouble. It is found frequently enough in children, and adults, in the form of simple denial: "I didn't do it." ("*He* did it" is something else.)

This is the lie used in dealing with the perhaps old-fashioned example of incriminating lipstick on the collar. It is the lie found in the police station and in high political office—wherever there is a need to try to undo some part of the past by stating that it never happened.

3. The lie for gain—for positive gain as distinct from avoidance of the negative. An example of this is the lie of the politician on the campaign trail. He lies and makes false promises to gain votes, which lead to office, which leads to power.

Beyond counting are lies for simple financial gain. Mail-fraud schemes, the selling of gold bricks or the Brooklyn Bridge, confidence games, many real-estate deals, and thousands of other demented transactions belong here.

And malingering—feigning illness to escape duty or work—also fits into this category.

4. The compulsive lie is one uttered because the liar simply must lie. This is a complex category including liars who lie because of organic brain damage, because of irremediable constitutional defects, or because of causes so deeply rooted in unconscious processes that the liar has no access to the causes.

Consider the lying found in Korsakoff's syndrome, a well-known clinical entity found in chronic alcoholics whose indulgence has produced brain damage. To cover memory gaps, the victim compensates with wild fabrications—which are easily identified as such by the listener, though the liar gives every appearance of believing his fantastic tales.

A somewhat similar condition is the Ganser syndrome, also known as the "syndrome of approximate answers." Here the vic-

tim, asked the sum of two plus two, is likely to respond with nine—
or any number other than four. These people lie because they have
to, and we don't know why they have to. The cause and nature of
the Ganser syndrome are matters of considerable dispute, but because this condition is most characteristically found in accused
persons awaiting trial, we suspect that this state of severe dissocia-
tion has to do with the avoidance of responsibility for one's past
actions.

Delving further into psychoanalytic theory we find another liar
who lies because he must. In general, one would suppose that the
liar lies to make someone believe something that isn't true or to
disbelieve something that is true. This is indeed the obvious and
superficial reason, but the psychoanalyst suggests that the true and
covert aim may be to produce—altogether unconsciously—that result in himself. The liar lies to deceive himself, an intrapersonal
lie. A very simple example of this kind of self-deceptive operation
is that of the patient who presents his physician with a false medical history, either to conceal symptoms he can't face or to fabri-
cate an illness.

And there is the psychopathic personality, or constitutional psychopath. (There are other labels, also, for the same condition:
constitutional psychopathic inferiority, antisocial personality, so-
ciopathic personality disorder, and so on.)

These individuals are unable to respond to the ordinary demands of life in ways most people would, in a commonsense
way, accept as "normal" or rational. Their deficiency is not mental, but rather "an apparent constitutional lack of response to the
social demands of honesty or truthfulness or decency or consideration for others, which incapacitates the patient from settling
down to any permanent standardized activity."[3]

These people lie, day in and day out. They are often quite lika-
ble, and they are persuasive. They take people in with the most
outlandish tales—and thus we have an interest in them in relation
to tales of unidentified flying objects. Interns in psychiatric hospi-
tals, before they learn better through experience, are easily duped
by these smooth-talkers, frequently becoming emotionally involved
in helping them get out of the hospital in which they have (un-

fairly, they cry) been incarcerated. They are believable, to the uninitiate, no matter how fantastic their tale. Faced with incontrovertible proof of lying, they say something to the effect of, "I'm sorry you don't believe me." The almost-standard retort of saucer seers, "I know what I saw," has the same ring and displays the same unshakability.

We do not set forth the view here that the psychopath is an important part of the UFO picture. Indeed, as we shall mention later in this chapter, psychopathology in general does not appear to be much of a factor at all in the world of the flying saucer. But we include this psychiatric entity here since it is most likely that some UFO hoaxes have been perpetrated by psychopaths. The psychopath will always be lying or faking about something or conning somebody into something, and in times when interest in UFOs is high, that area is a natural target for his attention.

5. The malicious lie. This is a self-explanatory category, in which reposes the lie intended to cause harm to one's enemy. Examples need not be given.

In the above classification of lying we have made no provision for *error*. Again we point out that hundreds upon hundreds of UFO sightings have been based upon honest reports and honest errors—misidentifications of meteors, weather balloons, planets, space shots, a wide variety of recognized natural phenomena. We emphasize, however, that error and lying can become inextricably mingled when the committer of the error manifests a need or wish to believe in the error. The need to consider this fact, in UFO sightings, is apparent.

We conclude this discussion of lying, frauds, and hoaxes with a brief account of N (for Nancy, France) rays—a nonexistent form of radiation whose "discovery" created a great stir in the early twentieth century.

N rays were "discovered" in 1903 by Prosper Blondlot, a physicist at the University of Nancy. These rays, which were said to emanate spontaneously from many metals and a number of other substances, had properties more arresting even than those of x-rays. The literature soon filled with papers describing the alleged prop-

erties of N rays, though scientists elsewhere were unable to reproduce the results reported by their French colleagues.

The remarkable N rays came to the attention of an eminent
American physicist, Robert W. Wood—an unfortunate circumstance for Blondlot, since Dr. Wood delighted in the exposure of
fraud. (He pinched the ectoplasm of the famous Boston medium
Margery, and he set a trap for Eusapia Palladino, another famous
medium, in New York. William Seabrook's biography of Wood is
a beguiling story of a remarkable wizard of physics—an American
small boy, as Seabrook put it, who never grew up.[4])

Wood visited Blondlot's laboratory in 1904. One of the essential
pieces of apparatus involved in studying N rays was a spectroscope, one of extremely unorthodox design in that both its lenses
and its prism were of aluminum. Using this instrument in a dark
room Blondlot was able, he said, to delineate a spectrum of lines
analogous to those seen in the visual spectrum as displayed by
conventional spectroscopes.

While Blondlot was demonstrating the apparatus, reading off
numbers by the light of a darkroom lantern, Wood, in the darkness, removed the aluminum prism and asked Blondlot to repeat
the demonstration. Blondlot did so, calling out the same numbers!
Wood replaced the prism before the lights were turned up.

The game was up, and Wood immediately communicated his
findings to the British journal *Nature,* alerting the scientific community to the nonexistence of N rays. Blondlot later became psychotic and died soon after. His sincerity and integrity were never
impugned. He probably suffered from some kind of self-induced
visual hallucinosis, generated by his need to make a major
scientific discovery—and thus, all unconsciously, perpetrated a
hoax.

How the other French experimenters in other laboratories came
to achieve the same results as had Blondlot, while others elsewhere could not, we do not know. Perhaps the French ones shared
a need to believe, or to attract attention and celebrity. The situation is precisely analogous to that of the observers who claimed to
have seen the nonexistent UFO discussed earlier.

WHY PEOPLE BELIEVE

"There's no use trying," she said: "one
can't *believe impossible things."*
"I daresay you haven't had much practice,"
said the Queen. "When I was your age, I always
did it for half-an-hour a day. Why, sometimes
I've believed as many as six impossible things
before breakfast."

Lewis Carroll[5]

Having discussed the liars, we must now consider those lied to, particularly those who are lied to and believe. How is it, the voice of reason asks, that so many people really do believe that their lives are determined, to a significant degree, by the planetary configuration obtaining at the hour of their birth? Why do so many people believe that the Israeli magician Uri Geller can bend metal without touching it? Why do people believe they can communicate with their "loved ones" who have "passed over"? Why do so many people, perhaps millions of them, believe that Earth is under constant surveillance by extraterrestrial observers? Why do some people believe that the Air Force harbors, and conceals, a captured extraterrestrial spacecraft at Wright-Patterson Air Force Base in Ohio? Why will people believe that Earth was visited in past millennia by superbeings from outer space? And so on, and on, and on.

Consider astrology. This nonsense was a flourishing business during most of the Middle Ages. Then came the Age of Reason and, as Charles Fair, Resident Scientist at MIT's Neurosciences Research Program, points out, astrology and similar pursuits began, as one would expect, to fade into the shadows.[6] But astrology and other nonsenses have staged a remarkable recovery in the twentieth century. Science and technology have advanced sufficiently to make space flight a reality—and the nonscience of astrology has kept pace. So much so, indeed, that very recently

(1975) a group of 187 distinguished scientists, including eighteen Nobel laureates, addressed themselves to the problem of public credulity in some alarm.[7] They were concerned, they said, about the "continued uncritical dissemination of astrological charts, forecasts, and horoscopes by the media and by otherwise reputable newspapers, magazines and book publishers."

They noted that since the gravitational and other effects produced on Earth by the planets and the far more distant stars are infinitesimally small, "It is simply a mistake to imagine that forces exerted by stars and planets at the moment of birth can in any way shape our future."

Quite so. But more than 1,250 daily newspapers in the United States carry astrological columns.

Charles Mackay, who noted that "each age has its peculiar folly; some scheme, project, or phantasy into which it plunges," was an early student of public credulity.[8]

One of Mackay's examples of an entire nation being swept off its collective rational feet was the "tulipomania" that flourished in Holland in the first half of the seventeenth century. Tulips were probably introduced into northern Europe from Turkey in the mid-sixteenth century. Their popularity increased over the years, and in Holland, in the 1630s, this popularity exploded into what can only be viewed as mass psychosis. The entire population became involved in tulip speculation. A fortune could be invested in a handful of bulbs. A single root of a rare variant commanded the present equivalent of thousands of dollars. The everyday business of Holland fell apart; everyone was in the tulip trade. Mackay recounts how "people of all grades converted their property into cash, and invested it in flowers. Houses and lands were offered for sale at ruinously low prices, or assigned in payment of bargains made at the tulip-mart." The mania eventually ended in collapse and panic, and the economy of the country did not recover for years.

If each age and perhaps each nation has its own peculiar folly, ours seems certainly easy to identify: an astonishing potpourri of irrationality, unreason, and nonsense, including beliefs in astrology, UFOs, parapsychology, pyramidology, exorcism, scientology, numerology, and witchcraft. To name a few.

As this is being written, in October 1975, the First World

Congress of Sorcery has recently been held in Bogotá, Colombia.[9] And a few days ago a group of fifteen to twenty people vanished from the Oregon countryside—disappearing from sight in order to join what the news media referred to as an "UFO religion."

This most recent UFO caper began in September 1975 with the appearance of crudely printed handbills in the vicinity of Waldport, Oregon:

UFO'S

Why they are here.

Who they have come for.

When they will leave.

Two individuals say they were sent from the level above human, and will return to that level in a space ship (UFO) within the next few months. This man and woman will discuss how the transition from the human level is accomplished, and when this may be done.

. . . If you have ever entertained the idea that there might be a real PHYSICAL level in space beyond the Earth's confines, you will want to attend this meeting.

The meeting was announced for 2:00 P.M., September 19, 1975, at the Bayshore Inn, Waldport, Oregon. Those who showed up were addressed by a persuasive couple, a man and a woman identified only as "The Two," who claimed to be millions of years old. The listeners were told that they could qualify for a trip to a better world, on a higher level, if they would abandon their families and worldly goods. The Two, they discovered, were working on behalf of HIM—human individual metamorphosis. Come with us, they said, and you will be on the same level with Jesus Christ.

Some fifteen or twenty followers thereupon abandoned their material possessions and left for parts unknown, presumably to prepare themselves for a ride in a spaceship. This curious incident was well covered by the news media, including CBS evening news on October 8, 1975.

Since that time a number of followers have defected from the movement (the "Process"), and sporadic accounts have from time to time appeared in the press, reporting sketchily on some of the flock's migrations. Our most recent source of information about this bizarre caper is from a rather lengthy article by James S. Phelan in *The New York Times Magazine*.[10]

The Two have now been identified as Marshall Herff Applewhite and Bonnie Lu Trousdale Nettles. Before they became space shepherds he was an opera singer with the Houston Grand Opera and musicologist at the University of St. Thomas; she was a nurse in a Houston hospital. They first met in that hospital in 1972 and discovered before long that they had known each other in previous lives. Both were interested in astrology and reincarnation. They refer to each other as Bo and Peep, and their flock is now said to number between 300 and 1,000.

The general idea is that they are messengers from a heavenly kingdom, whose advance men were the writers of the Book of Revelation: "And I will give power unto my two witnesses, and they shall prophesy a thousand two hundred and threescore days, clothed in sackcloth . . . And if any man will hurt them, fire proceedeth out of their mouth."

The witnesses will be killed, according to the biblical account, and then will be brought back from the dead and will ascend (with their followers, in the contemporary version) to heaven. In the new mythos, this rising from the dead is referred to as the "Demonstration"—which, in turn, is part of the Process.

The followers of Bo and Peep, scattered here and there about the United States, are told to keep in touch with the news, so they will know when the Demonstration has begun. They will have three and a half days to reach the site of the rising and then be carried aloft to a higher level.

In the meantime, Bo and Peep are busily writing a book, which they hope to finish before the Demonstration terminates that project. And their book will not be the only one to be generated by these events. Joan Culpepper—a disenchanted defector, according to the *Times Magazine* article—is writing her own book about The Two. She allegedly contributed $433 to the movement and says she has paid for an UFO trip and been defrauded. At the time the *Times* article appeared, the Los Angeles district attorney's office had initiated no action in aid of Ms. Culpepper's complaint.

When we first heard of the Waldport episode in the press and on national TV news we thought that though we had no knowledge of what had happened to the abandoned possessions (including, in at least one case, a family), the operation appeared to involve religious mania or a confidence game—or both. On the basis of the information presently known to us, we will stand on that statement. On the one hand, according to Phelan, no material gain has been traced to Bo and Peep; on the other, according to some defectors, followers have tossed up to $60,000 into the Process. It is perhaps not irrelevant to mention that two years ago both Bo and Peep were in jail in Texas—Bo on a charge of auto theft and Peep for credit-card misuse.

In any case, rational explanation of the Bo and Peep operation seems easier to come by than a rational explanation of the gullibility of those wishing to be taken aboard the celestial spacecraft. What can we believe except that, as someone once said, the average person will believe *anything?*

Robert Low, co-ordinator of the Colorado Project, addressed himself to another aspect of the problem of public credulity:

My observation was that the UFO crowd carries around a revolving showcase of the sightings regarded as most convincing. As soon as you or anybody else solves one of them, the UFO people would throw it out of the collection and substitute another, and there is always another available, to put forward when asked to give evidence that something is really going on. One cannot solve them all. There are too many; the data are too few and too inaccurate; and none of the events can ever be repeated.

An even more troubling problem is the impossibility, in my opinion, of dealing with belief systems. If the UFO believers employed any of the recognized methods of science and they were trying to demonstrate the existence of extraterrestrial visitation, they would gather together their evidence, reduce it, analyze it, draw conclusions, and present the material in a scientific journal. They would invite other scientists to examine it and see if they confirm the results and interpretation. The conclusion of the Condon study was that, while we were left with many unexplained sightings, we found, despite a diligent search, no evidence of extraterrestrial visitation. No evidence of visitation, not no visitation.

If the believers had the evidence, they would present it and say, "Here it is. You examine it, and I'm sure you will reach the same conclusion I have." Since they can't do that, they retreat to the use of a word like "believe." If there isn't any evidence, one must take it on faith—believe—and the less the evidence, the stronger the belief. The UFO advocates, having no evidence, hold strong beliefs. Indeed, I find them unshakable. It is not, it seems to me, the job of science to deal with beliefs at all. That is something for philosophy or theology. My preference is to leave it to them.[11]

Attempting to track down the believer, we search in vain for a clear-cut psychological or psychiatric entity or concept to account for belief in the extraterrestrial origin of unidentified flying objects. This is not surprising, since the believer in UFOs seems almost to be Everyman. Thirty-two million Americans believe in astrology. *More* people than that believe in UFOs. We don't see as much daily evidence of this belief, because ufology has nothing to offer comparable to the addictive daily horoscope.

But a Gallup poll indicated that in 1966, 96 per cent of individuals questioned said they had heard or read of flying saucers, and that of these, 48 per cent thought they are "something real." Just about half of the population.[12]

A study conducted under the aegis of the Colorado Project in 1968 came up with similar findings.[13] Among the populations queried was a national cross section of adults. The study found (to give but two examples) that 41 per cent of those queried believed that UFOs have landed and left marks on the ground and that 40 per cent believed that people have seen spaceships of extraterrestrial origin. In both cases cited, teen-agers as a group were the most credulous (54 per cent and 61 per cent, respectively).

It will be recalled (p. 83) that before the Colorado Project got under way, Robert Low, later project co-ordinator, suggested to university officials that the psychological and sociological aspects of ufology be emphasized in the Colorado Project. We have said that this was not done, as a matter of deliberate choice. The reason for that choice was stated succinctly:

This decision was buttressed by the evidence that we rapidly gathered, pointing to the fact that only a very small proportion of sighters can be categorized as exhibiting psychopathology and that, therefore, there is no reason to consider them any more suitable for study than psychotic or psychoneurotic individuals who belong to any other statistical class of the population as a whole.[14]

We believe that Low's view is probably right—that the question of belief is not the concern of science. Still, the question remains: Why do so many people believe in the extraterrestrial origin of UFOs?

Charles Fair suggests that man believes in nonsense "just because." He says: "A certain amount of claptrap seems almost necessary to our mental health, and so flourishes even in ages when it shouldn't."

The roots of the problem of belief in the unbelievable go deeper than that, of course. Consider the findings of a group of MIT scientists, sponsored by The Club of Rome to inquire into The Predicament of Mankind. The results of this ambitious inquiry were published in 1972, and they are disquieting.[15] Unless things change, and change *now,* apocalypse will be upon us. The basic thesis is that events in our world are happening exponentially, as distinct from linearly, and that this will lead us to the end of the world.

World population, for example, one of our greatest problems, is growing exponentially. And it should be obvious to all that this kind of growth of population on a finite planet cannot continue indefinitely. It just can't, and that's all there is to it. And it won't. The question is, what is going to stop it? The possibilities of war, famine, revolution, and anarchy come at once to mind.

Part of the trouble is that people tend to think in linear fashion, whereas the problems that must be solved involve nonlinear phenomena. The authors of the MIT study give us a sobering example of exponential growth, in the form of a French riddle for children. Say you have a pond in which water lilies begin to grow. The lilies double in size every day, in such a way that the pond will be covered in thirty days. They are small at first. You don't want them to take over the pond, but you're not in a hurry to do anything about it. You decide to delay action until half the pond is covered. The question of the riddle is, on what day will that happen? The answer is, of course, on the twenty-ninth day. You have one day in which to save your pond.

It has taken many hundreds of generations for the human race to reach its present numbers. At the current rate of growth, our numbers will double within the next thirty years. And during this time we will, presumably, be depleting our resources proportionally. That puts a lot of writing on the wall for anyone brave enough to read it. As Frank Herbert, the well-known science-fiction writer, says, "the end of the Vietnam war has changed very little in respect to a world balanced precariously on the edge of an explosive finale . . . You can smell a crisis coming."[16]

Granted, the standard or garden variety of UFO believer no doubt has never heard of the harrowing MIT study, let alone read it. Yet, the trends the MIT scientists extrapolated are here to be seen by everyone, to be absorbed into awareness, consciously or unconsciously. There is a sense of closing-in—of walls coming closer; of people, and more of them, coming closer; of the potential and irrecoverable loss of the world as we have known it.

It makes a kind of desperate sense, then, to turn to nonsense. In the astrology columns, if you overlook the demented assumptions involved, you will learn how to protect yourself in your perilous day-to-day activities. And for the Waldport believers the problem is solved more immediately and directly by departure from the threatened planet and their personal elevation to a status equivalent to that of Christ. With millions of years in which to enjoy salvation. Tempting and beguiling—if one can suspend sapience and function on a midbrain or thalamic level.

We live in an age of stupendous scientific and technological achievement and at the same time seem surrounded by an almost all-pervasive lunacy. An apparent paradox—but, there has always been some point to lunacy. The schizophrenic's psychosis is his means of survival. The believer's belief in nonsense is his attempt to survive in a world threatening to blow up any minute.

The current interest in occultism and nonsense is an attempt, by a substantial segment of our population, to survive in a world that would otherwise be too difficult and too threatening to cope with.

THE HILLS REVISITED

Absolutely not!

> Response of the psychiatrist who worked with the Hills,
> when asked if he thought the "abduction" had been real.[1]

The Betty and Barney Hill case, referred to earlier in Chapter 13, has been considered for many years, by the believers, as a classic "close contact" UFO sighting. The details have been related many times. The most widely distributed early account was in a 1966 book called *The Interrupted Journey,* by John Fuller, whose journalism we have mentioned, in a different context, in Chapter 7.[2] We reconsider the Hill incident here because it has recently become once again a matter of interest.

First came the publication in the magazine *Astronomy,* in the December 1974 issue, of an article by Terence Dickinson entitled "The Zeta Reticuli Incident." This was followed, in October 1975, by a two-hour NBC special called "The UFO Incident" on nationwide television, which we discussed in Chapter 13. Let us briefly give the facts of the "interrupted journey" of Betty and Barney Hill.

The Hills, both middle-aged at the time of the incident, were partners in a mixed marriage. She was white, he was black. In September 1961 they returned by car from a vacation in Canada to their home in New Hampshire. On the way home, at night, they saw a bright "star" or some other light source in the sky that seemed to move in a strange pattern. They stopped to have a better look. They thought they saw a spacecraft. Eventually they drove on, after being much frightened by the apparition. Betty subsequently had a number of dreams in which she and Barney were taken aboard a spacecraft by alien, humanoid beings. They were also troubled by a missing two-hour period in their memory of that night. Eventually they consulted a psychiatrist, Dr. Benjamin Simon of Boston. While under hypnosis they both recalled that alien beings had taken them aboard their spaceship. They recalled also that while aboard the vessel they had been subjected to physical examination. They had been released, they said, after being told, presumably under hypnosis, that they would remember nothing of the "abduction."

While on board the spacecraft Betty Hill asked one of the humanoids where they were from. She was shown a three-dimensional map which showed a number of stars, with connecting lines that represented routes of star travel. The memory of the map, together with the other memories of the abduction, were recovered only under hypnosis with Dr. Simon.

A two-dimensional sketch of the map as recollected by Betty was published in Fuller's book, and in 1966 it caught the attention of a Marjorie Fish—an Ohio schoolteacher and amateur astronomer. Fish discussed the map with Betty Hill in August 1969. Barney Hill had died earlier that year. Then Fish proceeded, with what must be viewed as admirable persistence, to construct many three-dimensional models of the stars in the vicinity of our sun to see if she could find a pattern similar to that of the Hill map.

And she did find such a pattern.

The Fish model suggested that the home base of the humanoids that had taken the Hills aboard their spacecraft was Zeta Reticuli —actually Zeta 1 and Zeta 2 Reticuli, a pair of faint stars in the relatively obscure constellation of Reticulum. This constellation is near the south celestial pole and cannot be seen from the United States. Zeta Reticuli is a close neighbor of Earth's, as closeness goes in the galaxy, being only thirty-seven light-years (about 200,000,000,000,000 miles) away.

Dickinson's article in *Astronomy* presented a computer-generated map, which is also somewhat similar to the Hill map. The stars of the computer map are the sun and fourteen other stars selected from a group of forty-six stars relatively near to our sun and similar to it in spectral type.

The slant of Dickinson's article favors the view that the Fish and computer maps are significant—i.e., that they tend to substantiate the reality of the Hill abduction. In the text of the article the views of Stanton Friedman and David Saunders are quoted at some length. Both are well-known as staunch supporters of the ETH. And, as noted in Chapter 7, we recall that Saunders was summarily dismissed from the Colorado Project because of what Condon saw as his attempt to undermine that investigation.

In general, however, the tone of the article is moderate. Dickinson, in his conclusions, entertains the possibility that the similarity between the Hill map in Fuller's book and the Fish map may be due to coincidence. This is eminently reasonable. He also doubts that the Hill map is the result of a hoax. So do we—though, as will be seen, we do not think it offers any evidence for the reality of the Hill abduction. Dickinson also notes that exobiologists are of the opinion that the chance of us having neighbors so close to us in nature and in space is "vanishingly small."

"The only answer," Dickinson concludes, "is to continue the search."

The publication of "The Zeta Reticuli Incident" generated, as expected, a considerable response. The issues of *Astronomy* for July, August, and September 1975 published some of the resulting correspondence. In the July issue two Cornell astronomers, Carl Sagan and Steven Soter, challenged the main burden of the Dickinson article, as did Robert Sheaffer. Both Sagan and Sheaffer are known in the ufological field as having scientific approaches to the problems. Sheaffer, as we mentioned in Chapter 16, was instrumental, for example, in demonstrating the fraudulent nature of the McMinnville photographs.

In the same issue Soter and Sagan were answered by Dickinson and Sheaffer was answered by Fish, and Jeffrey Kretsch, a student of astronomy at Northwestern University (whose astronomy de-

242 THE UFO ENIGMA

partment is headed by J. Allen Hynek) briefly discussed the Zeta
Reticuli system and verified the findings of Fish. In the August
issue David Saunders responded to Soter and Sagan. And in the
September issue, Michael Peck, another astronomy student at
Northwestern University, also responded to Soter and Sagan. In
the same issue, apparently concluding the debate, Soter and Sagan
responded to Saunders and Peck.

If that seems a little confusing, it is because the order of publication was to some extent dictated by space limitations for the various issues of the magazine.

The arguments ran as follows:

Soter and Sagan presented the Hill map and computer map
without interconnecting lines and showed that there was little similarity between them. They wondered how the stars had been
selected for the computer map and suggested that the statistical
fallacy of "enumeration of favorable circumstance" had been at
work in the construction of the map. They pointed out that some
selection had been made even from the original Hill map in
Fuller's book. This map contained a number of dots apparently
sprinkled at random to indicate a starry background; only three of
these stars had been selected for the construction of the Fish map
and the computer map. This selection, Soter and Sagan said, allowed great freedom to contrive a resemblance. Finally they
pointed out that Betty Hill had once thought she saw a close similarity between her map and a map of the constellation Pegasus
published in *The New York Times*. They concluded that the Fish
and computer maps did not even suggest a verification of the Hill
case.

Dickinson replied that the connecting lines in the computer map
joined the stars in a logical distance progression and that the stars
were all of the solar type. The three selected dots, he said, had
been put on the map because Betty Hill had said that they were
more prominent than the other background stars.

Sheaffer, as had Soter and Sagan, mentioned Betty Hill's reaction to the Pegasus map in the *Times* and presented a Pegasus
map, including connecting lines, which was, as he said, "impres-
sively similar" to the original Hill map. Sheaffer also presented an-

other map, the work of Charles Atterberg. This map, all of whose stars lie within 18.2 light-years of the sun (compared with fifty-three light-years for the Fish map), is an even closer approximation to the Hill map than is the Fish map. Sheaffer concluded that the Fish interpretation of the Hill map was by no means the only possible one.

Fish's reply to Sheaffer stated the ten restrictions she had enforced in the construction of her map—such as, for example, that our sun had to be a part of the pattern and had to have a line connected to it. She pointed out that Betty Hill's interpretation of the Pegasus map disregarded all of her (Fish's) criteria.

She complimented Atterberg on his accurate work, but noted that the base stars of his map are very near the lower limit for life-bearing planets—if we assume that life will develop only on stars of spectral types F8 to K5 or, more likely, F8 to K1. Further, she said, Atterberg used red dwarf stars for some of his points but bypassed others. Also, the base stars in Atterberg's map were not the largest or brightest ones on the map. The principal thrust of Fish's riposte was that the Atterberg map was defective in that it did not meet the criteria she had established for hers.

Kretsch said that he had constructed a model similar to Fish's and had verified her work "in terms of the astronomy used."

David Saunders accused Soter and Sagan of failing to treat the matter with quantitative objectivity. He then stumbled into a serious trap of what must be called "astronomorphic thinking." He pointed out that the sun belongs to a closed cluster of stars which includes just six other "admissible" stars, two of which are Zeta 1 and Zeta 2 Reticuli. In support of the Hill map, Saunders then ventured into the minds of the humanoids traveling about the star cluster. An explorer starting from any of these seven stars in his spacecraft, Saunders said, should visit all of them before venturing farther! Who says they should? Saunders says so, but we see no way whatever in which this statement can be justified.

Saunders then presented a murky statistical argument to the effect that the star map results are "exceedingly interesting."

Michael Peck used standard statistical procedures to show that the degree of resemblance between the Hill and Fish maps is "fairly high." He further said that the probability that a random set of points would fit the Hill map as closely as the Fish map did was one chance in one million billion.

Soter and Sagan replied to Peck that he had missed the point of their original criticism, which was that the stars in the Fish map had been preselected in order to maximize a correlation with the Hill map. They pointed out that if one *selected* fifteen points from a random set of forty-six, distributed in three-dimensional space, it would be no difficult matter to find another map showing the same degree of correlation to the Hill map as did the Fish map.

In reply to Saunders, Soter and Sagan chose, wisely, not to get into a discussion of how travelers from Zeta Reticuli should arrange their itinerary. Instead, they challenged Saunders's statistical procedures, pointing out that they were invalidated by numerous *ad hoc* adjustments made in the course of his argument.

They pointed out the importance, when establishing a correlation, of stating how many correlations had been tried before finding the one in question. This is, in our judgment, the most cogent part of Soter's and Sagan's criticism of the star maps. We shall briefly enlarge upon this point, and then approach the maps from a different point of view.

The Zeta Reticuli star map situation and controversy are remarkably reminiscent of a great deal of parapsychological research, beginning with the so-called ESP experiments conducted at Duke University by J. B. Rhine and others in the nineteen-thirties. In a "standard" experiment, a subject was asked to guess the symbols on a deck of twenty-five cards. In the usual deck of what were called "Zener cards" there were five each of five symbols: star, cross, circle, triangle, and wavy lines.

The probability of getting any particular card right is one in five. Chance expectation for a single run through the deck is five correct guesses, or telepathic responses, or whatever. (We do not consider here the controls or lack of them of the experiments; our interest lies only in the statistical aspects of the research.) The chance of getting two cards in a row right is one in twenty-five, and the chance of getting ten cards in a row correctly is approximately one in ten million.

An experimenter obtaining, in a laboratory session, a run of ten correct calls could easily think that something other than chance was at work. After all, one shot in ten million represents rather long odds. But the crucial point is that the run of ten correct calls cannot be evaluated except in terms of the total number of calls made by the total number of subjects, working in comparable conditions, with the total number of experimenters, over the entire time span during which such experimentation takes place.

Odds of one in ten million are long odds. But, in a single run through a deck of Zener cards there are sixteen opportunities to achieve this apparently remarkable success. For one run through the deck, then, the odds reduce to about one in 625,000. If a subject does fifty runs a day for ten days the chance of finding a run of ten correct calls is approximately one in 1,250 such series of runs, a manageable number. If we avoid the enumeration of favorable circumstance, i.e., selection of data, a one in ten million chance becomes unimpressive.

The same logic applies, of course, to more extraordinary runs of correct calls. The odds are longer, and they reduce more slowly, but the same principles apply.

Apart from all other considerations that cast doubt upon the Hills's contact with alien humanoids, the star maps simply do not stand up. The statistical counts against them are too many. Each three-dimensional star model can be viewed from many directions. Fish constructed hundreds of such models, each of which could be looked at from hundreds of viewpoints. It is entirely predictable that such a procedure would produce a map similar to the original Hill map. No doubt many other such maps can be found. We may approach the problem in two ways—the empirical and the purely mathematical.

It seemed to us almost an intuitive certainty that a random, three-dimensional pattern of forty-seven points would contain at least one pattern of fifteen selected points that would closely resemble the Hill map when projected upon a plane. Accordingly, we used a standard table of random numbers to generate a forty-seven-point two-dimensional pattern. Restricting ourselves to two dimensions would, we understood, make it more difficult to find a "Hill pattern," but we thought there would be no problem.

Our random-number pattern is shown in Figure 7, together with

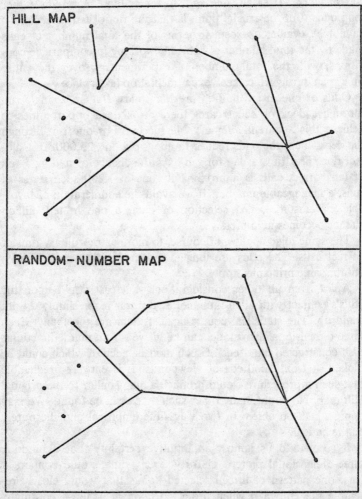

Figure 7. Hill map compared with map generated by random numbers. *Hill map courtesy of* Astronomy *magazine, random-number map by Ernest H. Taves*

the Hill map. The resemblance between our pattern and the Hill map is considerably closer than that between the Hill map and the computer map. And we generated *only* one such map. (The procedure we used to construct our random-number map is given in detail in the Appendix.)

A more rigorous approach to the problem of matching one pattern against another is that of mathematical statistics. We shall reduce the problem to its simplest form.

Everyone concedes that the stars nearest the sun are randomly distributed through a volume of space. A two-dimensional star map represents the apparent positions of these stars as seen from some arbitrarily selected point in space, well outside the space occupied by the stars. The distribution of the stars, as points projected on a plane, varies when the point of view shifts from one place to another.

Betty Hill's original map contained fifteen stars, one of which was our sun. The lines connecting the stars, supposedly representing interstellar trade or travel routes, are inconsequential to the problem of pattern matching, where the question is whether the stars, viewed from some arbitrary point in space, conform closely enough to the Hill map to justify the claim that the resemblance cannot be accidental or coincidental.

Although the basic problem is one for statistics to solve, we commend Fish for an ingenious and imaginative attack. She used a standard astronomical catalog of nearby stars and constructed numerous three-dimensional models, using glass beads on strings to represent stars. Viewing these models from various directions, she found one viewpoint from which fifteen stars seemed to fall into a pattern resembling the original Hill map. She did not select just any star; she used a list of ten criteria, as mentioned earlier.

It is not surprising that the flying-saucer enthusiasts, lacking statistical sophistication, seized upon the Fish map as evidence supporting the reality of the Hill abduction. It is more surprising that a few scientists, including David Saunders, entertain the idea that the Fish map provides support for the Hill incident. We have already noted that Soter and Sagan dismantled Saunders's statistics. Even so, they (Soter and Sagan) did not themselves present a convincing quantitative argument. We give in the Appendix a precise evaluation of the probabilities involved in map matching, based on elementary but well-known statistical procedures.

Those procedures may be described in less technical language. Betty Hill's map, drawn years after the alleged incident, contained fifteen stars. Marjorie Fish, after constructing many three-dimensional celestial models, based upon star catalogs, found a pattern that bore a resemblance to the Hill map. Then other researchers, presumably in an attempt at greater accuracy, fed into a computer the positions of forty-seven stars near the sun, plus the position of the sun, and from these selected fifteen to construct another star map. This one also bore a resemblance to the Hill map. Many ufologists interpreted the similarities between the Hill, Fish, and computer maps as having probative value in support of the reality of the alleged Hill abduction.

It seemed to us that from any randomly distributed assemblage of forty-seven points in space, fifteen could be found to match the Hill map, the Fish map, or, indeed, any other set of fifteen randomly placed points.

Our very first attempt, as described in the Appendix, demonstrated the validity of this supposition. We translated a table of random numbers into forty-seven points on an abstract "star map." By selecting the fifteen points closest to the points on the Hill map, we produced a very close approximation to the Hill map —thus demonstrating the speciousness of the argument that the resemblance between the three maps tended in any way to substantiate the reality of the Hill encounter.

What, then, are we to make of the famous Hill incident? Our suggestion is that the alleged abduction is based upon externalized dreams and fantasies of Betty Hill. As they were driving home that night the Hills had what is quite a common experience: they saw, from their car, a bright star or planet. We have shown that such objects have many, many times been misidentified as UFOs, even by trained observers (recall DHM's perception of Sirius, complete with flashing lights and small propeller, discussed in Chapter 10 (p. 133). The Hills stopped the car, got out, watched the object, and were afraid—as have been many people, before and since the Hills's experience, in the same situation. They drove on, and the object appeared to follow them—again a common phenomenon, which we have discussed on p. 175. Eventually they got home safely, and went to bed.

In their recollection of their experience the next morning *there was no memory of abduction aboard an alien spacecraft*. The abduction came into being only some days later—in the dreams of Betty Hill. She discussed these dreams with her husband and with others. Some of the content brushed off on Barney.

Later, reliving their experience under hypnosis, Betty's recollection of the "abduction" was filled with detail, whereas Barney could remember very little. Both of them had become unable to distinguish between dream and reality.

Plate 20. Seventeenth-century woodcut showing the sky filled with flying objects—positive and negative after-images of the sun. *From the Department of Prints and Drawings of the Zentralbibliothek, Zürich*

Plate 21. *below:* Internal lens reflections masquerading as an UFO. *Photo by Chuck Baker of the Central Oklahoma Astronomy Club, Purcell, Oklahoma*

Plate 22. *top:* Fake UFO photo taken by multiple-exposure method. *Photo by Robert Sheaffer*

Plate 23. *bottom:* Fake UFO photo, actually of a lens cap on a string. *Photo by Ernest H. Taves*

Plates 24–25. Photos of fake UFOs. The numbered points in the photographs were used in the photogrammetric analysis that established conclusively the fraudulent nature of the flying object. *E. L. Merritt*

Plate 26. Hot-air flying saucer made from a kit. *Photo courtesy of the Edmund Scientific Co., Barrington, N.J. 08007*

CHAPTER 19

UFOs AND PARAPSYCHOLOGY

CHEATING IN ONE FORM OR ANOTHER IS
ONE OF THE COMMONEST HUMAN ACTIVITIES.

C. E. M. Hansel[1]

In October 1974 the prestigious British scientific publication *Nature* carried an article bearing a somewhat cryptic title: "Information Transmission Under Conditions of Sensory Shielding."[2] This research was written by Russell Targ and Harold Puthoff, both laser physicists at the Stanford Research Institute (SRI) in California. The article described a number of parapsychological experiments they had performed. In some of these the subject in a visually and acoustically shielded room had apparently been able to duplicate, with startling success, target drawings located outside the room—drawings of which he supposedly could have had, by normal sensory channels, no knowledge.

In a typical experiment the subject would be isolated in the shielded room, whereupon the experimenters would choose, by one of three different methods, a target drawing which the subject would attempt to duplicate. (In a few experiments the procedure was reversed; the experimenters were in the shielded room, the subject outside.) The report of Targ and Puthoff describes thirteen experiments. Ten of the target drawings were prepared by the experimenters, three by SRI scientists not involved in the experiments.

The similarities between some of the target drawings and the responses were remarkable—so spectacular, indeed, that four days after the publication date of the report on October 22, in *Nature,* they appeared in *The New York Times.* That usually level-headed newspaper later published an editorial, headlined PARANORMAL SCIENCE, in which it informed the scientific community that it had been put on notice that it had best pay more attention to the possibilities of extrasensory perception. The editors of *Nature,* said the editorial writer of the *Times,* had taken an important step in publishing the results of the Targ-Puthoff research. The only cautionary note sounded by the *Times* was in mentioning that the major subject of the research was the well-known Israeli Uri Geller, the self-styled psychic whose reputation was clouded by suspicions of fakery.[3] Nevertheless, the editorial writer was clearly impressed by the apparent significance of the *Nature* report.

Although the *Times* editorial was published in the month following the appearance of the Targ-Puthoff article in *Nature,* we must charitably assume that the *Times* editorial staff was then unaware of an able and penetrating analysis of the Geller phenomenon by Joseph Hanlon, which had appeared in *New Scientist* contemporaneously with the Targ-Puthoff article in *Nature.*[4] Before turning to Hanlon's analysis, however, let us examine more closely the experimental procedures of Targ and Puthoff.

Both men are physicists, and it might be said at the outset that, historically, physicists don't have very good track records in investigating the paranormal. One thinks at once of Sir Oliver Lodge and of Sir William Crookes. Both were eminent physicists. Lodge made valuable contributions to the early art of wireless telegraphy, and Crookes invented the electron tube that bears his name—the grandfather of the television screen of today. Both, however, were hopelessly naïve and gullible in their investigations into spiritualism, psychical research, and the survival of the human personality after death.

Targ and Puthoff appear to be equally ill-equipped for such investigation. According to Hanlon, they both joined SRI primarily to do psychical research. As reported in their article in *Nature,* their research was sponsored by The Foundation for Parasensory Investigation.

Nevertheless, if the Targ-Puthoff results were obtained under what an unbiased scientist could fairly call controlled conditions, the scientific community would certainly have to sit up and take notice—and revise large segments of its thinking. We must, then, scrutinize the experimental conditions under which the Geller results were obtained.

Thirteen experiments with Geller are reported in the article. In three of these, Geller "passed"—no response drawing was made. In nine of the remaining ten experiments Geller was in the shielded room and the experimenters were outside; in one experiment these conditions were reversed.

The shielded room used in the experiments had been constructed at SRI for electroencephalographic research. It was a double-walled steel room with inner and outer doors, both of which were secured with refrigerator-type locking mechanisms. So, to a degree, the subject in the room was isolated from the outside. We know, however, that there was at least a one-way audio channel from the room to the outside, for we are told in the article that this means of communication was used to monitor Geller as he plied his trade inside the EEG room. The reasons this link was thought necessary or desirable are not mentioned in the article, nor is the precise nature of the audio link described.

And one searches in vain for assurance that, apart from this audio link, the room was indeed rigorously isolated. There is no mention or description of other wiring entering and leaving the shielded room, though if it was an EEG facility such wiring was certainly present. It is curious that the presence (or absence, if that was the case) of such wiring was not mentioned by the experimenters, since it is common knowledge that ordinary house wiring can be caused to function as an intercom link.

More importantly, there is no mention of any thought, even, of monitoring the radio frequencies in the vicinity of the room—a serious oversight.

As Hanlon points out, Geller had been brought from Israel to the United Kingdom and to the United States by Dr. Andrija Puharich, a specialist in medical electronics, who holds more than fifty patents primarily in the field of hearing aids. One of his patents, be it noted, is for a radio receiver small enough to be placed within a tooth. Be it also noted that Geller never allows himself to be searched or x-rayed. In this situation we must, with Hanlon, invoke Occam's Razor—a maxim that dictates we must not accept a paranormal explanation of Geller's feats without first having excluded all plausible normal explanations. These explanations have by no means been excluded in the Targ-Puthoff research.

This raises, of course, the question of fraud, of hoax. As Hanlon thoughtfully notes, there are a number of means by which the security of the shielded SRI room could have been breached. Ultrahigh radio frequencies (in the gigahertz range) would easily pass through the cracks around the doors and between the steel plates of the shielded room. These cracks could, in fact, act as wave guides—channels of microwave radio transmission from Geller to an accomplice. Or the ordinary power supply lines into the room could have been used. Or the intercom link between the shielded room and the outside. These possibilities seem to us more reasonable than turning to the paranormal.

We level no accusation of fraud against the experimenters, whom we think were disastrously outmatched by a skillful magician. The accusation we level against Geller is that he won't admit that his effects are accomplished by easily duplicated normal physical means.

Would an accomplice outside the shielded room be necessary? No. Geller himself (a tornado in action, a person almost no one can keep under continuous observation) could no doubt have bugged the space outside the shielded room, deftly deploying the transmitter while directing attention elsewhere. An accomplice would no doubt be helpful, though, and we learn from Hanlon that Geller's constant companion, Shipi Strang, was very much underfoot while the experiments were being conducted, a fact unmentioned in the Targ-Puthoff report.

One finishes reading the papers by Targ-Puthoff and Hanlon with a strong impression that the SRI work with Geller was minimally controlled, unscientifically organized, and incompletely reported. Granted that while the editors of *Nature* published their paper with some trepidation, it seems apparent that the cause of science would have been better served had the paper been refused.

A final point, and a devastating one: Of the thirteen experiments, in the three cases in which the target drawings were prepared independently by SRI scientists not concerned with the Geller experiments—when these targets were as blind to the experimenters as they were to Geller—in these three experiments and in these three only Geller declined to respond to the drawings.

Quod erat demonstrandum.

What, then, do these well-publicized experiments have to do with the world of the flying saucer? A great deal, we think. The Geller experiments and, say, the Pascagoula case (Chapter 16) reveal remarkable parallels. In each case mind-boggling events occurred which, if they had indeed happened as described, would overturn a great deal of currently accepted scientific thinking. In both cases, we think fraud was involved. In both cases there was, and still is, a widespread eagerness on the part of many people to believe in "far-out" explanations for strange phenomena instead of in normal, and plausible, explanations. And in each case, we submit, scientists were taken in, hornswoggled, and misled. Which shows once more that scientists are fallible, along with the rest of the population.

Thus ufology and parapsychology are closely related fields. Indeed, it should be said that Geller claims to get some of his "power" from flying saucers and that Dr. Puharich claims frequent contact with extraterrestrial forces. In both fields we suggest that rigorous use of Occam's Razor will dissipate ambiguity.

Perhaps a *New York Times* correspondent, in response to the "Paranormal Science" editorial, said the final fitting word on the Geller matter when he (a physicist) asked, "Incidentally, what makes you think that a handful of West Coast Ph.D.'s is any match for an Israeli magician?"

We agree. Many years ago, in fact, Raymond Birge, an eminent physicist of the University of California at Berkeley, with interests in many fields, observed that magicians can fool the average scientist more easily than they can the general public![5]

In both ufology and parapsychology one cannot fail to be impressed by innumerable examples of an utterly overwhelming need to believe, a need so strong as to make rational judgment impossible. Witness the example of the French physiologist Charles Richet, Nobel laureate (1913) and parapsychologist.

Like Crookes and Lodge, one of Richet's interests was spiritualism. In the middle of the nineteenth century two young girls of Hydesville, New York, the Fox sisters, aged eight and six, discovered a way of producing "raps" whose origin was shortly attributed by others—with financial gain in mind, as Birge points out—to "spirits."

The Fox sisters produced "spirit raps" for decades, with much recognition and success, and reports of their exploits attracted Richet's attention. Forty years later one of the sisters, Margaret, confessed that it had all been a hoax; they had produced the raps by a rare (in adults) ability to "crack" the bones in their big toes! Margaret (then Mrs. Kane) demonstrated how she did this on the stage of the Academy of Music, in New York City.

Richet, writing in 1923 in his *Thirty Years of Psychical Research,* acknowledged Margaret's confession—and stated his belief that the raps were genuine, while the confession was fraudulent![6] The objective student will find this difficult to believe, and it is; it shows the unbelievable tenacity with which the believer must grasp his belief.

Finally, it should be added that one of us (EHT) is directly and intimately aware, because of several years of experience in parapsychological research (while both an undergraduate and graduate student at Columbia University), of the extent to which the entire enterprise has been tarnished by fraud, deceit, trickery, and gullibility.

At the present time one reads much about a resurgence of interest in parapsychology, about parapsychology's right to a respectable place in the academic community. Our response is *Caveat legens*—let the reader beware!

CHAPTER 20

VON DÄNIKEN?

THE PAST TEEMED WITH UNKNOWN GODS WHO VISITED
THE PRIMEVAL EARTH IN MANNED SPACESHIPS.

Erich von Däniken[1]

Any book pretending comprehensive coverage of the subject of
unidentified flying objects must take some account of the von
Däniken phenomenon. In case any of our readers are unfamiliar
with von Däniken's name—not a likely probability—we mention
that he is the author of, together with other books, the 1970 best-
seller *Chariots of the Gods?*

His *modus operandi* is to confront the reader with a wide variety of ancient artifacts and structures and then declare that ancient
man could not have produced these without outside help. The outside help, he postulates, came from "gods"—visitors, of superior
intelligence, from outer space.

One example of the ancient structures that von Däniken in-
vokes in support of his hypothesis is the striking configuration of
straight lines and animal figures sighted from the air in arid table-
land on an elevated plateau near the desert coast of southern
Peru, the home of the Nazca people. The lines, to von Däniken,
suggest an airport. Since the Nazca civilization dates from the first
millennium A.D., these structures must have been built, von Däniken
argues, to convey to the "gods" a message to the effect that "this

is the place to land; we have built it as you directed." We shall discuss the Nazca lines and figures shortly.

We note that the question mark in the title of the book is misleading. Inside the book, as evidenced by the epigraph to this chapter, von Däniken says that unknown gods did indeed, and in large numbers, visit Earth in manned spacecraft. Period, not question mark.

Using the von Däniken method, Ben Bova, well-known science-fiction writer and now editor of *Analog,* has shown, whimsically, that a good case can be made for the view that modern Manhattan was planned long ago by extraterrestrial visitors.[2] The perfectly geometrical open space in the center of the island, he says, is clearly meant to be seen from the air. The skyscrapers point heavenward toward other worlds, of course. And so on.

It should be said that von Däniken's book is ill written (or ill translated). Most of the startling statements sprinkled throughout the book are not referenced. The book does contain a bibliography, but there are no references in the text to the works listed in the bibliography. This is an unprofessional way to go about writing a book meant to establish an entirely new archaeology and a new Earth history.

We are told, for example, that in the Baghdad Museum in Iraq are on display electric batteries that work on the galvanic principle. Though it is not so stated, it is implicit that these are ancient artifacts. We would like to know the provenance of these artifacts. We would like a reference to the scientific study or analysis that established both the age and the electrical or other nature of the artifacts. We are left with only the bald and entirely unsupported statement that electric batteries, presumably ancient, are in the Baghdad Museum. The book abounds with similar statements, similarly unsupported.

Von Däniken attributes the apparitions described in the Bible—Ezekiel's wheels and so on—to visitations by extraterrestrial spacecraft. We believe that the presence of these phenomena in our myths, religions, and legends is better accounted for by naturally occurring meteorological events (see Chapters 3 and 10).

As for the Nazca lines and figures in Peru, von Däniken's implication is that the Nazcas could not or would not have produced such structures on their own, that they required guidance from gods in spaceships. We find this, on the face of it, absurd. The Nazcas had a sophisticated civilization. None of their buildings remain, but we know they produced remarkable textiles and ceramics. Certainly they were capable of constructing straight lines upon the ground; this is a simple business and does not require surveying instruments. The purpose for which the lines were constructed could have been religious, aesthetic, or astronomical, or combinations of these.

The animal figures are, we agree, meant to be seen from the sky. Why not? Societies, tribes, and civilizations beyond counting throughout the centuries have placed their gods in the skies. Why not communicate by constructing figures large enough to be seen from the heavens? This would pose no particular problem for an imaginative people, which evidently the Nazca were. We invoke Occam's Razor once more, to obviate the need to bring in von Däniken's spacemen.

Let us now examine von Däniken's approach to another of his prime targets—the Pyramids of Lower Egypt generally, and the Great Pyramid of Cheops, or Khufu, specifically. Von Däniken's predictable position is that the ancient Egyptians could not possibly have erected the structures on their own. They needed, again, help from extraterrestrial visitors.

They could not, he says, have cut the stones to the degree of accuracy manifested by the stones of the Great Pyramid, to a fineness of a thousandth of an inch. They could not have transported them from the Nile to the building site on wooden rollers, since they had no wood. They could not have pulled the stones along on rollers in any case, for they had no rope.

And did they have the mathematics to construct the Pyramids so that, for most of them, the perimeter of the base of one of them divided by twice its height equals π? Is it only coincidence that the Great Pyramid's height multiplied by 1,000,000,000 approximately equals the distance to the sun?

Nor, von Däniken states, could the Egyptians, without assistance, have built the Pyramids in any practicable length of time. He concludes that the Great Pyramid alone would have required at

least 664 years to build. He suggests that the Great Pyramid
existed long before Khufu came along to claim it as his own in
2680 B.C.

The Pyramids are rather precisely oriented to the cardinal
points of the compass. The Egyptians couldn't have achieved this
orientation, says von Däniken, because they were interested in
only a few stars, one of which was Sirius.

Is it coincidence, he asks, that the bedrock upon which the
Great Pyramid rests is carefully and accurately leveled? Could the
Egyptians have placed the Pyramid in such a place as to divide the
continents and the oceans into equal halves? Is it only coincidence
that the Great Pyramid lies at the center of gravity of the continents?

Von Däniken offers other reasons why the Egyptians, unassisted
by gods, could not have erected the Pyramids, but these are
sufficient to illustrate his method, his thinking, his work. Let us examine his position in some detail.

First we shall deal with the questions of rope and wood, both of
which are conventionally assumed to have been used to transport
the stones from the Nile to the building sites. Von Däniken states
flatly that the ancient Egyptians had neither. This statement is,
simply, preposterous. Von Däniken must be unfamiliar with a
great deal of evidence, including an illustration of heavy transport
found in the tomb of Djehutihotep, a nobleman of the Middle
Kingdom (2133–1786 B.C.), reproduced in a study of the Pyramids by I. E. S. Edwards, an eminent British Egyptologist.[3] It
shows an alabaster statue, which probably weighed about sixty
tons, being transported by 172 men pulling ropes. The statue is
mounted upon a wooden sledge. The illustration also shows men
carrying wooden timbers. The statue is held firmly to the sledge
with heavy ropes, made taut by a method used today by cabinet-
makers. Probably these ropes were made of palm fiber. Further,
wooden timbers have been found in the ramps of at least one ancient Pyramid. Von Däniken's statements about the nonexistence
of rope and of wood in ancient Egypt are false.

Now for some mathematics. The ancient Egyptians were not sophisticated mathematicians, to be sure, and certainly had no ac-

quaintance with π. How is it, then, that this transcendental number clearly emerges from the dimensions of the pyramids?

Π is related to the circle, so rather than invoke extraterrestrial visitors, let us see how the circle might have been used in the construction of ancient Pyramids. Let us assume, with Kurt Mendelssohn, that, because the palm rope that might be used for measuring horizontal distances would be subject to stretching, "a much more accurate way of measuring long horizontal distances as, for instance, the base of a large pyramid, was required. One such method is to roll a drum and count the number of revolutions. The royal cubit . . . would immediately suggest itself as the standard diameter of the drum, and one revolution—we may call it a 'rolled cubit'—corresponds to the circumference of the drum stretched out horizontally."[4]

The height of the pyramid would be predetermined as x number of royal cubits—say, for example, forty, which would mean forty diameters of the drum. The drum is then rolled from the spot marking the center of the pyramid outward ten revolutions, to the center of one of the four sides. This done, the Egyptians have done nothing more than establish a simple 4:1 gradient—four cubits of height to one rolling cubit horizontally. This leads inexorably to an angle of elevation of 51°51'14"—as close as can be expected to the 51°52' found in the Great Pyramid. The ratio of height to perimeter of this pyramid is, then, $1:2\pi$. The ancient Egyptians discovered and used π, and were, no doubt, entirely unaware of it!

This theory is supported by the presence in Egypt of at least two pyramids with angles of elevation approximating 43°40'—the expected angle if the 4:1 gradient is changed to 3:1.

A measuring drum, then, is surely a more reasonable explanation for the appearance of π in the dimensions of the pyramids than is the invocation of gods from outer space.

Von Däniken claims that the Egyptians could not have cut the stones accurately to a thousandth of an inch. Though he does not so state, he no doubt refers here to the facing stones, rather than the core stones, which are cut more roughly. But he overstates his case. The Great Pyramid is indeed a marvel of construction, but the stones, even the facing ones, are not cut accurately to a thousandth of an inch. The average thickness of the joints is more like two hundredths of an inch, which was indeed within the capability of the Egyptians.

Though we agree that the Pyramid is a marvel, one would suppose that gods from space would have gotten the dimensions better. The difference between the longest and shortest sides of the Pyramid is 7.8 inches. This was an excellent result for the Egyptians to have obtained, but surely the gods, superior beings capable of space flight, would have done better than that.

Nor are the compass orientations entirely accurate. The most accurately oriented side, the south side, deviates to the west by about two minutes of a degree; the side most off, the east side, is awry by about five and a half minutes of a degree. Gods would have done better.

Von Däniken asks if it is a coincidence that the height of the Great Pyramid (481.4 feet) multiplied by 1,000,000,000 equals approximately the distance from the earth to the sun and comes up with 98,000,000 miles. Von Däniken doesn't even get the arithmetic right. The correct figure is 91,170,000 miles. Now, if we take the average distance of the sun from the earth as 93,000,000 miles, the pyramid makers were off by about 2 per cent—which means they missed the correct height of the pyramid by more than nine feet! Had superbeings capable of navigating through interstellar space wished to use the Great Pyramid to indicate the distance to the sun they surely would not have missed the correct height by almost ten feet. In any case, this is nothing but arrant numerology. What is sacred about the number 1,000,000,000?

Von Däniken argues that it would have taken the Egyptians about 664 years to build the Great Pyramid, assuming they knew how to do so, and that this, for a number of reasons, is too long a time. Mendelssohn, by contrast, argues persuasively, citing evidence, that not only the Great Pyramid, but *all* of the six major Pyramids were erected during a single century—without the invocation of supermen from space.[5]

According to von Däniken, the Great Pyramid is so placed that a meridian passing through it divides the continents and oceans into two equal halves. The same meridian for the continents and the oceans or separate ones for each? One for each continent, another for each ocean? He further states that the Great Pyramid lies at the center of gravity of the continents. This seems even more meaningless to us. How is the center of gravity of a continent, or of the total continental mass, determined? Who did it, and how? Von Däniken's assertions are gibberish.

Von Däniken asks if it is coincidence that the Pyramid is built upon a carefully leveled site. No, it is not coincidence. It was necessary, of course, to level the site, at least around the periphery, to construct an accurate pyramid. Mud dikes and water would be used for this. No difficult engineering problem is involved.

Von Däniken expresses doubt that the Egyptians could have lined up the Pyramids with the points of the compass, since they had no magnetic compass and were interested in few stars. This is nonsense. They were interested in stars, and they used them to orient their Pyramids and other structures. Edwards describes a text in the temple at Dendera, in Upper Egypt, which describes the king as "looking at the sky, observing the stars, and turning his gaze toward the Great Bear" in order to establish a temple orientation.[6] No doubt the astronomers (priests) had already done the surveying and the king was but going through motions. But there can be no doubt whatever that the Egyptians used the stars to orient the Pyramids.

The star we know as Polaris, the Pole Star or North Star, was not at true north 4,500 years ago, nor was any other particularly bright star. That is of no consequence, however. Theoretically, *any* star bright enough to be seen can be used to determine true north. It is necessary only to note the rising and setting points of the star on the horizon, and then bisect the angle formed by those two points and the observer's position. To produce an accurate fix, an artificial horizon would be required, but mud and water could conveniently be used for this purpose. Edwards describes in detail how this may be accomplished.

Here, then, we have seen von Däniken at work, and we have given our response to his allegations. We find that he supports his hypothesis with error, misstatement, fabrication, and wild surmise. His work is a veritable farrago of nonsense.

CHAPTER 21

THE BERMUDA TRIANGLE

THIS AREA OCCUPIES A DISTURBING AND
ALMOST UNBELIEVABLE PLACE IN THE WORLD'S
CATALOGUE OF UNEXPLAINED MYSTERIES.

Charles Berlitz[1]

Another sign—or symbol, or effect—of the need in our times for
nonsense is the presently flourishing legend of the so-called Bermuda Triangle. This dread place is the watery area bounded by a
triangle with Miami, Florida, Bermuda, and San Juan, Puerto
Rico, at its corners. This region is known by many other names as
well, including the "Devil's Triangle" and the "Graveyard of the
Atlantic."

A number of books have been written about mysterious happenings in the area—disappearing ships, lost aircraft, compasses gone
wild, and so on—but the Triangle was really put on the map, so to
speak, by Charles Berlitz's enormously popular best seller of 1974,
The Bermuda Triangle.

The relationship between the current access of interest in the
Triangle and in UFOs is, we suggest, close: in both fields of interest we find the construction of elaborate and unnecessary mystery
around phenomena more readily explained by normal laws of nature; in both cases there is a manifest need, or wish, on the part of
the public to believe in the farfetched rather than the natural; and
in both of these areas we find works set forth—on the one hand, by
imaginative authors with a casual attitude toward objectivity and

accurate reporting and, on the other, by thoughtful, scholarly writers.

The scholarly inquiry is, in the case of the Bermuda Triangle, provided by Lawrence Kusche, whose findings have recently been set forth in *The Bermuda Triangle Mystery—Solved*.[2]

It is clear, of course, that since men first sailed and flew, ships, aircraft, and crews have disappeared mysteriously in all parts of the globe. What sets the Bermuda Triangle apart, then, is what appears to be a remarkable concentration of such happenings within this relatively small part of the earth's surface. The trouble is, as Kusche has shown, that there is more (or less) here than has been revealed by the enthusiastic purveyors of mystery.

We give a few examples, paraphrased, of the kind of reportage upon which the legend of the Triangle is based, together with the results of Kusche's inquiries.

BERLITZ ACCOUNT

On February 2, 1952, a British York transport aircraft, carrying thirty-three passengers and crew, vanished on the northern edge of the Triangle while on its way to Jamaica.

KUSCHE'S FINDING

Kusche corrects the date to February 2, 1953, and notes that though the plane's eventual destination was indeed Jamaica, its disappearance occurred on a flight from the Azores to Gander, Newfoundland! Failure to note the site of the disappearance, while mentioning that the plane was on its way to Jamaica, suggests to the unwary reader that this is another mystery for the Triangle; the fact is that the plane went down hundreds of miles north of the Triangle. The incident is brought into the legend only through purposefully incomplete and misleading reporting.

BERLITZ ACCOUNT	KUSCHE'S FINDING
	Further, the weather was bad in the area where the plane went down. Kusche reports that strong winds and torrential rains restricted search operations. This is an important observation, because whenever the weather is mentioned in the "legendary" accounts of disappearances, it is usually described as "fine"—thus making the disappearances the more remarkable.
On November 9, 1956, a U. S. Navy Martin Marlin patrol seaplane vanished while on patrol "in Bermuda."	The aircraft wasn't "in" or over Bermuda, nor did it simply vanish; it exploded in flight hundreds of miles north of Bermuda and crashed into the Atlantic off the Maryland coast. The explosion was felt, and the flaming aircraft was seen, by the crew of a merchant freighter. There were no survivors, and no debris was found. Again, this unfortunate accident has nothing to do with the Bermuda Triangle.
Berlitz, writing of disappearances in the western Atlantic, mentions the loss in May 1968 of the submarine *Scorpion* about 460 miles southeast (*sic*) of the Azores—thus (for the uncritical reader) bringing the	Kusche points out the obvious fact that, although the loss of the *Scorpion* is often considered to be a part of the mystery of the Bermuda Triangle, the incident occurred much closer to Africa and Portugal.

BERLITZ ACCOUNT   KUSCHE'S FINDING

Scorpion into the Bermuda Triangle.

The *Cyclops,* a U. S. Navy   Kusche argues persuasively, cit-
collier with 309 Navy personnel   ing evidence, that the *Cyclops*
aboard, disappeared in March   sank during a severe storm in
1918, with a cargo of manga-   180 feet of water 70 miles east
nese ore, en route to Norfolk   of Norfolk. A major tragedy,
from Barbados. No trace of the   but one having nothing to do
ship was ever found. Berlitz   with the Bermuda Triangle.
writes that the only sure thing
about the *Cyclops* is that it disappeared within the Bermuda
Triangle.

Many more examples could be given, but these are enough to
show how thin the legend wears when subjected to objective scrutiny.

To one possessed of even a modicum of skepticism and rationality, the legend of the Bermuda Triangle is a tempting target
for satire, and a number of delightful spoofs have appeared.
Walter Sullivan, a normally level-headed writer about science for
The New York Times, brought forth the horrendous Hatteras
Hexagon—a six-sided area off Cape Hatteras beneath whose waters
lie no fewer than 697 wrecks, including those of the United States
battleships *Wyoming* and *New Jersey.*[3]*

James Stevenson, a cartoonist for *The New Yorker* magazine, produced the frightening Bruckner Octagon, another dread
area, this one bounded by a number of metropolitan New York
City access roads, including Bruckner Boulevard and the Cross
Bronx Expressway.[4] This geometric construct lies over land, and
the disappearances here involve solid and relatively immovable objects, including a Howard Johnson restaurant, a power station, a
motel in Pelham, and an apartment building. Stevenson's account

---

* Sullivan's data are correct. He uses them to show how established fact
can be manipulated to mislead the credulous.

was illustrated with amateur snapshots, and though the photographs were ominously fuzzy and vague they were nonetheless, Stevenson points out, disturbing. Perhaps the most disturbing of the lot is a dark portrait of the historian of the Bruckner Octagon, one E. Powers Jackson, taken (by his wife, in front of his garage) a fiftieth of a second before he disappeared from Earth.

Light-hearted spoofs, yes, but we wonder how many serious letters were written to the authors in consequence.

Why do some writers write books like *The Bermuda Triangle* and why do readers buy them in such impressive quantities?† The writer knows what the public wants (thrills, magic, mystery) and is happy to give it to them. Hundreds of thousands of readers buy books like *The Bermuda Triangle,* because the books say what they want to hear.

The Bermuda Triangle was on the best-sellers list for months on end, but *The Bermuda Triangle Mystery—Solved* never made it. Autism wins again!

We have discussed the why of this elsewhere (Chapter 12), but it is fitting to append here Sullivan's suggestion: "Why the vogue? Perhaps because the gullible preceded P. T. Barnum and will outlive him into perpetuity. Many, no doubt, simply wish no more than to enjoy the delights of the improbable."[5]

---

† One might ask also why the publisher publishes such books. He publishes them for profit. *Publishers Weekly,* for March 24, 1975, listed *The Bermuda Triangle* at the top of the nonfiction best-sellers list and noted sales to that date of 288,946 copies. Sales of this magnitude, it is said, make it possible for the publisher to bring forth books of more redeeming value but of lesser salability. The alert reader will have noticed that the publisher of *The Bermuda Triangle* is also the publisher of this book.

A SUMMING UP

We have shown that the broad grouping of phenomena we call "flying saucers" has always been with us. These objects are with us now and will no doubt continue to be with us until the dawn of a new and better Age of Reason.

Flying saucers have no probative value for establishing the existence of extraterrestrial spacecraft. Many are hoaxes; most are misidentifications of a very wide variety of natural phenomena.

Yet, belief in the extraterrestrial origin of flying saucers is widespread. A cult has arisen around the flying saucer, with an attendant array of organizations and publications. Most adherents to the cult are uncritical in their acceptance, as evidence of extraterrestrial spacecraft, of any visual sighting of anything not immediately identifiable. Some are scientists who should know better, but who seek explanation for "unexplained" sightings in new physical laws or phenomena that are yet to be discovered. The fame to be gained from such a discovery, or perhaps even a Nobel prize, may provide motivation for some of these UFO researchers.

The prevalence of belief in flying saucers is but one manifestation of a pervasive denial of reality—which in turn is probably occasioned by what has aptly been called "The Predicament of Mankind." The earth, measured by whatever parameter, is growing smaller at an alarming rate. Population is increasing explosively. Resources are being depleted. A sense of crisis is in the wind, and that sense is seeping into the minds of many who are unable to articulate it and might well, at the conscious level, even deny it.

In a time when we need science most, there is much (misguided) antiscientific animus around. This stems from a number of causes, including the development of atomic weaponry and the economic burden of the space program.

Because of the predicament our planet is in, it is tempting for people to invoke the concept of rescue by a superior civilization. This idea is not altogether unreasonable, in view of the highly probable existence of life on many other planets in our galaxy. It is extremely likely that "human" or humanoid creatures live contemporaneously with us somewhere in our own or other galaxies. Their chemical and physical construction is probably quite similar to our own, because atoms are the same everywhere.

If we could visit one of the other inhabited planets of our galaxy, assuming that there are such planets, we should probably not be much surprised by what we would find. All of the complex molecules that have thus far been found out there are entirely familiar to terrestrial chemists. The sun of the planet we visit will probably not be a great deal hotter or colder than ours. The planet itself will most likely have oceans and tides, and its axis of rotation will probably be tilted like that of the earth. It will probably be, in short, a kind of copy of Earth. If the inhabitants have not yet achieved a degree of space travel, they probably will in the future. Or they might have in the past.

Many ufologists point to the huge number of inhabited planets that may exist in our galaxy as an argument that we are currently being visited by beings from outer space. While affirming the high probability of the existence of intelligent life elsewhere in the universe, we deny that such visitations are now occurring or have occurred in the past.

Why are we not being visited? The major considerations are time, energy, and the enormous distances involved. As we have shown, the energy requirements for interstellar travel are truly stupendous and would tax the resources of any planet. The problems in respect of time are, as we have seen, enormous. The magnitude of interstellar distances is almost incomprehensible.

Interstellar travel is, however, by no means an impossibility. Such travel may even be commonplace where stars are relatively close together, as in the galactic center or in the globular clusters. But we are far from such parts of our galaxy.

It seems to us most unlikely that we have been, or shall be, visited by aliens from other planetary systems. "Unidentified flying objects" are normal phenomena of our physical world. It is alluring to many to interpret these phenomena as evidence of visits to our troubled planet by superbeings in saucers from a superior culture. We have shown that there is no scientific justification for such interpretation or belief.

As a matter of research priority, we suggest that all scientists can spend their time to better advantage than in the study of UFOs. Taxpayers' monies, certainly, should not be diverted into this activity. Until and unless evidence of flying saucers of a kind not yet forthcoming appears, our energies should be directed elsewhere.

The planets will continue to orbit the sun; let us identify them as such. There will be mirages; let us understand them. There will be hoaxes; let us recognize them for what they are. There will be meteors and parhelia and aurorae; let us enjoy these spectacular apparitions—as natural phenomena. But as for flying saucers, let us bring them to a deserved and prosaic end—down to Earth.

The original Hill map contained fifteen stars, if we discount the "background" stars except for the three bright ones. Let us assume that the basic map is in the form of a rectangle of n squares. Make the squares small enough so that merely indicating fifteen of the squares will serve to represent the Hill map—whose star positions, admittedly, are only approximate. We denote the number of catalog stars as r, where $r = 47$, the 46 from the catalog, plus the sun. Let p be the number of stars on the map, i.e., 15. The number of stars not used in making the map, 32, we denote by q. In general, now, $p + q = r$.

The problem is now reduced to the common statistical one of dropping seeds at random upon a rectangular board containing squares (or, to use a different analogy, dropping marbles into cells). Let us, however, use the analogy of a checkerboard, with black (b) and white (w) squares, though not arranged as on a checkerboard, for this board will contain p white squares (the star map) and q black squares (the background). The a priori probability that a given seed will fall upon a white square is

$$P_w = p/n, \tag{1}$$

and the probability it will fall upon a black square is

$$P_b = (n-p)/n. \tag{2}$$

The average number of seeds falling on white squares, in r tosses, is

$$W = rp/n, \tag{3}$$

and in black squares

$$B = r(r-p)/n. \tag{4}$$

But deviations from these averages will always occur. A general statistical theorem states that when r seeds are randomly tossed upon a board having p white squares and $(n - p)$ black squares, the probability, P_o, of finding exactly p seeds on the white squares and q on the black is

$$P_o = \left(\frac{p}{n}\right)^p \left(\frac{n-p}{n}\right)^q \frac{r!}{p!q!} \tag{5}$$

where ! denotes "factorial." Thus $5! = 1 \times 2 \times 3 \times 4 \times 5$ etc.

Let us consider four possible random-number maps:

1. An 8×8 square, 64 squares.
2. An 8×10 rectangle, 80 squares.
3. A 10×10 square, 100 squares.
4. A 10×12 rectangle, 120 squares.

For our problem, as noted above, $p = 15$, $q = 32$, and $r = 47$. The table shows the results of applying the above data and formulas to the random positioning of points on four different grids or, in this case, star maps.

TABLE I

Probabilities of matching a given pattern of points on a grid with a pattern of points produced by a random procedure.

	n	P_w	P_b	W	B	P_o	P_s	P_t
Map 1	64	0.234	0.766	11.02	35.98	.05166	0.919	353
Map 2	80	0.188	0.812	8.81	38.19	.01217	0.245	118
Map 3	100	0.150	0.850	7.05	39.95	.00182	0.0409	25
Map 4	120	0.125	0.875	5.88	41.13	.000298	0.00731	5

P_w is the probability that any given random point will lie on a white square, i.e., will fit the star map. P_b is the probability that any such point will lie on a black square, i.e., will not fit the map. For a set of 47 random points, W and B are the numbers of points that will, on the average, lie on the white and black squares, respectively.

P_o is the probability that, given 47 random points, exactly 15 will be on white squares, 32 on black. P_s is P_o multiplied by a factor, the effective circumference of the map, which may be rotated to seek a fit of the random pattern.

P_s is simply the probability of finding a match from some one specific point in space. To obtain P_t, the total probability, we have to multiply P_s by a factor representing the number of points from which we can view the stellar array and expect to find a different pattern. Imagine our star group to be surrounded by a parallelepiped of six faces, each face having n squares, or $6n$ squares in all. We can view the star array and see a different map from each square. Thus the total number of probable matches, P_t, becomes

$$P_t = 6nP_s.$$

The high probabilities in the last column show that the match obtained by Fish was by no means unusual. As our single empirical experiment proved, matches are easy to come by and have no significance.

One source of error in Saunders's argument is immediately apparent. He states that space has three dimensions, and hence multiplies the factor P_o by 3, instead of by $6\pi n^{3/2}$, to allow for the different orientations and possible viewing angles. The remainder of his statistical argument, including his arithmetic, is utterly wrong from start to finish.

Our final conclusion may be stated very simply. A high probability exists that a map constructed from random points will provide an adequate match for the Hill map. In fact, a careful search, either of random patterns or of star models based upon star catalogs, will discover dozens of such maps.

Dickinson's "Zeta Reticuli Incident" is a tour de force, and a product of vivid imagination, but it is not of statistical significance.

This statement is in no sense a criticism of Marjorie Fish, who is to be commended for her industry and her imaginative approach to an interesting problem. But her map does not withstand critical scrutiny, either by a common-sense empirical approach or by routine statistical analysis. The Hill case remains an interesting psychological and psychiatric phenomenon, but it provides no evidence for visitation of the earth by beings from interstellar space.

The random numbers used in constructing our "star map" were taken from *A Million Random Digits with 100,000 Normal Deviates,* published by the Rand Corporation. For convenience, we used the first forty-seven four-digit numbers in the first column of numbers on the first page of the Rand tables.

The first and second pairs of digits of each four-digit number provided the x and y co-ordinates for each point on the map. The scale for each co-ordinate was from 0 to 100. To make our map conform to the general shape of the Hill map, we adjusted our co-ordinates so that the ratio of x to y was 3 to 2.

The random numbers used are given below. If the reader will plot this map according to our co-ordinates, rotate it 180°, and select the fifteen points most closely coinciding with those of the Hill map, he will have constructed the random-number map shown in Figure 7.

1009	6606	9852	6548	9149	6119	0449	3217	9808	7402
3754	3106	1180	8012	8033	1547	0054	6923	3318	5417
0842	8526	8345	7435	4410	9455	3596	1956	8095	
9901	6357	8868	6991	1255	4248	5980	4515	7975	
1280	7379	9959	0989	6360	2352	4605	9486	1863	

Chapter 1

1. This quotation refers to Jacob. The remark was made after his vision of the ladder extending to the heavens, with angels ascending and descending.
2. U. S. Air Force files. (These files have been transferred to the National Archives, and are now available for public inspection.)
3. This viewpoint had been proposed many years earlier by Charles Fort, a collector of stories about mysterious events. He wrote about unidentified air-borne objects, suggesting they might be great ships from distant planets, manned by beings who were "fishing for us." He also coined the stunning phrase, "I think we're property."

Chapter 2

1. *The Lady's "Yes"* (1844), st. 1.
2. J. P. C. Southall, *Introduction to Physiological Optics* (Dover Publications, New York, 1961), pp. 231ff.

Chapter 3

1. R. L. Dione, *God Drives a Flying Saucer* (Bantam Books, New York, 1973).
2. Genesis 7:11.
3. Genesis 8:2.
4. Genesis 9:13–16.
5. Exodus 3:2,3.
6. A. B. Fraser, "Theological optics," *Applied Optics* 14 (April 1975), A92.

7. 2 Kings 2:11.
8. Daniel 7:1–8, Isaiah 6:1,2, and Revelations 4:1–3, 13:1, 14:14, and 15:1.

CHAPTER 4

1. Roger de Wendover, d. 1236, *Flowers of History*, trans. from the Latin by J. A. Giles (H. G. Bohn, London, 1849; reprinted by AMS Press, New York, 1968).
2. A. D. White, *History of the Warfare Between Science and Theology* (D. Appleton, New York, 1901).
3. F. Reinzer, *Meteorologia Philosophico-politica* (Peter Detleffsen, Augsburg, 1709).
4. See Note 1.
5. *The New York Times,* May 30, 1877.
6. New York *Sun,* September 21, 1877.

CHAPTER 5

1. *Hamlet,* I, v, 166.
2. C. J. Norcock, "An atmospheric phenomenon in the North China Sea, *Nature* 48 (May 25, 1893), 76–77.
3. "Ball Lightning" (in Notes by the Editor), *Monthly Weather Review* 26 (August 1898), 358. (U. S. Department of Agriculture, WB #176.)
4. R. S. Lambert, "Flying saucers—their lurid past," *Saturday Night* 67 (May 17, 1952), 9, 18.

CHAPTER 7

1. Letter from a private citizen dated April 29, 1969. Condon papers, Library of the American Philosophical Society, Philadelphia, Pa.
2. E. U. Condon et al., *Scientific Study of Unidentified Flying Objects* (Bantam Books, New York, 1969).
3. It is to Condon that we owe the pronunciation "oofo." He said that the subject was a goofy one, and UFO should be pronounced accordingly.
4. This correspondence, both pro and con, is most interesting. The hard-core lunatic fringe wrote at length, of course. One woman suggested that the inquiry be called off forthwith, as the UFOs

they were studying—all of them—happened to be her personal property.
5. J. G. Fuller, "Flying Saucer Fiasco," *Look* 32 (May 14, 1968), 58ff.
6. Condon papers, see Note 1 above.
7. E. U. Condon et al., op. cit., Appendix U, pp. 905–21.
8. Letter from a private citizen to Condon, 1969. Condon papers.
9. P. Morrison, *Scientific American* 220, no. 4 (April 1969), 139–40.

CHAPTER 8

1. J. A. Hynek, *Bulletin of the Atomic Scientists,* April 1969, 39–42.
2. P. Klass, *UFOs Explained* (Random House, New York, 1974).
3. The plane was actually an RB-47—a B-47 modified to provide ECM (electronic countermeasures) capability.
4. The emphasis here and throughout this chapter is ours.
5. The autokinetic effect is discussed in more detail in Chapter 13.
6. M. Sherif, "A study of some social factors in perception," *Archives of Psychology* #187 (1935).
7. "Apperception" is the process by which one relates something newly perceived to the totality of his previous experience and knowledge.
8. Letter, J. A. Hynek to R. J. Low, December 8, 1966, Condon papers.
9. The test results were compatible with a diagnosis of either psychopathy or schizophrenia. In the tests, the witness manifested a tremendous need to be important. His credibility, the psychologist reported, had to be seriously questioned.
10. Klass has similarly conjectured.
11. Condon papers.
12. See P. A. Sturrock, "UFOs—a Scientific Debate," *Science* 180 (1973), 593–95.
13. J. E. Oberg, *Official UFO,* October 1976, and scheduled to be reprinted November 1976 in the more accessible *Space World.*

CHAPTER 9

1. H. Gernsback, *Ralph 124C 41 +*, serialized in twelve parts in *Modern Electrics,* beginning with the issue of April 1911. This novel is quite unreadable today, but it teems with imaginative technical innovations.
2. In U.S. military parlance, "Joint" signifies the chiefs of the various

services of the United States. "Combined" included, additionally, the chiefs of the allied forces of Great Britain, Canada, and Australia.

3. V. G. Plank, *Spurious Echoes on Radar, a Survey,* Geophysical Research Paper No. 62, Air Force Cambridge Research Center, May 1959.

4. See Note 2, Chapter 7 (pp. 170–71, 310–16).

5. *Final Report on the Investigation of FAA Phenomena, Andersen AFB, Guam, 2–9 August 1966.*

CHAPTER 10

1. *Antony and Cleopatra,* IV, xiv, 3.

CHAPTER 11

1. *The Vision* (1786), II, st. 18.

2. F. L. Whipple, "Do comets play a role in galactic chemistry and γ-ray bursts?" *The Astronomical Journal* 80 (July 1975), 530.

3. J. Baxter and T. Atkins, *The Fire Came By* (Doubleday, Garden City, N.Y., 1976).

4. This report and the following ones relating to this case are from Air Force files.

5. We are indebted to Vic Hessler of the University of Alaska for these photographs.

6. See Note 3, Chapter 4.

7. E. W. Maunder, "A strange celestial visitor," *The Observatory* 39 (May 1916), 213–15.

8. Numerous letters from observers of the "beam" were published in *Nature,* for November 23, 1882, and following weeks. It was upon these that Capron's discussion was chiefly based.

9. J. R. Capron, "The auroral beam of November 17, 1882," *The London, Edinburgh, and Dublin Philosophical Magazine and Journal of Science* 15 (May 1883), 318–39.

CHAPTER 12

1. G. M. Whipple, *Psychological Bulletin* 6 (May 1909), 153.

2. D. H. Menzel and L. G. Boyd, *The World of Flying Saucers* (Doubleday, Garden City, N.Y., 1963).

3. See Note 2, Chapter 8.
4. Cited in J. P. C. Southall, ed., *Helmholtz's Treatise on Physiological Optics* (Dover Publications, New York, 1962, pp. 422–23).
5. R. Buckhout, "Eyewitness testimony," *Scientific American* 231 (December 1974), 23–31.
6. A. Hess and D. Didricks, and T. Sato, cited in A. Av-Shalom et al., "Prevalence of Myopia in Africans," *American Journal of Ophthalmology* 63 (June 1967), 1728–31.
7. F. V. Malmstrom, R. J. Randle, and R. J. Weber, *Perceptual Tunnel or Perceptual Sphere? Accommodation and Stress.* Personal communication.
8. See Note 6, Chapter 8.
9. T. M. Reade, "Curious apparent motion of the moon seen in Australia," *Nature* 38 (May 31, 1888), 102.
10. H. L. F. von Helmholtz, *Treatise on Physiological Optics* (1867; Optical Society of America, Ithaca, N.Y., 1924–25).

CHAPTER 13

1. "Two-Day UFO Mystery Was Just a Flash in the Pond," Philadelphia *Inquirer,* November 12, 1974.
2. We are indebted to Colonel Robert W. Clement, vice commander of Wright-Patterson AFB, Dayton, Ohio, for the information that these reports, which swept the North American continent, bore an uncanny resemblance to the plot of a science-fiction novel, *The Fortec Conspiracy,* by R. M. Garvin and E. G. Addeo, published in 1966 by the Sherbourne Press. The authors of the novel insist that the book is indeed pure fiction. Yet someone apparently read it and, impelled by any of a number of motives, set forth fiction as fact—thereby initiating a widespread, media-fed barrage in support of the validity of extraterrestrial UFOs and of the existence of a cover-up of their existence by that old whipping-boy, the U. S. Air Force.
3. This chapter is written by EHT, though both authors share responsibility for this and for all chapters in the book.
4. Philip Klass, author of several books on UFOs, has been the one other investigator (in addition to DHM) who has adopted an unfailingly scientific approach in his inquiries. J. Allen Hynek, though a scientist (chairman of the Department of Astronomy at Northwestern University and quondam consultant to Project Blue Book), manifests a much softer scientific approach to UFO studies than those of DHM and Philip Klass.
5. UFO Newsclipping Service, 3521 S.W. 104th, Seattle, WA 98146.

CHAPTER 14

1. A. Adams, *Ansel Adams—Images 1923–1974* (New York Graphic Society, Boston, 1974).
2. D. Leslie and G. Adamski, *Flying Saucers Have Landed* (British Book Centre, New York, 1953).

CHAPTER 15

1. W. Sullivan, *We Are Not Alone* (McGraw-Hill, New York, 1964).
2. Some years ago a newspaper science writer, observing the moon with his small telescope, thought he saw a bridge on its surface. Although the writer's overindulgence in alcoholic beverages was well known, this announcement was grist for the mills of the believers. Donald Keyhoe, a well-known UFO enthusiast, featured this discovery as proof that flying-saucer inhabitants had taken over the moon and were about to invade the earth. High-resolution photographs of the area have disposed of the myth. Keyhoe claimed, however, that Mount Wilson astronomers had turned their spectrographs on the alleged bridgelike structure on the moon and found it to be composed of iron. This statement exhibited a gross ignorance of the facts of spectroscopy, since light reflected from a metallic object does not in any sense disclose its chemical composition. But Keyhoe's pronouncement was, at the time, a seven-day wonder. Keyhoe later admitted his error, excusing it on the basis of having accepted without checking a statement made to him by some friend.
3. R. N. Bracewell, *The Galactic Club: Intelligent Life in Outer Space* (W. H. Freeman, San Francisco, 1975).
4. Ibid., p. 63.
5. Scientists are not in total agreement about the effects of time dilation in relativistic space flight. These figures are from Bracewell (p. 108).
6. I. S. Shklovskii and C. Sagan, *Intelligent Life in the Universe* (Holden-Day, San Francisco, 1966).
7. Much of the biology of this chapter appeared in a paper by DHM, "Life in the Universe," *The Graduate Journal* (University of Texas), vol. 7 (1965–66), no. 1. We also gratefully acknowledge the help and advice of Dr. Bernard D. Davis, Adele Lehman Professor of Bacterial Physiology, Harvard Medical School.

Chapter 16

1. R. V. Jones, part of a lecture published in *Bulletin of the Institute of Physics* 193 (1957), quoted in R. L. Weber, *A Random Walk in Science* (Institute of Physics, London, and Crane, Russak, New York, 1973).
2. See Note 2, Chapter 8.
3. E. U. Condon et al., *Scientific Study of Unidentified Flying Objects* (Bantam Books, New York, 1969).
4. Condon papers, Library of the American Philosophical Society, Philadelphia.
5. Klass, op. cit.
6. Philadelphia *Inquirer*, November 12, 1974.
7. *Gray Barker's Newsletter*, April, May, June 1976.
8. R. Hancock, *The Compleat Swindler* (Macmillan, New York, 1969).
9. F. Vere, *The Piltdown Fantasy* (Cattel, London, 1955).
10. *The New York Times*, October 27, 1974.
11. J. S. Weiner, *The Piltdown Forgery* (Oxford University Press, London, 1955).
12. This story appeared in *The Rocky Mountain Herald* (Denver) on October 26, 1974, under the by-line "Merlin." We are pleased to report that "Merlin" is Maurice B. Mitchell, now chancellor of the University of Denver.

Chapter 17

1. A. Klein, ed., *Grand Deception* (Lippincott, Philadelphia, 1955).
2. A. M. Ludwig, *The Importance of Lying* (C. C. Thomas, Springfield, Ill., 1965).
3. E. A. Strecker and F. G. Ebaugh, *Practical Clinical Psychiatry* (Blakiston, Philadelphia, 1925).
4. W. Seabrook, *Doctor Wood* (Harcourt Brace, New York, 1941).
5. L. Carroll, *Through the Looking-Glass* (1872), Chap. 5.
6. C. Fair, *The New Nonsense* (Simon and Schuster, New York, 1974).
7. B. J. Bok et al., *The Humanist* (September–October 1975), 4–6.
8. C. Mackay, *Extraordinary Popular Delusions and the Madness of Crowds* (1841, 1852; reprinted by L. C. Page, Boston, 1932).
9. For an interesting article recounting this bizarre meeting, see A.

Weil, "A Bunch of the Brujos were Whooping it Up," *Rolling Stone* No. 198 (October 23, 1975), 56.

10. *The New York Times Magazine,* February 29, 1976.
11. Letter, R. J. Low to DHM, November 19, 1975.
12. Condon Report, p. 212.
13. Ibid., p. 217.
14. Ibid., p. 46.
15. D. H. Meadows et al., *The Limits to Growth* (Universe Books, New York, 1972).
16. F. Herbert, "Science Fiction and a World in Crisis," in *Science Fiction Today and Tomorrow,* R. Bretnor, ed. (Harper & Row, New York, 1974).

CHAPTER 18

1. See Note 2, Chapter 8.
2. J. G. Fuller, *The Interrupted Journey* (Dial Press, New York, 1966).

CHAPTER 19

1. C. E. M. Hansel, *ESP: A Scientific Evaluation* (Scribner's, New York, 1966).
2. R. Targ and H. Puthoff, "Information Transmission Under Conditions of Sensory Shielding," *Nature,* 251 (October 18, 1974), 602–7.
3. *The New York Times,* November 6, 1974.
4. J. Hanlon, *New Scientist* (October 17, 1974), 170–85.
5. R. T. Birge, "Parapsychology: Fact or Fraud?" Address given at Marietta College, Marietta, Ohio, October 24, 1961.
6. C. Richet, *Thirty Years of Psychical Research* (Macmillan, New York, 1923).

CHAPTER 20

1. E. von Däniken, *Chariots of the Gods?* trans. by Michael Heron (Putnam, New York, 1970).
2. B. Bova, "The Whole Truth," editorial, *Analog* (October 1974), 5.

3. I. E. S. Edwards, *The Pyramids of Egypt* (Viking, New York, 1972).

4. K. Mendelssohn, *The Riddle of the Pyramids* (Praeger, New York, 1974).

5. Mendelssohn, address to annual meeting of the American Association for the Advancement of Science, New York, 1975.

6. Edwards, op. cit., pp. 198ff.

CHAPTER 21

1. C. Berlitz, *The Bermuda Triangle* (Doubleday, Garden City, N.Y., 1974).

2. L. D. Kusche, *The Bermuda Triangle Mystery–Solved* (Harper & Row, New York, 1975).

3. W. Sullivan, "The Bermuda Triangle Isn't Playing Square," *The New York Times,* April 6, 1975.

4. J. Stevenson, "The Bruckner Octagon," *The New Yorker,* April 7, 1975.

5. Sullivan, op. cit.

290   INDEX

Condon Report case 22, 104
Condon Report case 42, 107–8
Condon Report case 52, 111–12
Condon Report case 56, 113
Forkenbrock experiment, 181–84
Gemini 7 photograph, 116
Maury Island, 211–12
McMinnville (Oregon), 109–10, 193, 216
Pascagoula (Mississippi), 213–15, 255
Piltdown skull, 218–20
Roseville (Ohio), 193, 215–16
Trindade, 194
Holloman AFB, 11–13
Hynek, J. Allen, 5, 10, 85, 89–90, 93, 99, 109, 145, 180, 242, 283

I

Ice crystals. *See* Meteorological optics
IFO, 10
Ignis fatuus, 46
Interrupted Journey, The, 239

J

Jacob's ladder, 21, 279
Japan, unknown lights of, 43, 51–58
Jeremiah, 30
Jokii, Maurus, 75
Jones, R. V., 211

K

Kepler, Johannes, 155
Keyhoe, Donald E., 84, 284
Klass, Philip, vii, 90, 93–95, 110, 180, 213–16, 283
Korea, rotating lights of, 134
Korsakoff's syndrome, 227
Kretsch, Jeffrey, 241, 243
Kusche, Lawrence, 266–68, 287

L

Lambert, R. S., 280
Land, Edwin H., 172–73
LeMay, Curtis, 142
Leslie, Desmond, 191
Levine, Norman E., 83–85
Levy, Jay, 221
Lilley, A. E., 199
Limits to Growth, The, 286
Lodge, Sir Oliver, 252, 256
Look magazine, 84–85
Los Alamos, 11–12
Low, Robert J., 82–86, 99, 104, 124, 221, 235–37, 286
Lowitz, Johann Tobias, 24
Lubbock (Texas) lights, 192
Ludwig, Arnold, 226
Lycosthenes, 36–37
Lying, 225–30

M

McClure, Frank D., 93–95
McDivitt, James, 115
McDonald, James E., 84, 112, 135, 141
Mackay, Charles, 232

S

C